GILLIAN MONKS is a Quaker, Theosophist and practising Druid. She was born and brought up in Lancashire. She trained as a teacher and graduated from Lancaster University. She is developing a spiritual retreat on a five-acre plot where she also leads and facilitates workshops in self-development and spirituality. She lives with her husband and son, five cats and two dogs in the heart of Snowdonia.

**Read the blog at
Merrymidwinter.com
and visit
gillianmonks.com**

Merry
MIDWINTER

How to Rediscover
the Magic of the
Christmas Season

Gillian Monks

unbound

First published in 2018
This paperback edition first published in 2019

Unbound
6th Floor Mutual House, 70 Conduit Street, London W1S 2GF

www.unbound.com

Text Design by Patty Rennie

A CIP record for this book is available from the British Library

ISBN 978-1-78352-842-4 (trade pbk)
ISBN 978-1-78352-707-6 (trade hbk)
ISBN 978-1-78352-709-0 (ebook)

Printed in Barcelona by Novoprint

1 3 5 7 9 8 6 4 2

For my son, Dafydd, without whose advice, vision and
encouragement this book would never have come to fruition.

*

For my husband, Holger, whose loving understanding
and support has meant so much.

*

For Jenn, dearest friend, whose love and enthusiasm
has constantly inspired and spurred me on.

*

For my mother, Joan, whose singular lifestyle,
outlook and beliefs have taught me so much.

*

To you all I dedicate this book, with much love.

Contents

ENDMATTER

Introduction

Christmas is to remind us of the importance of love… not just to provide a reason for expressing it for a few days in December each year, but to spur us on in our endeavours to give it full rein ALL year round.

MIDWINTER FALLS UPON 21st December and humanity has celebrated on that day for many thousands of years. The whole relevance and success of the coming breeding and planting season, of growth and harvest, and the resultant well-being of all living things upon the face of the Earth, has always rested upon the pivotal point of Midwinter when the darkest days are experienced, and the light and warmth of the Sun begins to grow perceptibly stronger. This is the whole nub of the year, for if the heat and light of the Sun remain absent and the dark and cold continue life here on this planet will very quickly come to an end.

Many of our most cherished Christmas customs derive from a time when we all actively acknowledged, awaited and honoured this vital solar event upon which our survival so totally depends.

Festooning our homes with evergreens – holly, ivy, mistletoe and bay, among others – was originally done to provide literal and symbolic shelter through the worst of the winter weather for the woodland spirits which embodied the very essence of natural life. Our predilection for setting up a Christmas tree in our homes springs from the same source and is an important icon of twenty-first-century winter which is recognised (if not practised) all around the world.

Saint Lucy with her crown of candles and basket of sweetly spiced buns has her feast day on 13th December, the date of the original Winter Solstice before the calendars were changed and updated in 1752. She is just one of the remaining archetypes who originally represented the divine mother of bounty and nurture in the natural world. This archetype, in her many guises, returned the light to the land; as was ritually played out each year in Greek mythology by the characters of Demeter and Persephone. In some northern lands this archetypal female appears as Frau Holle (or in northern Britain as Mother Holly), causing snow to fall every time she shakes her feather mattress or plucks her Christmas goose, rewarding goodness and industry but punishing misbehaviour and laziness.

It is this generic female deity, embodied by such figures as Saint Lucy and Frau Holle who variously gave birth to or partnered the Wild Man of the prehistoric Boreal Forest – a masculine character who has undergone many changes of appearance and purpose but who now sits at the very heart of our Midwinter celebrations in the guise of our best-beloved Christmas archetype, Father Christmas.

The 25th December is the first day after the Winter Solstice when, in the Northern Hemisphere, the length of daylight can be perceptibly measured as having grown longer, and has been revered as a singularly special day in many cultures and geographical areas throughout the history of mankind. The Ancient Egyptian god Isis, the Greek god

Apollo, the Persian god Mithras and the Roman god Sol Invictus are just four among many divine solar entities whose birth was celebrated on 25th December, long before the coming of Jesus and Christianity. Jesus is the last in a very long and dearly loved line of divine archetypes who have always held the highest place in their peoples' spiritual beliefs and affections.

As such, Midwinter has always been a time for people to set aside their differences, lay down their weapons, and come together in a sense of community and celebration. We all share a spiritual heritage which reaches back into our primordial beginnings.

My hope is that once again, we can learn to level all barriers of place, social standing, genetic heritage and religion, demonstrating a way to bring everyone together in the celebration of winter, the rebirth of spring, and humanity's place within the scheme of things. In so doing perhaps we can show how to transcend all our lower, baser feelings and behaviour and use Midwinter and the celebration of the rebirth of Light as a focus to bring out the very best in all of us, not just for Christmas, but as a pattern for honouring, respecting, living and loving all the year through.

I wish to inspire, to help people redirect and re-understand the whole reason for celebrating Christmas and Midwinter. I hope to reach out to people on many levels and that everyone will find something in these pages to relate to and bring new joy into their lives.

I have included reminiscences from my childhood which I hope might jog older readers' memories and possibly entertain younger children. Parts of each chapter are certainly written so that they can also be read aloud and shared between parents and their little ones.

There are also lots of accounts of how my family and I go about our preparations and celebrations now. There are ideas and instructions for how to make your own decorations, your own entertainments, and re-write your own winter songs and carols to more genuinely reflect who you are and what is most important to you.

Then there are the simple seasonal recipes (for the whole of winter, not just Christmas!) which have been taken from my mother's own manuscript cookery book, and her varied observations, which appear as 'Comments from Joan'. Faithfully reproduced in her own words just as they were written many decades ago, they reflect some of the difficulties and shortages of the 1940s and 1950s onwards, but they also provide a snapshot of the hopes and dreams of an ordinary hard-working young wife and mother. Here you will not find dishes which cater for dietary preference or medical requirement – such things were almost unheard of then, and in the years immediately after the Second World War the focus for many people remained on finding enough of anything to eat. Consequently her recipes (and sometimes her comments) reflect my mother's endeavour to do the best she could with basic or poorer ingredients, nonetheless managing to produce nutritious, tasty and satisfying meals.

So often I hear people criticising 'Christmas'; the frantic shopping sprees, the over-spending, the massive consumerism and rivalry in giving, wearing, eating and drinking. We are all helping to create this gross distortion... so stop it. Now. These modern practices merely serve to mask – and ultimately degrade – our original resonance with and connection to something of great beauty and joy.

At the same time, try not to throw the metaphorical baby out with the bathwater! Take the best from modern convenience and manufacture and marry it to older values and customs – have the best of both worlds. *Merry Midwinter* shows you how this is possible, and it is not as difficult as you might think.

Just consider the title of this book; in the eighteenth century, the word 'merry' meant bountiful and prosperous (rather than very happy or having drunk too much alcohol). To wish someone 'Merry Christmas' was rather like saying 'God look after you and continue to make you successful and prosperous.' So in turn, 'Merry Midwinter' should convey the greeting 'A Pleasant and Bountiful Midwinter!'

While so many are denigrating Christmas consumerism, I have to admit that I absolutely love all the glitz, bustle and lights! Also spare a thought for all the many people whose only experience of Christmas will be the decorations, lights and piped music of the shops and streets this winter. Helping to care for an elderly neighbour last Christmas I realised that she didn't have any seasonal decorations, so I bought a very reasonably priced little tree – about two and a half feet tall – a box of baubles, a couple of strands of gold tinsel and a little set of multi-coloured fairy lights and set it up for her beside the fireplace in her living room. Her face would light up with joy each day when the tree lights were switched on again and she never seemed to tire of looking at it. It was only some time later when she confided to me that this was the very first time that she had had a Christmas tree in her own home. Nor will I forget the look of loving peace on her face when I called in to see her on the evening of Christmas Eve and we ended up singing 'Away in a Manger' together as I tucked her into bed. No consumerism here – unless you count the buying of the little tree and decorations – but a great deal of magic... and love.

It is time to turn away from this frenetic consumer competitiveness and peel back the layers to rediscover the authentic and meaningful realities of this, the oldest and most precious celebration in our human calendar. Time to become aware of the dark and the cold, the land and the solar splendour above our heads; to reach out in celebration of our shared experience of life.

The true relevance of Midwinter is not based upon any individual spiritual or religious belief or practice. It is an observation of planetary movement, which every single living thing on Earth is subject to and reliant upon. In these more uncertain times of global warming and more extreme natural occurrences, we might do well to pay greater attention to what is really going on around us... and why.

Underlying the explanations and suggestions in my book are the concepts of simplicity, personal endeavour, the importance of service to others, the magical properties of mundane actions when approached with the right intention, and the vital importance of realising and reconnecting ourselves to the natural world and the wider rhythms of life. The main message running throughout is that Midwinter/Christmas is not at all what you do, buy, eat or spend, but is an attitude to life.

There is absolutely no reason why ALL people cannot go beyond the boundaries of their faith, belief and practice and extend their hands to one another in a shared experience which goes right to the very root of our life and continued survival on this planet. For them to give of their time and goodwill as we all bear witness to this vital natural phenomenon.

In the Southern Hemisphere, people will be celebrating Midwinter in the middle of our summer, but that doesn't matter – it just means that somewhere on Earth, people are able to focus on hospitality, community, service and love twice within the year instead of just once.

This is no academic pontification, sounding good but baffling everyone as to just how they should try and apply it to their ordinary lives. I am offering suggestions and examples of very down-to-earth, realistic, relevant and simple ways of bringing changes into your life. It is up to *you*.

So this year, look afresh at what Midwinter and Christmas really represent and what they truly mean to you. How can you step back from the commercial jamboree and rediscover – and share – the authentic joyful significance, beauty and relevance of the season?

Remember, Christmas is a state of mind and a way of life, ALL year round.

A merry Midwinter to you all!
With my love.

Gillian Monks

NORTH WALES, 2018

The Approach of Winter

The object of a new year is not that we should have a new year.
It is that we should have a new soul.

G. K. CHESTERTON

IF ONE FOLLOWS the natural cycle of the seasons and relates to the old Celtic calendar, autumn drifts to a close with the falling of the withered leaves on the hillside and road verge, in garden and woodland. This often corresponds with the celebration of Hallowe'en at the end of October. But this over-commercialised pantomime is but a mere pale reflection of the true significance of this time of year. For the Celts, this was *Calan Gaeaf* (in Wales), *Samhain* (in Ireland), *Oidhche Shamhna* (in Scotland), *Oie Houney* (in the Isle of Man) and *Allantide* (in Cornwall), and marked the end of autumn and the beginning of winter. In Britian this is also now when our time changes from British Summer Time and we put our clocks back one hour, giving respite to the rapidly darkening mornings but, fittingly, plunging our early evenings into premature darkness and bringing home to us the fact that winter has truly arrived.

This is the time of year when it is good to slow down, to take stock of all the 'busyness' of the past spring and summer and all that we have accomplished and harvested during the year. Now is the time to think about ourselves; where we have been, where we are now and where we might want to direct ourselves in the future. It is also a time to rest, to draw close to one's family and spend some time by the fireside, if only metaphorically. Humanity can afford to enjoy some breathing space, inner nurturing and regeneration, just as the plants out in the natural world are resting and consolidating their strength for the great explosion of life and growth the following spring.

LOOKING BACK

Hallowe'en! Like many people of her day, my mother was fascinated by the old customs and traditions, coupled with information and practices which had been passed down from generation to generation in the family. As a child she always helped to make Hallowe'en the most magical time for me, when most of my friends at school had never even heard of it, and those who had were reduced to discussing it in excitedly giggled whispers for fear that one of our (convent nun) teachers would overhear – such things were severely frowned upon, derided or outright forbidden back in the early 1960s! This just goes to show how much things have changed in the past half century.

Once home, I could enthusiastically and imaginatively live my dreams. As we then lived by candle and firelight, the darkness, shadows and pools of glowing living light naturally lent themselves to mystery and I populated my young world with friendly dragons and lovable, benign witches.

At the time, we lived in Lancashire, home to the famous Pendle Witches. Being a somewhat intense child, I took the association personally. Now I smile as I remember how my allegiance to the beautiful rural Pendle area continued into my adulthood, when my family and I became members of the Religious Society of Friends (Quakers), knowing that Pendle Hill was where George Fox, who founded Quakerism, first had his revelations and became moved to do so... but that is a story for another day! Suffice to say that certain natural places – lakes, rivers, hills, mountains – have always held special sacred relevance... this is just one of them.

My mother always made me jugs full of hot 'witches' brew', a deliciously warming beverage concocted from various spices, including ginger, and which I never did manage to discover the exact recipe for, or authentically replicate – perhaps because we each include a little of our own personal essence in everything we do. At Hallowe'en we rarely ate a normal meal but instead preferred to sit by the fire devouring basins full of hot buttery creamed potato (which contained a magic bean, a symbol of life which granted the lucky finder a special wish) or bowls of hot 'parched' (maple) peas. I bobbed for apples in a huge tub of water, desperately trying to catch one in my mouth without the cheating use of hands or half drowning in the process!

For the Celtic peoples (as for many other cultures) the apple tree is divinely sacred and is one of the many representations of the divine feminine/goddess. Cut an apple in two horizontally across the core and you will find the shape of a five-pointed star, a venerated feminine symbol.

At this time of year, when it was believed that other realms of life and afterlife draw close and are more easily accessed, it has long been a tradition for women to apply to this feminine energy in their search for a good and compatible mate. Placing an apple underneath one's pillow could bring dreams of a future husband; peeling an apple whilst keeping the coil of peel in one whole piece and then tossing it over one's shoulder might result in it falling to the floor in the shape of the first letter of your love-to-be's name; or if a girl sat eating an apple whilst gazing into a mirror, she might be lucky enough to see her future husband peering over her shoulder.

For the rest of society, it was usual to give gifts of the best apples of the crop to family members – especially children – or revered members of the community. In Cornwall this is still practised in some areas, where they are called Allen apples.

In other areas apples are suspended beneath wooden crosses on which lighted candles have been placed, the trick being to catch an apple using only your mouth and take a bite before hot wax, dripping from the candles, splashes onto your face or gets stuck in your hair. On occasion this practice has been more kindly changed to hanging up a honey-coated bread bun. Swung even gently it can be great fun trying to catch the bun with your mouth... also bearing in mind that bread and honey have their own sacred relevance and importance.

It is traditional to light bonfires on the night of Hallowe'en. My family and I would go out into the dark night and light our bonfire, roast potatoes and chestnuts at the edge in the hot ashes while I danced around the fire with a lit sparkler in each hand. On those occasions the shadows and darkness were always my friends, and yet even then, I sensed that there was something far more profound buried within them, away from the comforting warmth and light of the flames. Older, and hopefully wiser, I now know so much more about the true significance of this unique event which, love it or loathe it, still resonates so deeply within each one of us and our cultural psyche.

Nainie's* Recipe for Treacle Toffee

Particularly good for passing around a bonfire on a chilly late autumn evening or keeping in a coat pocket for any time you are out walking.

Gillian

INGREDIENTS:

3 tablespoons treacle

3 oz (85 g) sugar

2 oz (55 g) butter

1 good pinch of salt

'Clutter'† of vinegar

---

* 'Nainie' is the Welsh word for 'Granny'.

† The use of this word caused some debate at the time my mother was taking down family recipes from her mother just after she married in 1949, but I estimate that a 'clutter' probably equates to a dessertspoon of vinegar.

METHOD:

- Mix all ingredients in heavy-bottomed pan, otherwise your toffee might easily stick and burn.
- Bring to boil, stirring all the time and keep boiling briskly without allowing mixture to burn.
- Cook for about ten minutes. You can test toffee mixture any time you want – drop a little mixture in a cup of cold water; when brittle it is cooked.
- Pour into a flat, greased tray and, when cool enough, cut into squares and roll in castor sugar to prevent them sticking together.

THE ANCESTOR TREE

As the year turns and autumn dies away and winter settles darkly around us, it is good to remember our ancestors with love and thankfulness; not just the people who have passed on in the previous twelve months, or even our well-remembered friends and family from earlier times, but all our ancestors... all those who have gone before us and who (for good or ill) have helped to shape us and the world in which we live.

Following Celtic tradition, as the old year breathes its last gasps and passes away and a resting time creeps upon us through the lengthening shadows, the barriers of time and place begin to shift and dissolve and the veils which separate the different worlds and energetic levels of existence thin and temporarily melt away. This allows us to remember more clearly and for those who have gone before to draw close to us again and, if we allow ourselves to be truly open to them, also to our new friends and experiences and the inspiring and stimulating wonders of our potential future. It is from this that we draw the significance of remembering and respecting the dead and looking into or intuiting our futures; unfortunately it is also how we have developed the erroneous preoccupation with zombies, blood and horror.

Some time during the last week in October, I sally forth into the garden, or out onto our land, to ask which tree is prepared to donate one of its smaller branches to us for our *Calan Gaeaf*/Hallowe'en celebrations. Usually I choose a branch from one of our own elder trees, traditionally known as one of the 'wise mothers' of the tree world. I am looking for a small twiggy branch, between two and three feet tall, bare of any leaves – or nearly so – to set up in a decorative pot of sand or clean damp earth. On this we hang photos of our past family members and ancestors, usually photocopies so that the precious and often irreplaceable originals don't run the risk of getting damaged, which also means that we can cut them to size and shape as the fancy takes us. To these I add autumn leaves, ones which have dried out and turned beautiful shades of brown, red and gold, or pretty synthetic (but lifelike!) leaves made from silk, glass or wood which can sometimes be found among the Christmas decorations in shops and garden centres. If we wish to remember a person but have no picture of them, we simply write their name on one of the leaves.

Another little decorative touch is to make little paper tissue 'ghosts' to hang on the tree. They are very easy but effective – something which even quite small children can have a go at making and which underline the feeling of other-worldliness at this time.

How to Make Paper Tissue Ghosts

YOU WILL NEED:

Box of paper tissues

Black felt-tip pen

White or coloured thread

TO MAKE:

- Scrunch a tissue into a ball.
- Place the ball in the centre of a second tissue.
- Draw the second tissue tight around the first balled tissue, folding it down to make a smooth surface and leaving the ends open for the bottom of the ghost.
- Tie a length of thread tightly around the top third of the tissue ball to form a head with the thread around the neck, leaving enough spare length to tie in a loop with which to hang your ghost up by.
- Mark eyes / other features on face with black pen.
- Repeat as many times as you wish!

These little 'ghosts' are very easy and quick to make and are effective and appealing decorations to hang in windows, doorways and on the Ancestor Tree.

The Ancestor Tree stands upon our hall table, which is covered with a thick, protective orange cloth. We also add candles of orange and black in shiny brass holders. These are lit each evening over the festive period, renewing the candles afresh as they burn down. We also light incense and each time I pass the photos fluttering from the Tree, I smile and send love and blessings to all our loved ones who have gone before us but who have undoubtedly helped to mould us into what we are today.

Baskets of little red apples or iced fairy cakes and bowls of sweets accompany the Ancestor Tree, waiting for the flurry of children and youngsters who knock at the door to play 'trick or treat'. With anguish I have heard of neighbours who steadfastly refuse to open their doors to anyone who knocks at this time of year. I have to confess to putting hand drawn signs upon the gate encouraging Hallowe'en revellers to approach. I love the laughter and excitement, even though some of the younger children are sometimes a bit fazed by the full-sized skeleton (from my son's medical student days) which we sit on a chair near the front door and arrange to hold the basket of goodies from which the children must choose!

ORGANISED CHAOS

'Hallowe'en – isn't that just an imported commercial gimmick from America?' I am frustrated and saddened by how frequently I am asked this question, or hear it being repeated. The roots of this ancient festival to honour the dead and mark the beginning of winter originate in the dim and distant mists of our prehistory.

Many of us are now familiar with the Mexican Day of the Dead at the beginning of November, when whole families – whole communities –

will decamp to the cemeteries to spend the night beside the graves of their loved ones, quietly and respectfully feasting, sharing, and above all, *remembering*. They are not alone in their beliefs. Rituals that surround the return of dead spirits are to be found in many cultures throughout history. Three thousand years ago the Babylonians set out food for their returning dead at their new year festival. In ancient Egypt, the living lit lamps to guide the dead. In Greece a festival, Anthesteria, was held during the first month of the year and attended by ancestral spirits. The Romans held a nine-day Paternalia to honour the deceased before the new year began. The Lett of Latvia used to entertain the dead for four weeks at year's end, from 29th September to 28th October. In Sweden, food and drink is still set out for the ancestors.

This ancient custom of receiving and honouring dead ancestors at year's end is still to be found all around the globe, from Burma to Mexico, Germany to Africa, and was continued by the Catholic church in All Souls' day at the beginning of November. All these festivals reflect a mixture of welcoming anticipation and anxious dread. Society generally held the opinion that if their forebears were convinced that they were being sufficiently honoured, the dead would bless the family, tribe or nation and return peacefully to their graves. But if they were offended, they might curse their descendants and wreak all manner of frightening punishments upon them.

The universal honouring of ancestors was so important that some scholars believe that the origin of mumming (a type of short miracle play, further explained in 'The Twelve Days', page 272) – and of religion itself – is found in ancestor worship. Some support for the connection with mumming comes from Sicily, where the dead were considered the Christmas gift-givers. On the night of 1st November, old year's end, the dead supposedly left their graves, stole gifts from the rich shopkeepers, traders and merchants and redistributed them to their relatives.

Here in the Celtic lands of the British Isles, similar beliefs and activities are inherent in our culture – indeed, in our very genetics. From time immemorial people have dressed up, disguising themselves as ghouls and ghosts in order to confuse the real spirits who are said to roam the Earth during this season. It is also a time of orderly (or sometimes, especially in the past, not so orderly!) chaos, with many of the adults (*adults*, mark you, *not* children) of the community indulging in role and gender reversal – men would dress as women and the women would don their menfolk's clothes, landowners would give food and alms to the less fortunate or serve their servants a feast, and employers would work for their own employees.

To literally illustrate the opening of the barriers between the worlds at this time, it is traditional to open all doors and gates, and sometimes to take the gates away altogether and even hide them. When we first came to this village some thirty years ago now, the neighbours were outraged because the local youths had taken down the big six-foot-high metal gates to the coal yard and hidden them nearby. A naughty prank? A wicked act of vandalism? Or perhaps a more deeply embedded genetic memory?

Parkin

A delicious and sustaining tray-bake for any time throughout the winter.

Gillian

INGREDIENTS:	COST IN 1985
1 lb (450 g) wholemeal flour	12½p
(or fine oatmeal)	(or 25p if fine oatmeal)
½ lb (225 g) pinhead oatmeal	12½p
1 lb (450 g) sugar	24p
¾ lb (340 g) molasses	9p
6 oz (170 g) lard	15p
2 teaspoons ground ginger	4p
4 teaspoons baking powder	2p
Pinch of salt	1p

METHOD:

- Mix flour, oatmeal, baking powder, salt and ginger in a bowl.
- Rub in fat.
- Add sugar and molasses – treacle may be used instead but won't produce such a strong flavour and will be sweeter – and enough water to make a fairly stiff dropping consistency.
- Grease and line the bottom of a roasting tin.
- Place mixture in tin, smooth top, and bake in a moderate oven – 180°C / 350°F / Gas Mark 4 – for an hour. May still feel quite soft to the touch but try inserting a metal skewer and if it comes out clean it is cooked.

Usually, half the enjoyment of anything is in the preparation and providing for others... the baking of the cakes, boiling of sweets, the decoration and surprise. Personally, I still receive the most satisfaction from the darkness and shadows, the stillness and silence both within and without which sit at the very heart of the spinning life force we find even within the double helix of our very DNA. The sitting with the Ancestors... the lighting of candles and giving of blessings... walking or sitting in the woods watching the withering leaves drift to earth as the light fades and dies, or sitting beside a blaze of logs, scorching on one side and steadily freezing on the other in the chill night air, telling stories of those who have gone from us, sharing remembrances, toasting marshmallows and sipping hot spicy mulled wine, fermented from our own elderberries, brambles or damsons. For we *always* have a bonfire. *Calan Gaeaf* is one of the main ancient fire festivals of the year, after all!

There is still the dangerous, untamed, unstoppable element to the celebration too... faint echoes of far distant days when the Wild Man would tramp the land, sometimes in the form of a horned god galloping across the sky with his hounds of hell, sometimes as a shambling, hairy creature carrying a stick or whip and ringing a bell or bells – ah, possibly our first sighting of the true Father Christmas? In this part of the world, the goddess *Cerridwen* is firmly in charge, with her terrifying tailless black sow, *Hwch Ddu Gwta*, which, if you are unlucky enough to be spotted, will reputedly pursue you and if caught will gobble you up or carry you off to be plunged into the goddess's amazing cauldron of death and rebirth, endings and new beginnings, rest and rejuvenation (the boar – or sow – is both a symbol of fertility and an agent of death and resurrection in many mythologies).

For this time of year is when we first turn away from the activity of the light, sunny growing cycle of the spring and summer months; everything in the natural world that grows or gives birth has come to fruition and been harvested and now the time for wilting, fading and dying back into the earth begins in earnest as the life force descends into darkness and temporary death. It's a time of assessment of what has gone before, of stillness, healing and recuperation, of introspection and the first stirrings of possibilities for the coming new year. As the world of flora and fauna retreats back into the earth or withdraws into hibernation, so we too should seize this opportunity to take stock of our lives, our achievements and failures, our aspirations and new challenges.

But as well as all the inner work there is still the outer chaos to contend with, which can produce much laughter, fun, teasing and a recognised licence to push the boundaries of what is normally acceptable and allowed. Hence the evening of 31st October will often see my son donning his great black cloak and tricorn hat to answer the door when the children knock, and my shy, retiring husband running round our front garden to leap out with a flashing lantern or torches at any unsuspecting trick-or-treaters. One of the problems is that the youngsters of today don't expect anyone else (especially the older and supposedly more mature) to actually join in!

For me, Hallowe'en, *Calan Gaeaf*, is not just the start of winter, it is also the start of Christmas. In the way of the natural world, I like things to come and go gradually. As November gets underway, the pictures are taken off the Ancestor Tree and then each day I remove two or three of the leaves until the tree is left quite bare, exactly like all the trees outside, and so it will wait until mid-December, when it will take on new significance and a new lease of life. Sometimes I paint it partially white or silver to mimic frost and snow; other times I leave it just as it is, for we don't always have such cold and frosty weather over Christmas, despite what the carol singers tell us! By the middle of Advent (which is the period of time covering the last four Sundays before Christmas), I hang sparkly decorations upon it – white or silver balls, birds and icicles – and last year, my son added a little set of dainty silver fairy lights. This is our little winter branch, left by the door to guide and welcome the spirits of winter to our home.

PAGAN OR PATRIOT?

We don't usually celebrate Guy Fawkes night. The Gunpowder Plot and the subsequent capture of the desperate Fawkes must have been a god-send to the church authorities of the day, as it gave them an excellent opportunity to shift the public focus from bonfires celebrating ancient rites and beliefs at the end of October to the far more laudable fires a week later in commemoration of the foiling of a dastardly plot.

As a child, my mother didn't wish me to miss out – any excuse for a party! Whether it was for Hallowe'en, Guy Fawkes, my birthday, or all three, she would organise and host huge social get-togethers at our house for anywhere up to sixty people. I adored Hallowe'en but didn't enjoy Bonfire Night – the noise of the fireworks frightened me and I would often remain in the cottage, watching from the dining-room window with my hands clamped firmly over my ears until they had fin-ished, after which I would joyfully run out to join my friends around the colossal fire, the plates of steaming hot potato pie topped with home-pickled red cabbage or beetroot, with dishes of trifle, dark, moist parkin and sticky handfuls of treacle toffee or toffee apples for pudding. Sometimes we even played the traditional Hallowe'en games, like bobbing for apples, on Guy Fawkes night too – my practical mother maintained that getting all the children half drowned and totally wet was an excellent way of cleaning off all the toffee!

COMMENT FROM JOAN: OCTOBER 1959

I rather think that I will have to paint some more acorns, cups and fir cones if I wish to present each member of the Historical Society with a cluster broach to wear when they come to the Hallowe'en-cum-Bonfire party next Saturday. Last Sunday Jim built quite a substantial wooden and rubber tyer framework for the bonfire – paper, cardboard, etc. can be added later. Of course we will have to repeat the performance on 5th November with Jim asking Jerry and his family down. I certainly hope that it is better weather than last Saturday!

ANOTHER YEAR OLDER

The next event on my personal winter festival calendar is the celebration of my birthday, which occurs just after Bonfire Night at the end of the first week in November. From choice, this has taken the same format for the past ten years or so.

First and foremost, it is a day which is always spent with my beloved family. To begin, a long, lazy, *late* breakfast around the living-room table in the cosy warmth of the aga; and something especially tasty to eat like kippers, crispy bacon or smoked mackerel, accompanied by hot crusty home-made rolls and jams and preserves and seemingly endless pots of freshly ground steaming coffee. Sometimes I open my birthday cards at this stage – other years, I wait until teatime, or even the evening when it is quieter. Then we all go off to our local garden centre, which by this date has assembled and opened its annual display of Christmas decorations.

I never cease to be entranced by the overwhelming displays of baubles, balls, dolls, snowmen, elves, Santas, nutcrackers, fairies, birds, deer, bears, bells, ribbons, bows, synthetic greenery, twinkly lights and garlands of tinsel! Our garden centre always has Father Christmas (*Siôn Corn* in Welsh) sitting by a temporary hearth, surrounded by woodland creatures, telling fairy stories. Last year I completely lost my heart to a six-foot-tall animated model of a black bear which was standing nodding and waving from among a small forest of fir trees. Several years ago there were lots of traditional sweets made from coloured glass which I found poignantly reminiscent of the sweets and sugar plums in the Christmas ballet *The Nutcracker* – I am quite sure that if they had been available when I was a child, our tree would have been festooned with them!

One year I was fairly blown away as they had a gorgeous full-sized carriage with a Cinderella of ethereal beauty sitting inside it – the main theme of the display being pantomime stories. *Jack and the Beanstalk*, *Mother Goose*, *Aladdin* and others were also represented. If I had been a child, I probably wouldn't have slept that night from utter wonderment and would have insisted on visiting the display many more times in the lead up to Christmas.

Despite their consumer connotations these displays enchant me... re-enchant me... refocus my heart, mind and soul on all that Christmas truly is. I *buy* very little, but I use it to inspire me. It sets my mind thinking of how I wish to manifest our Midwinter celebrations this time around. I have even been known to sit down afterwards and write out my Christmas dinner menus and shopping list! But it also helps me to reaffirm my love and appreciation for what I already possess, and to know just how very lucky I am. We 'Ooooh!' and 'Aaaah!' over everything, choosing only a handful of shiny, glittering, twinkling enchantments to take home with us.

For me it is about the promise of other wonderful times that the displays bring to mind – the real bonus is all the ideas and potential uses that the wealth of decorations suggests, and not just for Christmas time either. There are always a small proportion of items which can be utilised for other things besides Christmas decorations, or used at other times of the year, like the gauze 'autumnal leaves' on the Ancestor Tree at Hallowe'en. I have found dainty bunches of very realistic silk snowdrops, creamy-headed silk roses and other flowers which have gone into posy bowls and vases at various times throughout all the seasons, and garlands and accessories which have helped to decorate rooms and doorways at other times of the year. For although I love natural living things around me, I also hate to see them fade and die in our warm airless rooms, away from the cool moist earth and fresh dampness which gave them life.

It is well worth carefully scrutinising the burgeoning displays as there are always items that can be utilised at other times of the year. Silk flowers for decorating head wreaths, birthday chairs, tables at summer garden parties or sales of work – even the dinner or tea table. Masks for the dressing-up box or village carnival; domino masks for New Year's Eve or that February or Summer Ball. Sprays of leaves in silver or gold to use as hair ornaments or even to re-trim a hat which, with a little tweaking, will make a quirky and unusual accessory to complete a new outfit. Sumptuous tassels and trims to embellish exotic evening wear or even supplement the soft furnishings in your house.

This is not to say that I endorse or in any way encourage a lot of wasteful, mindless buying of 'stuff'! Rather I am trying to maintain a balance between the old and the new and to demonstrate how we can all take the very best from both worlds. There are many beautiful decorations out there which we could not possibly hope to produce for ourselves. I wish to aim everyone in the direction of only choosing those things which are made from natural items such as glass, paper, card, silk or other fabrics, wood, etc. and/or which they could not possibly make for themselves.

There are also all manner of craft supplies which appear before Christmas, and it is fun to walk around and become inspired with potential projects and ideas for other times of the year. Things like cake decorating sets, biscuit cutters, fabrics and paints that actually have nothing specifically to do with winter – let alone Christmas – often only appear with the seasonal decorations. One of the things I like to do is to take our new purchases home and share our thoughts and ideas with each other, some items then being carefully put away for another time and others making an immediate appearance. There are, after all, an amazing amount of decorations these days which have nothing speci- fically to do with Christmas but everything to do with all four seasons including winter. So when you next go to a shop, store or garden nursery selling things for Christmas, don't just think '25th December' – think 'all year round'!

When we have all explored to our heart's content, we retreat to the restaurant, find a space in the area with comfy chairs near to the warm- ing stove, and order a full afternoon tea – three-tiered perfection in the form of savoury nibbles and sandwiches, pastries, iced fancies, clotted cream and chocolate, and not forgetting that most quintessential ingre- dient, lots of cups of piping hot tea!

Little Pleasures

Dark, dark days, November and December,
The dying time of year so pale and grey and still.

'WINTER SOLSTICE', G. MONKS

I ALWAYS THINK that the most important aspect of any event or celebration is the anticipation and enjoyment of dreaming, planning and
preparing. But once the stress of approaching dates and deadlines kicks
in and corners have to be cut because you no longer have sufficient time
or energy to do what you originally intended, excitement and pleasure
can rapidly turn to pressure and chores and everything begins to sour
and spoil. Many people fall into the perennial trap of thinking that they
have lots of time to make, bake and shop and then suddenly come to the
realisation that the time has gone, there are only a few days left and they
are unceremoniously plunged into a frenzy of panic and ill-considered

actions. We *all* do it at some time or other – some more predictably and frequently than others. It only results in ruining any fun or satisfaction and often leaves the person in question feeling resentful and bitterly disappointed.

One thing that is *really* easy to make well in advance is the mincemeat. I make ours when the apples have been harvested in late September or early October. Stored in an airtight container or screw-topped jars in a cool dark place it will keep for at least one year.

Mincemeat

INGREDIENTS:

3 lb (1.3 kg) raisins

1½ lb (680 g) currants

1½ lb (680 g) sultanas

1½ lb (680 g) apples

¾ lb (340 g) chopped suet*

1½ tablespoons mixed spice

3 lb (1.3 kg) sugar

6 lemons

---

* Suet may be left out – this does not detract from the taste and makes the recipe vegetarian / vegan friendly.

METHOD:

- Mince raisins, currants, sultanas, apples and suet.
- Grate rind from lemons and squeeze juice.
- Mix well.
- Put all ingredients together in a large crock and stand one month before using.
- Any spirits or home-made wines may be added in a quantity not to make mixture too wet.
- Mince pies should always be oval in shape to represent the manger.

Be realistic about what you have time to achieve. Better to decide to eat more simply, party less and give less flamboyantly, but do so happily with good grace and temper intact! If you were planning a wedding, there is simply no way that you would leave it until the week before to write and send out your invitations, buy your dress, suit or outfit and choose gifts for the bridesmaids and best man, let alone book the venue or start thinking what to have on the menu. Christmas is no different. Try to aim to complete as much preparation as possible when you absolutely do not *have* to. If you feel that you have no choice in the matter then you are already late and your pleasure is dwindling with every tick of the clock.

Some of your preparations can be carried out much earlier in the year. For instance, in summer I like to candy citrus peel to chop up and use in the making of my mincemeat and Christmas cake. Home-candied peel bears no resemblance to the hard dry stuff that can be bought in the supermarkets. It is not difficult to do – it just takes about ten days to complete, with one simple process lasting a very few minutes every other day. You can use any citrus peel but orange is particularly good, and my very favourite is grapefruit, which produces thick, luscious peels. How syrupy or dry it eventually ends up simply depends on how long you leave the finished peel drying for. Left moister and cut into pieces or strips and dipped in dark chocolate, it makes an after-dinner treat to die for! Dried until the peel is dry to the touch and stored in an airtight container it will keep for at least twelve months, although ours never lasts that long before it is eaten!

CANDIED PEEL

- Save peel from breakfast grapefruits, squeezed oranges or lemons; make sure that all the pulp is cleaned from the inside of the peels.

- Boil peels anything up to three times, throwing away and covering with fresh water in between each boiling – each boiling should last approximately ten minutes, until the peel is more or less cooked.

- After discarding the third lot of boiling water, make up a syrup of ½ lb (225 g) sugar to ½ pint of water by dissolving sugar in the water over a gentle heat before bringing to the boil – if you have a lot of peels, double or treble the quantity of syrup.

- Place the peel in a bowl and pour over the syrup. Put a saucer or plate over the peels to hold them down in the syrup (the peels must be submerged), then cover the whole with a cloth and leave for 24 hours.

- The process now consists of reboiling the syrup and peels at intervals, the strength gradually being increased as shown in the following table.

DAY	SUGAR TO ADD TO EACH HALF PINT OF SYRUP	SOAK FOR
1	½ lb (225 g) sugar to ½ pint water	24 hours
2	2 oz (56 g) sugar dissolved in syrup and reboiled – I reboil peels for up to 10 minutes each time	24 hours
3	Ditto	24 hours
4	Ditto	24 hours
5	3 oz (85 g) sugar or more dissolved in syrup and reboiled with peel for 3–4 minutes	48 hours
7	Ditto	3–4 days
10-11	Drain peel from syrup and put on rack and dry slowly in a warm place or a very cool oven	

STORAGE: the syrup may be spooned over or into the peels as they dry. They can then be kept in airtight container in cool dry place for 12–24 months.

SYRUP: the syrup cannot be used for more candying or crystallising as the acid from the fruit peels will have altered its character, but it can be strained and kept in an airtight jar, used to pour over ice cream or steamed marmalade pudding, for fruit salads or to replace the sugar in Chorley cakes.

MAKE LISTS

Buy a little notebook or a five-year journal, and use it as a reference tool; jot down all your ideas and lists of things which can then be kept in one place and added to or changed as the year progresses. Of particular relevance to when approaching Midwinter / Christmas are several key areas which it is better to decide upon while you still have plenty of time.

Make lists of people you might wish to send Christmas cards to and people you would like to give presents to – helps avoid forgetting someone and the resultant panic buying.

Don't forget to pick up a list of last posting dates from your local post office or carrier. Buy extra postage stamps, but wait until the Christmas versions are released for sale for that extra festive touch!

Think how, where and when you might like to celebrate; what events you might like to attend and the people you might wish to ask to be with you for them, even who you might like to invite to a party, a drinks evening or Christmas dinner itself, and invite them early on in the autumn to avoid the disappointment of them having already made alternative arrangements!

Make a note of any restaurants or theatre tickets which will need to be booked and get it done in good time.

If you do plan to travel over the winter holidays, check out availability and book tickets and accommodation as early as possible.

Look through your cookery books – or treat yourself to a new one – and decide what you might like to try cooking and baking and think how you might wish to decorate your Christmas cake this year. Make lists of ingredients that you might need to accomplish your goals. Keep an ongoing list of where to find new recipes which you would like to try, or old favourites so that you can easily locate them if you wish to repeat them.

And don't forget:

- Prioritise.
- Ask for help.
- Be realistic about what you aim to achieve.

This next 'Comment from Joan' was compiled back in the early 1990s by my mother who originally set up home on her own when she was only seventeen years old in 1943 and war-time rationing was at its peak – items simply weren't available and she had little money to spend on them even if they had been.

COMMENT FROM JOAN: MAKING THE MOST OF LITTLE,
EARLY 1990S

Christmas can be an expensive time when there is so much extra that we suddenly wish to spend money on. Here is a list of suggestions for those who might need extra kitchen utensils to make all the new recipes you wish to try, or even extras for entertaining, without spending a lot of money that may be needed for other things. The whole object is to enjoy and not get stressed about it!

Pick up free cookery leaflets in supermarkets.

*

Cookery books in charity shops or at jumble sales.

*

Pans, oven dishes (Pyrex, etc.), baking tins from same places.

*

Dishes and extra plates.

*

Hand mincers and other helpful utensils from same sources.

*

Wooden and metal spoons; knives: carving, bread and table;
forks and table spoons from similar sources.

*

Candlesticks to decorate; odd lengths of material
to dress things up – covers, swags, etc.

*

If lacking a pastry board, roll out on table on thick plastic bag;
if no rolling pin can use an empty glass wine bottle.

*

Use pans in lieu of mixing bowls and basins, and well-washed
foil cases from bought pies and takeaways for pies.

*

Use cup as cutter for jam tarts and saucer or plate as pattern
for pastry circle, large or small.

*

Or, cut both ends cleanly from empty metal food tins and use
for cutters of all sizes. Just keep well washed and dried.

WHEN DO YOU BEGIN TO SING?

When I was a little girl, I attended a convent school run by the nuns in the neighbouring town of Leyland. In the mornings, my father would drive me into the main bus station in the centre of Chorley on his way to work from where, along with a whole throng of bottle-green-uniformed youngsters, all bound for the same destination, I would catch an equally green Fishwick's bus. We were serious little individuals, all sparkling tidy with not a hair out of place. Hardly recognisable were the lively tribe who travelled back to Chorley at tea-time, chattering and joking, satchels bulging, hair flying and ties and hats askew.

From the main bus station I would then have to walk across part of town, down into the main street, to catch the C2 town circular bus which ten minutes later would deposit me on the outskirts of town. A few more minutes' walk took me past the rows of individually designed detached houses to the top of our lane, where the houses and tarmacked road simultaneously and abruptly ceased.

From here I had another mile or so to walk, skirting around puddles, balancing along the ridges of ruts, or sloshing expeditiously right through all the mud and water that I could find, satchel banging, Wellingtons flapping. Eventually I reached the top of Rocky Hill, where our lane divided, the left leading away to Bill Green's cottage and Noblett's farm, and the right-hand track dipping between tall hedges as it traversed large stones and rocks – hence its name – off in the direction of the cottages at Primrose Hill and eventually our own dear cottage of Drybones.

It was at Rocky Hill that my mother would come to wait for me, sitting on the stile by the gate. Sometimes she would bring one or more of our dogs (we had six Alsatians at that time), who would be ecstatic with glee to see me again after our interminable separation of at least eight and a half hours and who would come bounding up to me, all bright eyes, pink tongues and damp fur as their greetings nearly bowled me off my feet.

We would all walk home together and at this time of year, our eager exchanges of news of the day would give way to singing. We would start around the middle of October, practising the 'Souling Song' for *Calan Gaeaf*/Hallowe'en/All Souls' day. This traditional song reflects the connection of this time of year to the more modern All Souls' day and the more timeless celebration of death and the dead generally. Until recently, doughy sweet soul cakes were still made and distributed to children on the Gower in South Wales and I am told that this practice is being resurrected and becoming more widely known and popular again.

A soul! a soul! a soulcake, please good Mrs, a soul cake!
An apple, a pear, a plum or a cherry, any good thing to make us merry

As soon as the month changed, this would quickly give way to Christmas carols. On we would march through the fast-failing light of the short winter's afternoon. Among my favourite carols for tramping home to was 'In the Deep Midwinter', which we could easily identify with, especially the bits about frosty winds moaning, earth as hard as iron and water like a stone, descriptive words which have held their personal significance for me ever since. Both my mother and I loved 'The Holly and the Ivy' and I innocently imagined that it must have been written about our own magical ancient woods. 'The Twelve Days of Christmas' was brisk, repetitive fun and saw us well on our way; 'The Wassail Song' also encouraged a quick march, while 'Good King Wenceslas' held more personal relevance for me, especially in bad weather when trudging through the biting wind and lashing rain, my heart might temporarily fail me too... I knew something about the night growing darker and the wind growing stronger and felt great affinity with the page, 'marking' King Wenceslas's footsteps, as I myself stepped carefully and exactly where my own mother had gone first, albeit frequently through the mud, but sometimes also in snow.

Upon reaching the cottage, and having divested ourselves of coats, boots, gloves, scarves, woolly hats and any other extra garment useful in keeping the cold and wet at bay, I washed my hands and face and then went through into the warm shadowy kitchen where tea was waiting for me.

Currently the family usually begin to notice me humming tunes to carols – if not openly singing the words – any time onwards from the Summer Solstice in June. I do try to curb the tendency, but it is difficult when some of the melodies are actually among my favourite music, regardless of their seasonal connotations. 'Joy to the World!' is amazingly stirring, as is 'Ding Dong Merrily on High' and 'Deck the Halls'... 'Please to See the King', 'The Cherry Tree Carol' and 'The Gloucester Wassail' are wonderfully earthy and full of life... the 'Coventry Carol' and 'O Come, O Come, Emmanuel' hauntingly beautiful. When my uncle was a small child he was so passionately fond of 'Once in Royal David's City' that my grandmother would sing it to him as a lullaby all year round.

And when do we, as a family, 'officially' begin to sing Christmas carols? On the return journey home from seeing the display of Christmas decorations at the Fron Goch garden centre on my birthday, of course! Now why shouldn't that surprise you?

CHRISTMAS CARDS AND 'ROUND ROBINS'

'Oh, I don't send cards at Christmas any more. It costs so much these days, and think of the environment!'

I have always had a lengthy list of friends and family to send cards to at Christmas, even when I was a little girl. Every year I make out a fresh list and carefully appraise at least some of the names there. But then I ask myself what I would do and say to any of these people if I came face to face with them – even slight acquaintances. Would I stare stonily ahead, ignore them, walk briskly by? My answer to myself is always the same. I would beam a joyful smile, give them a very cheery seasonal greeting and enfold them in a warm hug... and genuinely mean it. I would hardly do less for a total stranger on the street at this particular time of year! So why wouldn't I treat a loved one like that? Thus my list of recipients might vary for other, natural reasons, but no, it never gets any shorter.

First and foremost, although they are largely referred to as 'Christmas' cards, please remember that these are now more widely seen as non-denominational and non-religious; it's more a case of them being greetings cards for the season generally.

Decide who you might want to send cards to and write a list. Go through your address book (and if you don't have one then acquire one and *use* it) so that you don't leave someone out. Do this earlier in the autumn; then you are aware of roughly how many cards you may need and can keep an eye out for ones that you really like – the picture on the front is part of your message. It might be lovely to be honoured with a large sumptuous card with lots of gold on it, but it is more important for your communication to be meaningful, with a picture that you know will amuse or touch the recipient and a message inside it to match – then the size and quality becomes irrelevant, for it is the thought and meaning that it represents that matters so much. One year I made about fifteen of my own cards – small pastel depictions of the Midwinter sunrise – to send to friends who I knew would understand and appreciate what it meant to us both. I put time and effort into each one and thought deeply about each person that I was making the card for as I did so. Such thoughts are also a part of your underlying message.

Write your cards with authentic messages from your heart, really meaning what you say. You don't even have to send a card – write a kind or loving letter or note on plain paper.

But whatever form of communication you choose, stop and hold it for a moment; imbue it with your love before pushing it into its envelope. Thoughts and words (written or spoken) have a real energy all of their own, even though it can't be seen with the naked eye.

If you really aren't bothered about sending a nice message to a neighbour, work colleague or even an annoying family member, then *don't*! But perhaps it is better to cast aside your emotional grievances and extend the true message of Midwinter, which is that of unconditional love, and write something which you might (surprisingly – hopefully) really end up meaning.

The same applies if you subscribe to the inclusion of the ubiquitous 'round robin' newsletter. Don't groan! I think that they are wonderful and I love both writing and receiving mine. But as with everything, it isn't just what you do, it is the manner in which you do it that can make all the difference. I have always been a prolific letter writer but these days, like many other people, I don't have as much time to sit down and write. Therefore, towards the end of the year it is wonderful to be able to pour out all my news – and my feelings – to my dear ones. I try not to hold back. If I have had a good year I rejoice in sharing my good fortune with my friends. If I have had a terrible time, I gently let everyone know, but also try to balance my negative news with positive perspectives for the future. If I am sharing news about an event or person which might be of great relevance to some readers but not to others, I include a short sentence saying so, and perhaps also a brief explanation. I try to make my messages as genuine as possible, but I also try to include detail, humour and reality.

In a perfect world it would be lovely to be able to send out beautifully handwritten, personal letters, but it would take me so long that I would never achieve it – forty or fifty letters of 2,500–3,000 words each would be a colossal and daunting task. But as with writing the actual cards, while I am typing my letter I bring to mind as many of the people that I am addressing as possible. I also scribble (literally – you haven't seen my handwriting – another reason why I type these days!) personal messages somewhere on my duplicated letter.

I have heard many criticisms of 'round robin' messages; that they are nothing more than opportunities for people to show off, announce to the world how well they are doing, how clever and beautiful their children are, what fantastic long-haul holidays they have recently enjoyed. If you receive a letter like that, then see it for what it really is – a document written by someone who is so unsure of themselves that they need to feel everyone's approbation, or who has worked incredibly hard and is looking for some recognition of their achievements – and be generous and give them a little of what they crave... after all, it is the season of gifts.

The most important thing to remember is to absolutely mean what you think, write and do – and that applies to more than just writing cards or letters. As I said earlier, thoughts and words have a life of their own, an energetic resonance as real as any physical action, so make sure each thought and action comes straight from your heart for, be under no illusion, it will find its mark.

You might like to visualise all your seasonal messages zooming across the landscape, trailing fine red lines of loving connection between you and your dear ones. But you are just one person. Consider what the Earth would look like if *everyone* who sends out Midwinter cards posted them off with the same depth of loving intention. The Earth would resemble a great entwined ball of soft wool made up of love. Isn't this what Christmas is supposed to be all about? On an invisible energetic level, the whole world would be bathed in good wishes and love. How healing for the whole planet – not just for humanity but for everything, animate and inanimate!

I began by quoting what I have heard many people saying about not writing cards any more. This would be part of my reply to them. What price do they put on tangible world-wide goodwill? As for using the Earth's resources, you can buy cards made only from recycled paper or using sustainably sourced and managed trees. And you can then recycle them again after the Midwinter season has passed. I keep the very best in my journal, either the pictures I like best (which I sometimes put up on my bedroom wall to look at all through the year) or the precious messages that mean the very most to me. The rest I sort and cut into attractive seasonal gift tags to use on the next season's presents. Whatever bits are left after all that I recycle. No waste.

If people do not appreciate or understand your efforts that is their loss. You will have done your best in attempting to be genuinely loving, giving and authentic.

THE POST BOX

Throughout Advent, as my mother and I sat by the fire after tea, sewing, writing and listening to the radio together, I would make my Christmas cards. Sometimes I was given packs of line drawings to colour in with watercolour paints or my best Lakeland crayons. Mostly they were my own creations, given extra detail with coloured paper doilies and shiny paper saved from sweet wrappers. Back in the early 1960s you kept and used whatever you could. There was very little available then – no super craft shops in which to pick and choose. You had to use a lot of ingenuity, invention and imagination... no bad thing, I think! I even made all my own gift tags, using stencils for speed. But I never went as far as to print my own wrapping paper; that would have seemed far too laborious, patient though I was.

Nearer to Christmas came the writing of the cards. Sitting on a smaller chair at one side of the kitchen fire, I would nobly endeavour to make much of my comparatively few, while sitting at the little round table at the opposite side of the fire, my mother would rapidly and efficiently work her way down her amazingly long list as the piles of completed white envelopes grew. Those with red, blue and white edging or blue air-mail stickers were to be posted first to South America, the USA, Canada, Greece and Sri Lanka, while those that were being sent to more local destinations could wait until nearer the day.

Sometimes my mother would write – and receive – in excess of 200 cards, for she was a gregarious woman with many friends and acquaintances as well as business associates and family. We used to put them all up too, strung on ribbons and looped across the walls and along the black oak beams, or pinned behind the doors. Anyone visiting at other times of the year could be forgiven for thinking that we had developed a bad dose of woodworm in the backs of the downstairs doors, when in reality, it was the hundreds of holes left by all the drawing pins! I was allowed to put my cards behind the front door, but they rarely ever filled it, whereas my mother's spilled over everywhere and the latecomers would, in desperation, be relegated to a large flat basket.

Now, as a family, we have a 'post box' – a cardboard box simply covered with Christmas paper and with a slit cut out of the top of one side. I originally made it for my son when he was little and it is currently in its twenty-sixth year... same box with original paper! We stand it on top of a low cupboard in the hall. As soon as we begin to receive Christmas cards, rather than opening them willy-nilly as they arrive in dribs and drabs throughout the three or four weeks before Midwinter / Christmas, we pop them all into the post box. Late afternoon on 22nd or 23rd December, or even on Christmas Eve itself, the family comes together and while we enjoy tea by the fire we open the box of cards, taking it in turn to open each envelope and read the messages and letters aloud so that we all share in the goodwill and news.

Afterwards I attach the cards to lengths of broad ribbon which I hang in the hall from ceiling to floor. Often there are many lengths of ribbon to put up and the hall becomes a bower of bright pictures. Every time I walk through the room I am overwhelmed by the feeling of warmth and love which emanates from all those beautiful messages, connected to all my dear ones, and feel very truly blessed.

BY YOUR OWN HANDS

All of the above applies to making your own gifts too. I will look at this topic in more detail in 'Sacrifice, Service... and Shopping' (page 88), but for now let me just say that if you wish to make something to give, try to leave yourself enough time in which to do it... time when you feel inspired to make and give, not when you are stressed, rushed and desperate! Making can be done throughout the year and your creations can be put away in protective packaging until they are needed.

Whatever you make, whether it be food, clothes, decorations, gifts, cards or entertainment, there is something undeniably sweeter, more potent and infinitely more satisfying about a personally crafted and produced object than something that is impersonally manufactured. It is also absolutely unique because it contains a minute amount of you: your personality, your thought, time and effort, your very essence and energy. No amount of wealth, riches and expertise can be better than that.

But don't try and do too much! Better to decide to make one or two gifts than start out too ambitiously, scare yourself silly in the process and not actually make anything. Better to make *one* evergreen decoration and really enjoy and appreciate it than aim to dress your entire house like a woodland bower and never even put up a single leaf or twig.

First of all, aim to do what *you* want – then at least one person will be satisfied. Try to steer away from what you feel you ought to do. Then consider what you might like to have but either cannot find in the shops or couldn't afford to buy if you did. 'Home-made' is often used as a euphemism for 'amateurish', when in reality the standard of the result is often far superior to anything you can pay someone else to do (in other words, buy through a retail outlet).

GOING CRACKERS!

One such item which instantly springs to mind is Christmas crackers. They are not difficult to make or necessarily expensive to produce (depending on what paper, decorations and gifts you might like to include), but they are infinitely more satisfying for everyone to pull. And they can be personalised so that each person gets an appropriate present in his or her cracker. You may also wish to include mottoes or quotations, and again these may be tailored appropriately to your guests or the person who is going to read it. It is easy to unobtrusively mark each cracker with an initial or even a name.

You don't have to bear the whole brunt of choosing or paying for everything either. Get a family member to volunteer to be responsible for filling the crackers. Also bear in mind that if you don't have the time or ability to make your own crackers, you can always buy some and carefully open one end of each cracker to insert your own better quality contents!

It is also possible to make the main body of your crackers and leave one end open so that you may fill them with personalised gifts, jokes, hats or mottoes nearer Christmas when you know definitely who will be joining you for dinner. Again, store partly made crackers in a good strong cardboard box so that they don't become damaged and tired-looking in the meantime. And it is a good idea to have a couple of spare crackers in case you get last-minute unexpected visitors joining you.

Of course, if you make your own crackers you can use them at any time of the year – birthdays, Easter, weddings, anniversaries – either as more trivial table decorations or as a way of giving quite considerable gifts. Use pretty floral gift wrapping and decorate with silk flowers, or they may be colour-themed to tie in with the rest of your table/room decorations. The gifts may likewise be themed so they are all related to a specific age, anniversary or sporting event. The options are limitless.

How to Make Christmas Crackers

YOU WILL NEED:

Crepe paper – one colour or a selection of green, red, blue, yellow etc.

Thin cardboard

Coloured or shiny paper

Coloured cotton or ribbon

Pictures or little decorations

Tiny gifts or wrapped sweets, mottoes or jokes and / or paper hats

'Cracks' – can be bought at larger hobby shops

Scissors, glue, cellotape

Two tubular containers, one slightly smaller in diameter than the
   other (sweetie tubes, empty drinks cans, etc. can be used)

TO MAKE:

- Cut a rectangle of coloured crepe paper 8" wide by 12" long.
- Cut the 8" edges into a zigzag pattern.
- Cut two thin strips of coloured paper, 8" long and ½" wide, and glue
  them on the crepe paper about ½" below the zigzags at top and
  bottom. Turn the crepe paper over so that the inside is facing you.
- Cut a strip of card 8" long by 5½" wide, with the longer edge
  horizontal. Attach a 'crack' to the cardboard with a short piece of
  sticky tape so that it is aligned with the 5½" side of the card, about
  1" from one edge. It should stick out above and below the card.
- Lay the card with the 'crack' uppermost in the middle of the crepe
  paper. Place the larger tube on top of the card and roll everything
  round so that the decorated crepe paper is now on the outside,

with the 'crack' and card inside it and the tube inside that, holding the shape. Secure the crepe paper firmly with sticky tape.

- Insert the smaller tube into one end of the cracker, so that it holds the end of the cracker open. Tie a piece of cotton or ribbon firmly around the crepe paper between the two tubes, drawing it tight. Carefully remove both tubes.
- Fill the centre of the cracker with gift, joke motto, hat etc.
- Gently push the smaller tube into the unsealed end of cracker and firmly tie it tightly to match the other end. Remove the tube.
- Finally, glue small Christmas decorations onto the main body of the cracker, on the opposite side from the join.

NOTE: *Numerous variations on these basic instructions can be made. Crackers need not just be for Christmas. Using different colour themes and paper doilies, ribbons or lace, beautiful crackers can be made for birthday or anniversary celebrations. Cotton-wool chicks, silk flowers or tiny eggs transform crackers into Easter decorations. Red hearts make a Valentine 'card' or 'gift box' with a difference. Please note that if pulled by themselves, the 'cracks' can burn or damage eyes – adult supervision advised.*

BY CANDLELIGHT

After I had got in from school and we had eaten our tea, there then followed one or two precious hours when my mother (having already prepared the evening meal earlier in the day) would be free to spend what is now termed 'quality time' with me. And what quality time it was... the best!

This was the time when we would talk and plan our Christmas. My mother would lift down her ancient volumes of Charles Dickens and, sitting at the little three-legged table, by the light of one of the tall brass candlesticks, she would read evocative, touching, funny passages aloud to me to get us into the spirit of things: extracts from *The Cricket on the Hearth*, 'Christmas at Dingley Dell' from *The Pickwick Papers* and *A Christmas Carol* were favourites.

It was here at the little table before the fire that my mother first taught me how to make Christmas crackers – although she made crackers to pull for many other occasions throughout the year too. They were usually constructed from red crepe paper, without the definitive 'cracks' in them as when I was little I had a horror of bangs and loud noises. They were beautifully and ingeniously decorated and always filled with good mottoes and jokes, and proper little gifts. My mother also made the crepe paper hats that were folded up inside the bulging crackers, sewing the seams on her treadle Singer sewing machine and allowing me to decorate them afterwards. Crowns of every shape, size and design were favourites, sometimes so large and ornate that they wouldn't actually fit inside the crackers at all and would have to be distributed separately as everyone sat down to dinner or tea.

A really popular charity contribution were the huge single crackers that my mother would sometimes make, about two and a half to three feet long, constructed with several 'cracks' and filled with dozens of individual toys, to be raffled off or donated to a children's home or hospital ward. One can only imagine the wonder and excitement of the poorly children who received such a treat!

Slowly Building the Magic

Walls for the wind, and a roof for the rain, and drinks beside the fire,
Laughter to cheer you, and those you love near you, and all that
your heart may desire.

IRISH BLESSING

THESE DAYS I hear constant reference to the 'Big Day', meaning Christmas Day on the 25th of December. Apart from the fact that there is much more to Christmas than just one day (even in the Christian church), it is obviously courting disaster to place so much emphasis on a single event. Other days of almost equal importance are the Winter Solstice, Christmas Eve, Boxing Day, New Year's Eve, New Year's Day and Epiphany or Twelfth Night.

What people often fail to realise is that a lot of the pleasure is in the *anticipation*. Build the excitement and expected pleasure *slowly*. There is no reason not to also have a lot of fun in doing so along the way! Making and taking pleasure in smaller – and possibly quite trivial – occasions in the weeks and even months before Midwinter spreads the excitement and anticipation, diffusing some of the huge expectations placed upon 'The Day' and engendering a great deal of extra pleasure in the process. In other words, you can have a lot of fun while preparing and waiting for the main event.

I am not just referring to Advent either, which I will be looking at in another chapter. Like Hallowe'en and Bonfire Night, which occur in the month before Advent, there are lots of other occasions that are good to celebrate and enjoy which can be pleasurable in their own right and even temporarily remove the focus on Christmas altogether... at least for a short while. For throughout November and twice in the first half of December there are a number of saints' days (some of which, like Christmas itself, have other more ancient origins) which are good to mark and celebrate; there is also the festival of Diwali and Thanksgiving day. As there are at least eight separate occasions I am not suggesting that you try and celebrate them all – perhaps just two or three different ones each year so that you can ring the changes, keep it fresh, and not get bogged down in yet more weighty 'tradition'.

FESTIVAL OF DIWALI

This five-day festival is immensely popular and falls around the end of October or beginning of November, though the date changes every year. The festival of lights falls on the third day of the celebrations, which is set to coincide with the new moon and the fifteenth day of the Hindu month *Kartik*. This is the highlight of the festival, when many in India throw open all their doors and windows and light lamps to allow *Lakshmi*, the goddess of good luck and fortune, to find her way into their homes, which have been thoroughly cleaned and renovated beforehand and are then decorated with *Rangoli* artwork – patterns and designs made from coloured rice powder and flowers drawn upon the floor.

At this time Hindus, Jains and Sikhs celebrate the triumph of good over evil, hope over despair and knowledge over ignorance. People dress in new clothes, paint henna patterns on their hands, light many candles and lamps and participate in family prayers, followed by a grand feast. Music and dance performances take place and activities such as yoga are entered into. Little gifts may also be given.

SAINT CECILIA'S DAY: 22ND NOVEMBER

Cecilia was a noblewoman of Rome in the second century AD who was martyred for her Christian faith. She has long been revered as a patron saint of music, so it is good to make music of all kinds the focus of this day.

If you have young children, get them to make a simple percussion instrument (a drum or rattle of some kind); having a messy craft session on the kitchen table with Mum or Dad and ending up with something that can be played or used (and likely end up annoying the parents immensely!) can be huge fun. Or give them something to play – something that you have made yourself or even bought, like a wooden whistle or percussion instrument. But don't just give it to them. Make an occasion of it. Draw up a simple scroll on an ordinary piece of paper and present it to them with a flourish and glasses of celebratory fruit juice (perhaps one of the autumn berries, whether home-made or bought from the supermarket), which can be served hot. Play music together, sing together, find some music to listen to together on the radio or television.

I remember when my son was a very little boy, only two or three years old, I had found a cheap packet of plastic musical instruments at the local market. Arranging them in a nice little container I left them outside our front door for him to 'find', having first told him about Saint Cecilia earlier in the day. When he discovered them, I let him think that they were a special gift from her, after which he had quite a soft spot for the beautiful and tragic young lady for several years and had great fun making a lot of noise, which he appeared to find extremely satisfying!

For adults, find a concert or opera to watch on TV, or buy a DVD to watch and invite some friends and neighbours round, serve hot drinks and biscuits or snacks (bought or home-made) or glasses of wine and bowls of nuts. Or find a live performance to go to, either alone or as a party. It doesn't matter how much or little you do, how simple or inexpensive, as long as it is enjoyable, and if you have family or close friends, it brings you *together*.

Lemon Drizzle Cake

Something fragrantly sweet to celebrate Saint Clement's day —
any citrus fruit is appropriate to use.

Gillian

INGREDIENTS:

5 oz (140 g) butter or margarine

5 oz (140 g) sugar

8 oz (225 g) self-raising flour

3 beaten eggs

2 lemons grated and squeezed

1 oz (28 g) sugar for glaze

METHOD:

- Pre-heat oven to 180°C, 350°F, or Gas Mark 4 and grease and line a round 8" cake tin.
- Cream butter and sugar.
- Gradually beat in eggs, adding a little flour as well to prevent curdling if necessary.
- Gradually fold in the flour and grated lemon rind.
- Place in cake tin and smooth top.
- Bake in centre of oven for 30 minutes and test with skewer to see if it is cooked.
- Place lemon juice and 1 oz sugar in small pan. Stir to dissolve sugar and bring to boil for a few seconds.

- Allow both cake and lemon glaze to cool, then pierce top of cake all over with a fork and paint on the glaze with a pastry brush and dust with sugar.

SAINT CLEMENT'S DAY: 23RD NOVEMBER

Pope Clement I of Rome died a martyr *circa* AD 98. He is the patron saint of metal workers and blacksmiths and this day in November used to be taken as a holiday for workers in these professions.

Legend has it that Pope Clement was the first man to refine iron from ore and shoe a horse, but as we know that, historically, this happened long before Pope Clement lived, it is possible that there is some confusion between this pope and the mythical metal worker Wayland the Smith, who in Germanic and Norse mythology was a legendary master blacksmith who used supernatural powers/skills to make weapons and other magical items. He is reputed to have made Beowulf's sword. The story is told of how the king of Sweden captured him and forced Wayland to make many wonderful items. After taking a gruesome revenge upon the king and his family, Wayland escaped on magical wings he had fashioned for himself, and finally came to settle in Berkshire, England, where he built himself a house of stone now known as Wayland's Smithy but which is, in reality, a prehistoric burial mound. This perhaps gives a clue as to how old the stories of Wayland the Smith really are.

Interestingly, in England this day in November also used to be counted as the first official day of winter. There were various traditions involving the firing of anvils, gunpowder, marching in processions and drinking alcohol. The day was often represented by an iron cauldron and in rural areas, smiths went round visiting homes to beg for beer and wine. Children went 'clementing', calling from door to door requesting apples, pears or other sweet treats in exchange for singing songs: 'Clemeny, clemeny, clemeny mine; a roasted apple and some good red wine!' There is also the implication of citrus fruits from the old nursery rhyme about Saint Clement's church in London and the accompanying game which children used to play: 'Oranges and lemons say the bells of Saint Clement's!'

For children on this day, get them to help you make hot home-made lemonade, or bake an orange or lemon cake (see recipe) and eat it for tea together while you talk about the saint and the mythical smith. Find a story about Wayland the Smith or Beowulf at the library or online and read it aloud. Have a special basket or bowl full of citrus fruits and call it 'Clemeny's Bowl'. You may do the same for adults and older children too, but also possibly add to this, talking and learning more about metals and metalwork; find out if there is a smith local to you, visit an exhibition or craft centre which displays or sells metalwork, or simply find or buy an old horseshoe, paint it and hang it above one of your outside doors to bring you luck.

SAINT CATHERINE'S DAY: 25TH NOVEMBER

Catherine of Alexandria, also known as Saint Catherine of the Wheel, was an early fourth-century princess and noted scholar in Alexandria, Egypt. She became a Christian at the age of fourteen and converted hundreds of other people to Christianity before being martyred by the pagan emperor Maxentius. She is the patron saint of (among many other things) philosophers, students, librarians and preachers.

So this might be the day you want to enrol your child at the nearest branch of your public junior library, or make a special visit there. Give yourself time to read something you will really enjoy or read aloud to someone, perhaps the very young or elderly. For older youngsters and adults, you might like to organise a debate about something philosophical or moral – you only have to look at the day's issues in the national or international news to find lots to talk about! Or perhaps treat yourself to a new book and sit down with your favourite drink or snack and simply enjoy taking time out for yourself to relax while you read it!

When I was a child, this date signified something quite different. I attended Saint Catherine's Convent Junior School, so she was our particular (and what felt like very personal) patron saint. On this day the school always held its Christmas Fair and Open Day, for which parents and older children had been industriously preparing for weeks, and in the case of the nuns, most likely since the summer holidays, if the wealth of gorgeous hand-knitted baby clothes and lacy, herby accessories were anything to go by! It was a time of great bustle but also of pride in who and what we all were doing together, with a wonderful feeling of warm hospitality as children and teachers opened the doors of their otherwise private inner sanctums and welcomed everyone in.

My mother would spend days sewing gifts to donate to various sales of work, but especially for my school. Aprons, peg bags, needle-books and the like were made for the handicraft stall. For the toy stall (particularly popular at this time so close to Christmas) there were always bewigged dolls of all sizes dressed in gorgeous sets of clothes, complete with matching fur-edged bonnets and coats. I remember once when, through the course of his work, my father came across a huge box of twelve-inch-high plastic dolls which were being sold off very cheaply and which my mother took and redressed individually in pretty dresses and hats – ironically, all the dolls had originally been dressed as nuns! The day before the actual event, a massive bake would take place and I would come home from school to find a dozen coffee, chocolate, pineapple or orange gateaux marching down the length of the refectory table in the kitchen, flanked by dozens of fairy cakes and biscuits.

COMMENT FROM JOAN: THE AMAZING BAKING TIN…

Gill bought me an 18″ long bread loaf tin on the Flat Iron market yesterday for 7/.[*] I'm delighted! It will be fine for large cutting pork pies… just think of all those perfect slices for big Christmas parties! Ricky calls it a 'Rhubarb Pie Tin' – no need to cut up the sticks! ha! ha! Bread strike on Merseyside[†] this last ten days – everyone going mad for yeast and flour – needless to say, always making my own bread I am not affected.

---

[*] That is seven shillings in old money and 35p in our modern currency.
[†] Very early 1970s.

THANKSGIVING DAY: FOURTH THURSDAY OF NOVEMBER

Thanksgiving day is a North American holiday which has come to symbolise the sanctity of family and home. The popular belief is that the celebration is modelled on the 1621 harvest feast which the English colonists (pilgrims) and the indigenous Wampanoag people shared together. In fact there were other, earlier 'thanksgiving' events in the American colonies, and elsewhere – it was a recognised cultural and ecclesiastical thing to do and went hand in hand with the more general autumnal harvest thanksgiving. The modern American holiday is no exception but as well as giving thanks for the recent harvest safely gathered in, it also strongly focuses on our families and homes and the blessings of the past year which have affected us personally.

It was Sarah Josepha Hale who originally campaigned for a national Thanksgiving day to help promote national unity. Throughout the late 1840s and 1850s she canvassed five different presidents. However, it was only in 1863, during the American Civil War, that President Lincoln realised that this might be a very good idea and proclaimed a national day of thanks to be celebrated on Thursday 26th November of that year. Subsequently, the celebration changed dates and moved about a bit, but in the United States it is now fixed on the fourth Thursday of November, while in Canada it has been celebrated on the second Monday in October since 1957.

You don't have to have been born on the North American continent to appreciate the fundamental message of this major American holiday. A day on which everyone comes together with family and/or close friends to celebrate what is truly precious in our lives and give thanks for it is surely appropriate and applicable to *everyone*. I wonder why we aren't all celebrating a Thanksgiving day of our own – surely we all have a great deal to be thankful for. I cannot think of anything lovelier than taking the time and effort to come together with loved ones and give thanks for all our good fortune; to take stock of just how many good things we have in our lives and acknowledge how lucky we are.

If you don't think that you are particularly lucky or blessed, just look around you at some of the other people and places in the world. No matter how poor and stretched we may be, how stressed or depressed, most of us still have a roof over our heads with recourse to some kind of justice, medical relief and social welfare if necessary. We do not have bombs exploding in our streets or see our children starving, maimed or killed on a regular basis. If you really don't believe me, try writing down three things for which you can be truly, deeply grateful each night before you go to sleep. At the end of a week, read them back to yourself and see if you can still say that you can't find anything to give thanks for.

As with so many special times – including Christmas – the way the Americans celebrate is by cooking a special dinner. If this is the route you wish to go down you can prepare any foods you wish – perhaps traditional dishes of your homeland or particular dishes / recipes pertaining to your family. Or you might like to try an American-style meal with roast turkey, corn bread, potatoes, sweet potatoes, sweetcorn and cranberry sauce followed by pumpkin or apple pie. (I would just like to note here that although cranberries grow in Britain, until the 1970s I never heard of cranberry sauce except in American films – we traditionally ate redcurrant jelly with our turkey on Christmas Day, though this fruit seems to be largely forgotten now.)

As a family we usually have a nice meal of some kind and come together to eat it; we spend the day or even just the evening together. As we sit around the table at the end of the meal, we each share aloud some of the things that we are thankful for and sometimes toasts are proposed, both in gratitude for what has been and also for the coming year.

I have to say that any time and any excuse to lovingly celebrate with our dear ones and give thanks is an excellent idea!

SAINT ANDREW'S DAY: 30TH NOVEMBER

Andrew is the patron saint of Scotland, so if you have Scottish ancestry or connections of any kind, or simply feel drawn to all things Scottish or wish to acknowledge Scotland as one of the countries which make up our British Isles, this is one of the best days to do it.

Having shortbread with your elevenses or for your afternoon tea, cooking haggis and neeps for dinner, playing recordings of Scottish folk music or bagpipes, wearing a kilt if you own one, telling Scottish folk tales... I am sure that you can think of many ways you might wish to acknowledge this day, and indeed, it is good for us to join all our brothers and sisters across the northern border in their celebration. It is healthy to acknowledge our rich and diverse cultural differences while recognising that we are all closely connected – something we should all strive to promote and never forget.

SAINT NICHOLAS'S DAY: 6TH DECEMBER

Nicholas is the patron saint of many people, including sailors, merchants, archers, brewers, pawnbrokers, students, repentant thieves and, perhaps most significantly, children. There are many stories and variations on the origins of Saint Nicholas and how he came to be connected to the tale of giving out gifts to children.

Nicholas was a fourth-century Greek Christian bishop of Myra in Asia Minor (modern day Demre in Turkey). Because of the many miracles attributed to his intercession he is also known as Nicholas the Miracle Worker and had a reputation for secret gift giving. The best known example of this was the aid Nicholas gave to a poor man who had three daughters but couldn't afford a proper dowry for them, a serious matter in those times when money was required to ensure the future welfare and security of girls through a good marriage. Nicholas decided to help, but being too modest, or not wishing to humiliate the family by being seen to accept charity, he didn't offer the money publicly. He went to the house under cover of darkness and threw three purses (one for each daughter) filled with gold coins through the window opening into the house. Some say it landed in the girls' shoes, others say it became caught in their stockings, left hanging to dry by the fire.

In the Netherlands (and eastern European countries) children leave clogs or shoes out on 5th December (Saint Nicholas's eve) to be filled with presents. They also believe that if they leave some hay and carrots in their shoes for 'Sinterklaas's horse', they will be left some sweets. In the Netherlands much more is made of Saint Nicholas and his feast day than Christmas itself. Children gather in the streets with their families while

Saint Nicholas, accompanied by Struwwel Peder, (Shock-haired or Wild Peter), travels on his cart or sleigh through the community. If they have been good children, they will receive their rewards from a generous and benign saint, but if they have been naughty, they run the risk of getting a beating from Wild Peter, or at the very least, no present, or simply a lump of coal.

When I was a young child back in the late 1950s and early 1960s, not much was known about this tradition here in Britain. But my mother often found things to do or celebrate that no one else had heard of, and Saint Nicholas was no exception. While my playmates at school looked avidly forward to Christmas morning and opening their bulging stockings, I experienced a kind of dress rehearsal on 6th December. Similar, but totally different, it was all part of the general Christmas magic, but it cast a particular atmospheric spell of its own. All day long I would hug my marvellous secret to myself, positively glowing with excitement at what was to come when I reached home again. The main difference for me between Saint Nicholas and Father Christmas was that Saint Nicholas's day seemed very personal to me as no one else around me at that time enjoyed such a celebration and it all took place at teatime, in twilight and shadow, not the brighter early morning of Christmas Day.

If I was at home that day, I would quietly leave my slippers out on the living-room hearth early in the afternoon and then wouldn't dare to go back into the room again until the time was just right for fear of disturbing the saint and being left empty-handed. If it was a school day, which somehow made it even more special, I would leave my slippers on the hearth in the morning before I left for Leyland. Walking back down the lane in the failing winter light later in the afternoon was a journey into another world at any time, but on 6th December, my anticipation and excitement knew no bounds. The nearer we got to the cottage, the more my heart pounded and my legs would become quite wobbly. But do not mistake the reason for my barely controlled emotions – it wasn't really the prospect of the present I hoped to receive that worked me up into such a fever, but the evidence of 'magic' made manifest in my own home that awed and thrilled me – the actual gifts were only the end product, the proof.

On reaching the front door, my mother would unlock it and then allow me to enter first. Cautiously I would peer around the door and, having ascertained that I wasn't committing the unthinkable crime of actually disturbing Saint Nicholas at his work, I would carefully creep into the room and across to the hearth. In the cheerfully dancing shadows cast by the flaming fire, I could see... oh joy! Several intriguing little packages tucked into and spilling out of my slippers!

But I would have to wait until the kettle had boiled and the tea had been brewed and my mother and I were sitting comfortably beside the blazing fire so that we could share the magic and pleasure together. Then, with the candles lit in their heavy alabaster holders, I would begin to carefully unwrap each treat. Saint Nicholas always brought things which I could use in my preparations for Christmas: coloured crayons or paints, tubes of glitter and glue, Christmas cards to colour in or Christmas activity books and coloured paper chains that I could make in the coming weeks; but there was also often a little toy or soft rubber ball and fruit and nuts. And of course, most importantly, a big bag of coins – not gold this time, just gold-wrapped chocolate!

How to Make a St Nicholas or Christmas Stocking

YOU WILL NEED:

Red or other material

White nylon fur, Christmas ribbon, colourful braid or broad ribbon

Cotton, needle, scissors

Glue

TO MAKE:

- Cut two matching boot shapes from the material.
- Put the two boot shapes back to back, wrong side facing out, and sew together around edges (if using felt or some other non-fraying material, you can blanket stitch round edge on right side as part of decoration).
- Fold top of boot over into generous hem and sew down.
- Turn stocking right side out.
- A loop of ribbon, matching fur or braid may be sewn to the top of the boot so that it can be hung up – ensure loop is big enough to fit over bedknobs! Glue white fur around top of boot which completes it.
- The basic boot / stocking can now be decorated however you wish.

These days, with no children in the house, we still mark the day: afternoon tea by the fire as always, with the first stollen or particular kind of spice cakes or biscuits to enjoy and gifts on the hearth for all – usually things like rolls of gift wrap and matching tags or pairs of scissors and cellotape dispensers to help the two men in my life cope with organising their own Christmas preparations! But sometimes it is a new CD of carols or a book about Christmas or Midwinter, folklore or folk tales that also complement the time of year and stir the adult imagination.

We also have a charity float done up like a sleigh, complete with Father Christmas and elves, which visits all the rural outlying villages in late November or December. Christmas carols in both Welsh and English are loudly played as it slowly makes its way around the narrow village streets, giving time for people to hear it and run for their purses or wallets in pursuit of loose change to donate to the small army of bucket-wielding collectors who accompany Siôn Corn (Father Christmas). Occasionally, the local silver band will also come and play in the village streets, collecting for charity, and once or twice one of these occurrences has taken place on Saint Nicholas's day itself. No matter how loud and blaring the music might be, or strident the flashing coloured lights, a great shiver always runs down my back as I watch the man in the red suit ride slowly past me, waving and smiling. We all know that this is a volunteer, a perfectly ordinary human being like you or me from whichever charity is running the sleigh this particular year... and yet... and yet... once someone dons that red robe and assumes that role, something else entirely takes over, all my practical thoughts fly straight out of my head, and I am a child again!

SAINT LUCY'S DAY: 13TH DECEMBER

Lucy is now seen as another Christian martyr, this time dating from the third century, who according to legend brought food and aid to the Christians hiding in the catacombs in Rome wearing a candlelit wreath on her head to light her way and leave her hands free for carrying as much food as possible. Her feast day once coincided with the Winter Solstice before the Gregorian calendar imposed its reforms to our dates, and in Scandinavian countries is now viewed as the event signalling the arrival of Christmastide.

In Sweden, where she is known as Sankta Lucia (the name Lucia originating from the word lux or lucis, meaning 'light'), she is depicted as a lady wearing a white dress with a bright red sash and wearing candles on her head. In both Sweden and Norway, girls dressed as Lucy carry biscuits and bread in procession as traditional songs are sung. All across Scandinavia special buttery sweet buns known as Lussekatt (Saint Lucy's buns) are made with saffron and enjoyed as early in the season as the beginning of November. A Swedish source states that Saint Lucy's day used to be known as 'Little Yule' and was among the most important days of the year.

In Italy, Lucy (or Lucia) arrives on the evening of the 12th December in the company of a donkey and her escort, Castaldo, and she is said to bring gifts for good children and coal for naughty children. In return, children are encouraged to leave out coffee for Lucia, a carrot for her donkey and wine for Castaldo, but they mustn't watch out for her arrival or else she will cast ashes into their eyes, causing them to be temporarily blinded.

Lucia is the patron saint of the city of Syracuse where, legend has it, a famine which gripped the population was ended when ships loaded with grain entered the harbour on her feast day. In Italy, Sicily and Dalmatia, there is a popular tradition which involves the planting of grains of wheat that will eventually be several centimetres high on Christmas Day, representing the Nativity.

With her previous connection to the Winter Solstice, light and grain, Lucy is obviously an entity dating from much longer ago than the third century. On the one hand she is the grain mother, earth mother, white goddess who epitomises the bounty of the summer and good harvests, but who at the darkest time of the year also represents the Sun and the solar return or 'rebirth' of light and warmth. But in such a guise she has endured her share of discreditation; for example in Sweden, where on the night of 13th December they used to observe the Lussi night, which was the demonic embodiment of all that the newer religions were trying to disparage. Lussi was then seen as a female witch or demon with evil traits who was said to ride through the air with her followers, known as the *Lussiferda*, across northern, western and central Europe (similar to the *Oskoreia* or *Wild Hunt*). Trolls and evil spirits and even spirits of the dead were thought to be active outside between Lussi night and Yule. Naughty children must take care and behave well or Lussi might come down the chimney and carry them away, whilst certain tasks in preparation for Yule/Midwinter must be completed before this date or else Lussi might punish the whole household. (Notice here the reference of a spirit or entity using the chimney to gain access and also the name of Lussi and her companions *Lussiferda*, or could that be Lucifer, the discredited feminine angel who was cast out of heaven down to Earth – perhaps not because she was so very wicked but because she presented such a challenge to the newly established Christian religion?)

I am sure that there are numerous ways that you can think of celebrating Saint Lucy's day: candles, lights and special loaves or biscuits. But there is a much deeper theme here – one of thankfulness and gratitude for all the benefits of our life, wherever you are and however you are living. No matter what our situation, we can always find something to be glad and grateful for.

Here is a recipe for Saint Lucia's buns. Perhaps while you are enjoying them you can spare a thought for all the people in the world who are less fortunate.

Santa Lucia's Saffron Buns

INGREDIENTS:

300 ml milk, tepid

1 teaspoon saffron threads

500 g strong white bread flour

7 g sachet fast action bread yeast

½ teaspoon salt

100 g golden castor sugar

10 cardamom pods, split and seeds removed

75 g butter melted

1 large free range egg

1 small free range egg for glaze

24 raisins

METHOD:

- Grease one or two large baking trays. Soak saffron threads in the milk.
- Combine flour, yeast, salt, sugar and cardamom seeds in large bowl, make well in centre and add saffron milk, the large beaten egg and melted butter.
- Bring all together and knead dough for 10–15 minutes until smooth and elastic.
- Put dough back in bowl, cover with clean cloth and allow to prove (rise) in a warm place until doubled in size – approximately 1 hour.
- Pre-heat oven to 200°C / 400°F / Gas Mark 6.
- Turn dough onto floured board and knock back. Divide into 12 equal-sized pieces. Take each piece in turn and roll out into long strip, before twisting tightly into letter 'S' shape. Place buns onto baking sheet and again cover with clean cloth, allowing them to rise in the warmth for 30–45 minutes.
- Once risen, brush tops with beaten egg and then push a raisin into the centre of each scroll – 2 raisins per bun.
- Bake for 15–20 minutes until dark golden brown and they sound hollow when tapped underneath.
- Allow to cool on wire rack before serving – best eaten the same day, but can be frozen.

PLEASE NOTE: *This is the only recipe in this book which does not originate from the pages of my mother's manuscript cookery book. Practically nothing was known about the Saint Lucy celebrations in Britain fifty years ago. I found this wonderful* *recipe on the website of Karen S. Burns-Booth and recommend a visit – lots of other lovely ideas and wonderful recipes! www.lavenderandlovage.com*

REVERENCE AND RELEVANCE

After reading the basic derivations and emphases of the saints listed above it becomes apparent that the activities and beliefs associated with many such religious celebrations have long histories. There are deep, wide-spreading relevances which originated much further back in time than the current Christian era of the last 2,000 years. Maybe the Christian saints really lived the lives and performed the actions they are reputed to have done. Perhaps good spiritual people are periodically destined to repeat certain actions and events, making them seem familiar and similar to other older heroes and heroines. Or possibly it is a case of more recent heroic souls gathering in local approbation to themselves the heroic deeds of other earlier figureheads and archetypes that are reputed to have lived all around the world at different times throughout history. What does matter is that we all resonate to the ideals which they portray. It is enough that we become aware of the rhythms which connect and underpin both the natural world and humanity as a whole and honour and celebrate the resonance of life and divine spirit which runs through everything... regardless of what name, label or definition we attach to it.

Special Treats for Ordinary Days

'Oh Winter Hearth, where many sacrifices burn,
And Lords and Ladies of the Yule look on and smile.'

'WINTER FIRE', G. MONKS

IN CELEBRATING OTHER lesser feast days and occasions I am putting forward ideas of ways to make the connection between our mundane everyday existence and what is significantly special, divine, out of the ordinary. I would go further and say that there are no really special days, if we adjust our way of looking at life a little; that *all* days are special in some way, and religious or secular observation is simply a method by which to help us identify and express this.

We can most easily understand this when we first fall in love. Suddenly, for apparently no reason, the sky is bluer, the grass is greener, life is magical and we want to laugh and sing, feeling that we could almost explode with happiness. Most people will experience this sensation at some point in their life, sometimes when it is most unlikely or inappropriate; the rest of their world might be imploding or disintegrating, but that makes no difference to the couple involved. It can happen again with the birth of a child. Immediately, the rest of the outside world is seemingly irrelevant and all one's energies and whole being are absorbed by the utter miraculous joy of the new little person who has just arrived.

I am therefore suggesting that you utilise these other celebrations to bring an element of fun and appreciation into your life, indulge in a little true magic and learn to fall in love with life as it is, every day. And this does not just involve your life but many of the people around you as well. In modern parlance, you might wish to think of this approach as employing a form of mindfulness. It is a way of focusing or recalibrating your perception of the average and ordinary and turning it into something sparkling and magical. Learn to clearly see what is around you and appreciate it for what it is.

If you can't do this so easily for yourself, try doing it for your child or other children locally, or for your partner or family or close friends. When my own child was very small, I was a single parent, and even though I had amazing support from the rest of my family, there were still many times when I was lonely and alone. But putting aside my own feelings I conjured up many little times for my child and me to share. Sometimes it was just making tea and toast in front of an open fire on a wet afternoon... and we would sing, or I would read aloud poetry and children's stories.

There are lots of simple things that you can do that take neither a lot of time nor money. Share a pot of tea or coffee, or a jug of hot chocolate, or steaming mulled wine or hot spicy fruit juice. Make a food snack and set it out nicely on a cloth with a lit candle or little posy of flowers. Wrap a single sweet in pretty paper (or some other tiny offering) and present it ceremoniously, or make a game of it and play 'hunt the mystery item', calling out 'hot... hotter!' as they get close to finding it or 'cold... colder!' if they begin to move away from it.

An open fire makes a wonderful, cosy, comforting focal point to a room or home. Most people no longer have them, although a growing number now have wood-burning stoves instead. If you have neither, a table, no matter how small or battered, can be used to gather everyone around and can be transformed by throwing a nice piece of material over it. A group of lit candles can create the soft light and shadow reminiscent of an open fire – not to mention some of the heat as well! – and what kind of holders, and the size and colour of the candle you use, depends on the time of year and what atmosphere you are trying to create.

So give yourself and those around you a treat. Bring a dull day purposefully alive. Find something to celebrate. I have suggested the occassions in the previous chapter with fairly specific details and ideas for each one to start you off, but you might wish to make up your own – an anniversary of something or just something nice that happened to you that day that you wish to share. Have that special hot drink, mulled wine or honeyed herbal, just for yourself, or with your children, family or friends. Add a lovely squashy cake if you wish, or a plate of favourite biscuits, or hot buttered crumpets or toast dripping honey. Create your focal point with a table, throw, flowers, candles, or an old-fashioned hearth if you are lucky enough still to have one. Set the scene, if not for yourself, then for someone else. Giving to or for others is the very best way of getting satisfaction and enjoyment for yourself, and if you persist, you might just find yourself falling in love all over again... this time with life itself!

EDIBLE IDEAS

If you need ideas for simple snacks and treats for your Midwinter teas or suppers there are plenty of beautifully detailed books dedicated to just such themes, but to get you started here are some very basic suggestions.

SANDWICHES: traditional closed affairs made from two slices of bread or one slice cut a little more thickly and piled generously high with any combination of cheeses or salads – or cold cut meats if you aren't vegetarian – on any type of bread. A real favourite of mine is humus with chopped avocado. Or how about sausage rolls?

TOAST: hot buttered toast, cinnamon toast, hot buttered crumpets or teacakes.

HIGH TEAS AND SUPPERS: when something a bit more substantial is called for. Cheese on toast; beans on toast (delicious with a good knob of butter and some freshly ground pepper added); toastie sandwiches with any filling, savoury or sweet, that you can think of; eggs: boiled, poached or scrambled, added to fish (smoked mackerel, haddock or kippers makes a more substantial meal); savoury flans of many kinds, or why not try some kedgeree?

MORE FOR THE GROWN-UPS: a selection of cheeses and pâtés with an equally good selection of crackers and biscuits, coupled with fruit and a pot of good coffee – simple, easy and very satisfying.

SWEETS: anything that you fancy, either bought or home-made. But children love helping to bake their own biscuits and flapjacks and there are scores of marvellous recipes to be found in books or online. Fun and educational, they also taste all the better for the effort and resultant satisfaction!

ALCHEMY

Seeing food prepared and cooked and then eating it straight from the griddle or pan holds a fascination for everyone of all ages. These days kitchens are purpose-designed and constructed. All food preparation is relegated to a separate area within the living space but which is still set apart from the rest of daily life, and meals are magically produced like the magician's rabbit from a hat when finally required. But in days gone by, when enclosed ovens required time to heat and families were larger, it was the general habit for someone to sit by the fire and bake griddle after griddle of little pancakes (see the flannel cake recipe below) or unleavened (meaning un-risen) bread or cakes for the rest of a hungry family. There is something overwhelmingly comforting about the fragrant scent of warm spices as you sit and watch a griddle full of Welsh cakes slowly turn a golden brown before slathering them in butter and biting into them, hot, sweet and fruity.

Gathering around a fire together to participate in the preparation and production of food has been at the heart of our society for hundreds of thousands of years. It is the single most important action in the development of humanity and answers a deep and abiding need within us which we invariably respond to on the most fundamental level. Hence the fashion for restaurants to produce food within sight of the public, the popularity of booths, vans and carts cooking and selling hot food in the street, the craze for fondue parties in the 1970s, when everyone could gather round and dip their own pieces of bread into melted cheese, and the more recent trend for chocolate fountains and other forms of melted deliciousness in which to dip all manner of fruit and sweeties.

With the aid of a portable electric hotplate or a little camping gas ring which only needs to cost a few pounds, you can recreate the whole effect and ambience of a cave or campfire right in the middle of your living room. Use an old towel or tablecloth folded beneath a large thick chopping board to stand your burner on so that the surface beneath it is protected. Mix your dough or batter beforehand and then assemble everything else you will need on a tray. Let someone else prepare or brew and pour the drinks that you are serving while you get started on getting the first cakes, breads or pancakes on your griddle. For the griddle you don't have to buy a special utensil, you can simply use a thick-bottomed frying pan.

GRIDDLE CAKES

PANCAKES – of any size, large or small. Put out a selection of bowls of sweet (honey, fruit, yoghurt or crème fraîche) or savoury fillings (peanut butter, humus, grated cheese, cream cheese) so that people can fill their own.

OATCAKES – these aren't the hard biscuit type but the savoury oat pancake variety that were widely made and eaten throughout the ages. Again can be filled with savouries or sweets but are delicious served warm with just butter, rolled up into a sausage shape and eaten in the hand.

FLANNEL CAKES – small sweet pancakes served with butter or fruit preserves or jam.

WELSH CAKES – sweet, spicy, fruity little discs best made with the addition of nutmeg. Can be served cold but for the very best effect, serve hot with butter.

PLEASE NOTE *that all of the above are best served accompanied by copious amounts of napkins, paper towels or clean damp cloths!*

So you can only cook a very small number of cakes at a time and everyone is sitting waiting, wanting more? Do them good. Let them get to know what real food in real time takes to create; none of this fast convenience here. It will sharpen their appetite and taste all the sweeter when their second and third helpings eventually do come along! So the air gets a little smoky – that is all part of the cooking process too, just remember to temporarily disable your smoke alarm, but for heaven's sake DO remember to switch it back on as soon as you have finished.

Below are some recipes which you might like to try out on these occasions.

Savoury Potato Cakes

A great way to use up leftover cold mashed potato! They must be served hot with butter or some substitute spread. They can be plain or have a variety of things added to them before cooking, such as grated cheese or cooked chopped bacon, or can be made sweet by adding grated raw apple and a sprinkle of sugar. We prefer them savoury and plain. They also make a good lunch or supper dish with the addition of poached eggs and salad.

Gillian

INGREDIENTS:
Cold mashed potato
A little flour
Beaten egg to bind
Shake of salt
Vegetable oil to cook
Butter to serve

METHOD:

- In a bowl mix together the potato with a tablespoon or two of flour and one or two beaten eggs (depending on how much potato you are using). If you are using other ingredients, also add them at this stage.
- Roll potato dough out or form little flattened cakes with your hands.
- Sprinkle with salt, if making savoury cakes.
- Place as many as you can fit without squashing onto a hot well-greased griddle or pan. You may need to add a little more oil as they cook.
- Turn over after three or four minutes. You may need to turn them again before they are fully cooked – remember that although they are mostly made from ingredients which are already cooked, they also contain raw egg and you must be sure that this is properly cooked through.

NOTE: *if you aren't eating them immediately, they can be kept warm under a thick clean towel, in the bottom of a warm oven or under a hot dish cover. I find that they are actually better served warm rather than hot – their flavour is more developed – and eating them with fingers rather than cutlery also seems to enhance the enjoyment!* Gillian

Welsh Flannel Cakes

(Scotch Pancakes or Drop Scones)

INGREDIENTS:

2 teacupfuls (½ pint, 7 oz, 200 g) flour

½ small teaspoon bicarbonate of soda

1 small teaspoon cream of tartar

¼ teaspoon salt

2 eggs (1 will do if you add more milk)

¼ pint (280 ml) milk (more or less)

METHOD:

- Sift flour, soda, cream of tartar and salt all together.
- Beat up the eggs well. Then beat them with the milk.
- Mix egg/milk mixture with the flour, etc. to make a thick batter. (The size of eggs varies and some flour takes up more moisture than others.)
- Grease your girdle* well. (My ten-year-old product of the younger generation has herewith gone into peals of laughter, saying, 'The mind boggles, but you'd be able to do the twist!')
- Don't have the girdle too hot. Drop the batter on the girdle in spoonfuls. (Facetious remarks again.) When brown on one side, turn over and brown on the other.

---

*   Unbelievably, 'girdle' is another name for 'griddle'.

In spite of the family's hilarious comments, we all love eating these delicious cakes with butter and honey or jam, especially Gillian Nonita.[*] Oh yes, while still hot keep under a cloth (the cakes of course), so that they will be soft and not crisp when cool.

Lancashire / Staffordshire Oatcakes

Since I moved to Wales I have frequently heard these referred to as 'Staffordshire Oatcakes' but there were always large piles of these soft pale delicacies for sale on Blackburn market where we regularly shopped which were clearly labelled 'Lancashire Oatcakes'. Having said that, this is a very basic and ancient recipe which at one time was in widespread use before leavened bread (made with yeast) or ovens were easily to be had. It was quick and easy to make fresh, but larger quantities were also prepared and dried until hard / crisp on racks hanging from the ceiling. These could then be reconstituted by crumbling directly into soups and stews. *Gillian*

INGREDIENTS:

4 oz (112 g) strong white bread flour

4 oz (112 g) medium oatmeal

4 oz (112 g) rolled porridge oats

Pinch of salt

1 egg

Water or milk to mix

1 flat teaspoon dried yeast or 1 teaspoon of fresh yeast

---

[*] Nonita is the author's middle name.

METHOD:

- Mix all dry ingredients together, add egg and enough milk or water to make a pancake-batter consistency and leave to stand for at least 2 hours – longer if possible. The mixture thickens considerably while standing, so may need extra liquid added by the time you come to cook them.
- Heat frying pan or thick-bottomed girdle – must be fairly hot – and lightly coat with lard or vegetable oil.
- Measure mixture with a soup ladle and pour one full ladle onto the hot metal surface, tilting the pan to allow the mixture to coat the surface thinly – just like a pancake.
- When the edges begin to curl away from the sides of the pan, gently turn the oatcake over and cook on the other side for a couple of minutes.

Can be stored in the fridge for 2–3 days.

Welsh Cakes

INGREDIENTS:

6 oz (170 g) self-raising flour

6 oz (170 g) fat; can use half butter and half lard – I prefer all lard

5 oz (140 g) sugar

5 oz (140 g) currants

Half a nutmeg, grated (most important!)

1 egg, beaten

METHOD:

- Rub fat into flour.
- Add sugar, currants, grated nutmeg and combine with beaten egg – can use a little milk or water to achieve a soft pastry-like consistency.
- Tip onto floured board, knead gently and roll out to just under ½" (1 cm) thick.
- Cut into rounds using a 2½" fluted cutter.
- Place on a hot griddle – it is the right temperature if the Welsh cakes sizzle slightly when first put on; then turn down heat slightly so sizzling stops.
- Bake on both sides until golden brown. May be turned a second time if necessary.

Butter generously and serve hot with a pot of tea or coffee, but be aware, there is a joke in the family that regular consumption of these fragrant little cakes will give you the complete inability to see your knees! Also very good served cold. Enjoy!

AS ALREADY MENTIONED, it can be so cosy and relaxing to sit around your domestic focal point – even if it is just your little camping stove as you bake your griddle cakes, or a few lit candles in the middle of the table – talking and making things. One idea which doesn't take up too much space and is fairly simple to do is to make little winter gnomes from fir cones, beech masts, pipe cleaners and felt. Small and jolly (but definitely epitomising the essence of wild Midwinter celebration), they can be hung on Christmas trees, in windows, used to decorate festive yule logs, balanced among the leaves in jugs of holly or simply carried around in little children's hands.

How to Make Fir Cone Gnomes

YOU WILL NEED:

One fir cone for the body

2 × 2½" lengths of coloured pipecleaner

Small piece of coloured felt

Pink wooden bead for the head (size depending on size of fir cone)

Length of coloured wool or thread

Blue and red pens, markers or paints

Scissors and glue

TO MAKE:

- Take the two lengths of pipe cleaner and bend them in the middle to form a pair of arms and a pair of legs.
- Bend the legs again to make knees, and bend ¼" up at the ends to make feet.
- Bend up ¼" at the ends of the arms to make hands.
- Place a dab of glue in the centre of arms and legs and fix them to the 'spine' of the fir cone so that the hands and feet stick out at the front.
- Paint or draw features on bead to form head.

- Glue head onto top of cone. Often there is a stalk onto which you can slide the head, which provides a stronger connection.
- Cut out a triangle of coloured felt, roll into a cone and fix with glue on one straight edge to make a hat.
- Using a little glue on top of the bead, stick the hat onto the gnome's head.
- If you want to hang your fir cone gnomes on your tree or from window frames, tie a loop of coloured cotton loosely beneath your gnome's arms. Otherwise, sit your gnomes among the branches of your advent wreath or tree.

PLEASE NOTE: *If you do decide to try this out, please ensure that all hands are well washed after eating hot buttery treats before handling the craft items!*

Sacrifice, Service... and Shopping

Happiness does not come from having much,
but from being attached to little.

ANON.

WHATEVER YOUR BELIEFS and practices, there is always an element of sacrifice around the time of Midwinter. It is found in the dim and distant Neolithic times when people first began to husband animals and, through lack of resources, were forced to slaughter most of them in early winter each year; in the archetypal 'death' of the Oak King in the battle against his brother, the Holly King in western Europe; in the annual fight between the Persian god, Mithras, and the bull; or even in the death and resurrection of the sun god, Osiris, in Ancient Egypt. This is the time of year when the celestial Wild Hunt roams the skies, when in Celtic belief we metaphorically give ourselves back to the realm of Spirit to be reborn from Ceridwen's cauldron just as the natural world gives itself back to the Earth to grow again the following spring.

The very Sun itself 'dies' into the darkness of the Winter Solstice before it is 'reborn', in turn sacrificing the dark so that the Light may eventually be reborn anew.

Varying facets of sacrifice cling historically to the entire concept of Midwinter, on every level and in every sphere of society, and continue to do so.

Each year, millions of animals are sacrificed to provide us with a marvellous seasonal feast. Woodland evergreens are sacrificed as the holly and mistletoe are cut and brought to the December markets and ready-made wreaths and displays are found for sale everywhere. Millions of live trees are sacrificed each November and December to provide us with our Christmas trees, for even in this age of smart synthetic decorations, 60 per cent of us still opt to grace our homes with a live tree.

Also, think of all the many little sacrifices which we all make around this time, giving our time and energy to bring enjoyment and happiness to others. Think of all the parents who have little or nothing to spare but who will go to endless lengths of crippling over-work and self-denial just to provide some little treat for their child or children at this extra-special time.

OFFERING SERVICE

If you are going to give or do something then give or do it generously and wholeheartedly, otherwise don't give or do it at all. So if you are going to 'make' Christmas for your family (or anyone else), then give your time and effort without resentment or conditions. This is your gift. This is your service to them. This doesn't mean that you must break your health, destroy your emotional and mental equilibrium or ruin any chance of your own pleasure and enjoyment. Even people who know you well, who are close to you, will be wrapped up in their own busy lives and concerns and will often not notice what lengths you are going to on their behalf. Without appearing a martyr or a bossy-boots you need to let those around you know that you are prepared to put in the effort to provide certain things for their enjoyment and that by doing so you are showing how much you care for them.

At the same time, you must actively allow and encourage them to help you in making the celebration a truly joint effort of loving service to each other. If you have young children you begin when they are very young, showing them by example – not silently doing it all yourself, until your children, when grown to adulthood, simply look bewildered and declare that 'Mum... Dad... so-and-so... always did everything...' Explain what you are doing and why, and how they can help you to create magical times. As the twig is bent... If you are in a group of adults – whether they be friends, relatives or work colleagues – get them together and have a little chat. Ask them what they all most want from the celebration and then find out how each one is prepared to help or is capable of contributing. Encourage. Continue to re-enlist. Deputise. Delegate. Compromise. This in itself is as much a gift as anything you could buy in the shops – more so, as the feelings of achievement and satisfaction and strengthened community so engendered will spill over into the rest of the year and set a pattern of behaviour for everyone which will benefit you all.

WHEN SERVICE BECOMES A SACRIFICE

Your loving efforts – your service – becomes a 'sacrifice' when you haven't got the necessary resources: when you haven't got as much time to spare as you had anticipated; when you suddenly have extra bills to pay and so haven't got the funds you had counted on; when extra tasks are dumped on you at work; when you become unwell or something doesn't go quite to plan. Then you become stretched and stressed in your efforts to achieve what you originally set out to do. In this instance I am not actually saying beware of such situations – they frequently arise, that's life – rather I am suggesting that you offer up your struggles, worry, fears and hard work as a loving sacrifice to those around you, making the very best of an imperfect situation.

The act of achievement is in itself a 'gift', but so too is the act of sacrifice in stepping up to the plate and still coping. Realising your goals is an accomplishment in itself, but to do so while keeping your temper, while remaining calm and pleasant and not disseminating the desperation which you might suddenly be feeling is also your sacrifice: you are sacrificing your own natural reactions and needs with loving thought and consideration for others and control and thought for yourself.

Throughout our everyday lives – not just at Midwinter – we can offer this type of sacrifice, not just to other people but to our homes and the animals, plants and environment around us. Picking up litter, sweeping a path, scrubbing out the cat's dishes, mopping the kitchen floor or cleaning the bathroom might not be very appealing or seen as particularly heroic. It is what it actually *means*: you are investing your time and effort – your very life – in creating somewhere clean and comfortable, in nurturing so that others (as well as yourself) may live safely, well and happily. You honour the place and people by your gift, and in turn, that honour reflects back onto you, and so you also honour yourself.

WHEN SACRIFICE AND SERVICE BECOME A GIFT

Another word for 'sacrifice' is 'gift'. As it states in the *Oxford English Dictionary*, sacrifice is the act of giving up something valued for the sake of something else more important or worthy – the relief of suffering, perhaps. In this instance it is the giving of energy and effort to provide others with joy, fun, company and companionship, the giving of your love unconditionally.

The gift becomes a sacred service to what is around us, whether that be animals, people or the very land we live on. But somewhere along the way many of us have been sidetracked into only focusing on the idea of 'gifts', and some of us focus even more strongly on making sure that we receive as many and as much as possible, with little or no thought for the reciprocal act of giving, or what that truly entails.

The celestial mother 'gives' her son, the Sun, back to the Earth. God in Heaven gave his Son, Jesus, to humanity. The shamans gave their knowledge and wisdom to their people. Historically parts of the slaughtered animals were gifted back to the natural world. Father Christmas gives to children. Now is the time to show acknowledgement, appreciation and love to family, friends, those who work with or for you, and especially to remember those who are less fortunate than you.

There are many 'gifts' which we can bring to our Midwinter celebrations, including the gift of our intellect, our ability to visualise and execute our plans, bringing them into actual reality. There is also the gift of our passion to create, to give, to provide, and the gift of our emotion, when physical action is coupled with the added drive of our empathy and compassion, magnifying and deepening our achievements in the process. Our skills and abilities, our knowledge and experience, are all gifts which we bring to all situations, all aspects of life, and they are made extra special by our uniqueness, our singular 'self' which is unlike anyone else anywhere on Earth.

ALTERNATIVE GIFTS

Apart from the regular presents purchased from a retailer there are lots of different types of gifts that you can give these days.

TIME AND THOUGHT: Firstly, instead of leaving your gift-buying until the last minute and rushing around the crowded, depleted stores feeling nauseous with panic, sit down with yourself earlier in the year and make out a list of who you need or would like to get something for. Next to this column of names you might also fill in anything that you think a certain person might like – or even need – and then you can keep a lookout for it. If you go somewhere different – away for the day, or to visit an outdoor market that you don't usually frequent, or even away on holiday – keep your eyes open for something nice (within your price range) which you think any of those people on your list might appreciate. It is the thought and care that goes into a gift that makes it successful. Give yourself time so that you can take time.

KEEP IT LOCAL: You might also wish to choose gifts so that you simultaneously support local craft workers and businesses instead of mass manufacturers on the other side of the world. Whilst it is good to lend a helping hand to the economies of their countries, we owe some loyalty to our own working communities and the artists and inspired artisans around us. Also, bear in mind the environmentally healthier option of sourcing your purchases as locally as possible to avoid unsavoury modes of production and the accumulation of 'air miles' and 'carbon miles' and the disastrous emissions from transport vehicles.

CHARITIES: By this I do not mean go and do your Christmas shopping in charity shops – although considering some of the gorgeous things that they sell these days, that might not be such a bad idea; you can get lovely items at very reasonable prices and support a charitable concern at the same time. What I am really referring to is the kind of gift that you buy on behalf of someone and then give to someone else who needs it. For instance, buying a goat or some chickens or seeds and tools for a person or community in other disadvantaged countries, or contributing towards the funding to build a school or hospital or buy books or medicines, or simple transport for medics – that sort of thing. Then the person on whose behalf you have donated the money receives an official certificate telling them what has been given and to whom. There are scores of options for this type of giving now.

There are also smaller charities which organise financial funding to enable people to start small businesses, to which you can donate money (as much or little as you like) and then when that business is underway, the owner repays the loan. At this point, you can either take your money back or reinvest it in a similar appeal. But in the case of giving this process as a gift to a friend or relative, you would pay in an amount of money and then hand over the details to them so that they could have the satisfaction of choosing what they would like to fund and who they would like to help. (This is quite a good gift for a teenager as it teaches them just how much can be achieved from so little, and that those who are less fortunate than ourselves are real people and that we can all reach out and make a difference.)

OF YOURSELF: Many people really appreciate something that you have made yourself and it doesn't have to be huge or vastly complicated. We are now lucky to have so many craft and do-it-yourself books at our disposal and a positive plethora of programmes on television which show us how to cook, bake, make, sew and generally produce a bewildering array of exquisite items. But like children in school, our own attempts seldom look as professional as those demonstrated. We mustn't lose heart! We mustn't forget that the books and programmes are exactly that – produced by professionals with years of experience and/or qualifications. Just because your first – or second, or even fourth or fifth – attempt isn't quite what you expected, doesn't mean to say that you won't improve with practice, or that what you have already produced isn't charming in its own right and will still be cherished by the intended recipient. We are all amazingly talented, inventive and able – it is just a case of finding out what we are best at and building on that. Remember, you also need to *enjoy* doing whatever it is you are creating!

SETTING LIMITS: If you really feel that you need to buy something for your loved ones, then why not agree to set a limit on how much you all spend. It can be quite substantial, but the smaller the amount, the more ingenious and inventive you have to become and the more fun you will all have in doing it. For instance, you might decide to set the limit at £1 (or £5 if you are feeling extravagant!), especially if there are young children in the house. But if there are older children or adults, then this might encourage them to buy materials with their allotted allowance and make a gift instead. Or you might try writing everyone's name on a piece of paper. Each draws a paper and has to provide a gift just for that person alone.

Alternatively you might give everyone a small Christmas stocking – one that is only about five or six inches long – and tell them to provide something tiny to go in each sock so that everyone gets the opportunity to make/buy/give to everyone else, but is severely limited by size and space. One child might make and wrap a bookmark or an egg cosy or a plastic pen or over-sized paperclip for everyone, while Mum or Dad might find something much more expensive (but equally small in volume) with which to stuff the stocking... jewellery, tokens, or football or concert tickets for instance. Or not. Perhaps Mum and Dad need a rest from all that spending and they might be the ones putting in the new mobile phone cover (without the new mobile to go inside it!).

A LITTLE IMAGINATION: It is quite possible to spend very little money, but coupled with time, thought and effort turn a simple item into a really splendid gift. Buy a few packets of seeds – common culinary herbs like sage, thyme, parsley, marjoram – and paint/decorate/personalise some recycled yoghurt pots with a plastic bag of compost to give the beginnings of a garden... good for all ages but especially youngsters who you want to encourage to actively grow things and understand more about nature. For adults you might wish to buy a couple of packets of seeds which will produce something edible and include a couple of favourite recipes which contain the fruit or veg.

Thinking of the natural world and wildlife, you could give seed balls or packets of wild bird seed, or the recipe of how to make your own seed balls and encourage people to take an interest in their local bird population.

Another idea is to cheaply buy a second-hand book and write a lovely message inside the cover explaining why you chose this particular book for that person. Alternatively, frame a picture cut from a magazine (or advertising brochures) along with a loving or inspiring message, or a family saying. Or frame a piece of your own artwork, or that of your children.

Rum* Butter

Filling small decorative jars and adding pretty labels and covers makes rum
butter a very easy gift to make for friends and neighbours, but one which
is always welcomed and appreciated.

Gillian

INGREDIENTS:

1 lb (450 g) sugar

½ lb (225 g) fresh butter

1 small glass rum

Nutmeg and cinnamon to taste (a wee sprinkling of nutmeg,
    ½ teaspoon cinnamon)

METHOD:

- Beat the softened butter by hand with a wooden spoon, then
  beat in the sugar, then the rum, nutmeg and cinnamon. Put
  into one large basin and smooth the top.

- In Cumberland, a bowl of rum butter was always prepared
  before the coming of a baby. It was offered to visitors and a
  small piece was put in the baby's mouth as its first taste of
  earthly food.

---

* You can also make brandy butter in exactly the same way – simply substitute the
spirit you use.

GIFTS THAT MONEY CAN'T BUY

We hear a great deal these days about all the money that is spent at Midwinter, especially on gifts that are inappropriate and unwanted, or only given from a sense of duty or obligation. To some, this almost appears an obscenity; after all, in our Western society, so many of us already have so much. We have everything that money can buy. So what about giving gifts that money *can't* buy?

Remembering the service and sacrifice aspects of Midwinter, extend the hand of friendship to neighbours or people that you don't know very well. Spend time with a lonely neighbour. Offer to help someone who is struggling with pre-Christmas preparations, or who might be finding it emotionally difficult at this highly charged time of year. Invite someone who is lonely or unwell to spend time with you over the holidays. There are little intangible gifts that you can give too – complimenting a stranger on how they look or their lovely smile, or even just cheering someone up and making them laugh. And remember, no matter how busy or stressed you may become, try to remain good tempered and kind to everyone around you. These are 'gifts' that you can offer to the world at large – no one will ever really know, but that doesn't matter, the world will be just that bit better a place for it. Only you will be aware of what you have done, but even you might never truly understand the difference that you have made to someone else.

Then there are the very personal gifts that are unique to you or your close family. You might like to record a CD of yourself reading your favourite poems or pieces of prose, or singing your favourite songs. Or perhaps you might like to write down stories and memories of times you have shared together and why you love them. Getting the youngsters involved, you might record your child / children singing Christmas carols or other songs, and / or reading stories for grandparents or other family members who live further away. On this same theme, another lovely thing to do is to record an interview with your elderly parents / grandparents about their childhood memories, how they met, what they enjoyed doing when they were younger, etc., and give copies to siblings or children.

Alternatively, why not try giving pledges instead of presents? These are promises of actions, from cooking a nice meal to promising to put the rubbish bins out, without complaint, for the next 'x' number of months or years. Or perhaps someone might like to offer a pledge of cleaning out the hamster cage, fish tank or rabbit hutch for the next six months; or brushing the dog, weeding the vegetable beds, chopping the logs, doing the ironing, bringing you tea / breakfast in bed once a week... I'm sure there are lots of things that you can think of to make the lives of those around you easier and more pleasant. But it might be more to the point to actually ask everyone to write down the sort of things that they wish someone else would do for them – then people can choose from a list of suggestions which they can be sure will be appreciated.

I once heard a well-known film actor being interviewed. He was talking about his childhood, the big family he came from and the loss of his father when he and his brothers and sisters were only young. His widowed mother worked incredibly hard but they had very little to keep themselves with and when Christmas came around there was nothing to spare for treats or presents. So his mother invented the 'pledge box'. A few weeks before Christmas, she decorated a cardboard box with pretty paper and sealed it, leaving just a slit in the top. She then stood it under their little Christmas tree. Each child had to write down on separate pieces of paper what they were willing to do for their mother and for each other and post them into the box. The pieces of paper could be coloured, decorated or illustrated. These were their gifts to each other. On Christmas morning, they broke the box open and one by one drew out the pledges and gave them to the recipients, reading them aloud with much resultant laughter, teasing and not a few tears. The actor said it was one of his most powerful memories and just hearing about it certainly made an impression on me!

If you go down the route of pledges, they don't need to fit in a box. They can be written on large pieces of coloured paper or cardboard (or even framed if the promise is really serious!), worded officially and rolled up and tied with a beautiful coloured silk ribbon and presented on Christmas morning – or whenever – with a little speech and a flourish.

Just make sure that if you pledge to do something, you carry out your promise and see it through!

How to Make Your Own Calendar

YOU WILL NEED:
Calendar book for the new year
Stiff coloured card
Coloured ribbon
Image

TO MAKE:

- Image can be sourced from magazine, recycled from last year's calendar or pictures drawn / painted by yourself or your children – or maybe use a family photo?
- Glue the chosen image to the stiff coloured card.
- Attach the calendar book to the bottom of the card by sticking two short lengths of coloured ribbon to the back of the card and the calendar so that it dangles.
- Attach both ends of a piece of ribbon to the top of the calendar to create a loop with which to hang it.

SIMPLICITY AND ATTENTION TO DETAIL

Simplicity and attention to detail is the key to success in anything you attempt. Don't try to achieve a celebration that you haven't got the resources, finances, space, technical know-how or cast of characters for. Don't plan to decorate your house and / or cook a festive feast that you don't have the decorations, pans, dishes or tableware to pull off, or the space to accommodate. It is no use dreaming of decorating a twelve-foot-high fir tree with a dazzling array of baubles if all you have is a box of battered balls and a living room with an eight-foot-high ceiling. Or envisioning entertaining sixteen worthy souls around your festive board when you only have a tiny space which just about fits a small folding table for four. Similarly, someone who doesn't cook very often and isn't hugely skilled in the kitchen can't be expected to annually metamorphose into a Cordon Bleu cook simply because it is the middle of December. Nor does the fact that it is a certain date on the calendar suddenly give you more money in your pocket, or mean that grumpy old Uncle Joe is inexplicably going to become the genial life and soul of the party simply because you have invited him to Christmas dinner. No.

Keep it simple and utilise what you have, including the decorations you already have, the utensils in your kitchen, and the space, time and energy at your disposal. Try to resist the urge to over-spend, but if you keep it simple this should be easier to do. Making it yourself (whether it be food, decorations or gifts) is usually much cheaper financially but more expensive time and effort-wise; on the other hand you do get a far superior and absolutely unique result if you do it yourself. If you are going to cook your Christmas dinner – or any other special foods over the winter holiday – or make or do anything else, try to work within your capabilities... which is where keeping it simple comes in. Far better to eat a relatively simple Christmas dinner which has been beautifully pre-pared and tastes delicious than to aim for dozens of mind-blowing dishes which end up not being cooked very well, stressfully presented and which result in a row or tears because your nerves are frazzled.

You first have to ask yourself *why* you are doing all this for 'Christmas'. Because you feel you ought to – that it is expected of you? Because everyone else is doing it? Because you want it and no one else is going to do it for you? Or because you love your family / the group of people you are with and wish to give them a lovely time? Whatever the reason, there is absolutely no point doing anything if it isn't going to be something that the people you are doing it for are going to thoroughly enjoy.

CONSULT OTHERS

It might sound obvious and has previously been mentioned, but I cannot stress enough the importance of *asking* everyone what they are looking to get out of celebrating Midwinter / Christmas this year. They might not have even thought about it before, or be able to tell you, or even particularly care, but at least make them think. If they really don't know or care, then you can simply please yourself without any guilt.

I also usually ask if anyone has any particular preferences for what time of day / which day we have Christmas dinner, whether we want hot or cold food on Christmas Eve, whether we want to invite anyone or throw a party some time during the Twelve Days, if anyone might be coming to stay, or indeed away staying somewhere else for the whole or part of the holidays. Then I find out when everyone will not be working and what exactly comprises our 'holiday' for this year. I usually have this conversation sometime in September (which often elicits exclamations of 'Oh Mum, not yet!') or early October, giving me plenty of time to simply let the ideas drift around in my mind for a while and also to feel my way towards what resonates with my needs and wishes too.

Then begin by doing a bit of forward planning. Write down the main day(s) on which you plan to have all the family home or have people join you. Make out some simple menus of what you would like to serve on each of those days – you can cover the whole period from the Winter Solstice until after new year if you like, nothing is written in stone and can always be altered or dropped completely, but I have found that it is really helpful to be able to look at a list and see what I need to bake or prepare for that day or the following day and what I need to get out of the freezer and when. Try to work out days when you *know* you are going to be out (partying, walking, visiting or some other activity) and so won't need to cater for the family, or will have no time to produce a meal(s) so must rely on a simple snack, a takeaway or someone else in the family making a meal instead. Also factor in days when you might want to simply slouch in your pyjamas in front of the television; there is no reason why you shouldn't have something nice – a treat – to look forward to munching on while you do so, as long as you have had the foresight to buy or cook and freeze it first.

Once you have your menus, decide what you would like to try and make yourself and if you can do any of the preparation beforehand. Then have a look round the supermarkets and shops to see if there are any special ready-made desserts, cakes or dishes to supplement what you are prepared or able to do or can afford. Don't forget to involve others in your plans and execution of them, and if someone likes preparing or cooking something – or is willing to try something new – then let them do it!

Similarly, decide what you want to achieve with your decorations. Do you want to have a sophisticated look, or a natural woodland effect, or a certain colour theme? To me, the very essence of Midwinter celebrations is based on 'lots of everything and plenty of it', a sensory overload and a wholeheartedness which is anything but minimalistic or subtle! But if you want to try having more natural evergreenery and decorations don't try to make everything. Choose one or two pieces – perhaps an Advent wreath or a yule log as a centrepiece for your table – with extra sprays of greenery in jugs or vases (or jam jars!) and behind pictures or on window sills to go with your Christmas tree, which does not need to stand floor to ceiling but can be quite small, placed on a table to lift it up in line of sight. If you can't afford a real tree or haven't much space, or haven't much time or energy for lots of decorating, you might like to simply stick some fir branches in a decorated pot or bucket of damp sand and hang some pretty baubles on them, or simply string some coloured lights (or plain white ones) around them... extremely effective. Or make a kissing ball (instructions in 'Evergreenery', page 129) to hang above your sofa or dining table, or have one instead of a tree; hung from the ceiling it's out of the way but very decorative and festive.

When thinking about what you want to do and where you want to go over the Advent and Midwinter period, try and pace yourself and space your outings and treats with time in between. When I was a child my mother tried to arrange it so that we had alternate days/evenings out and therefore had time in between activities and events to rest, do our own thing or prepare for the next one. (More on that when we take a look at the Twelve Days of Christmas.)

You too need to pace your activities so that you too have time to prepare, to complete, and to take a breather or have a rest so that you don't get stressed out and do get as much enjoyment and pleasure as everyone else.

FROM FAMINE TO FEAST

In days gone by, the Christian church advocated that the forty days before Christmas should be observed as a period of abstinence from eating certain richer foods, similar to the period of Lent before Easter. One main aspect of the Midwinter/Christmas holidays that is responsible for bringing people out into the shops in droves is all the food and drink which is purchased. It is certainly very much easier to buy whatever you could possibly wish for at the click of a button, the swipe of a card or a quick jaunt down to your nearest big supermarket, although not as much fun.

When I was a little girl, my mother usually did her shopping in the nearby towns of Chorley, Preston or Wigan, and sometimes travelled down to Chester or London if she couldn't get what she wanted locally. She also purchased the harder-to-come-by delicacies by mail order, and from September onwards, catalogues and brochures would arrive almost daily through the post – large glossy editions smelling of crisp new paper and printer's ink, detailing marvellous festive foods and gifts from not just around Britain, but all over the world. My mother and I would then sit together by the dining-room fire and look at them together, discussing what she had chosen and why and sometimes allowing me to choose one or two treats for us all too. Hams from Grays of Worcester; caviar, stem ginger and crystallised fruits from Fortnum & Mason; tea from Jacksons of Piccadilly; truckles of cheese, wrapped like mummies, from Cheddar; and extra treats from Jenners of Edinburgh... our smoked salmon for new year always came from Scotland too.

As the autumn wore on, the goodies began to arrive and each was unpacked, exclaimed and enthused over, and then carefully stored away until nearer the time. Some fresh items, like the ham, had specifically agreed arrival dates, usually around 19th or 20th December – we had no large freezers then, and our small calor gas fridge would never have coped. I defy many modern fridges to accommodate such items. The hams alone were anything up to thirty pounds in weight, the largest we could get that would still fit in the oven – I believe that double that weight was available, but impossible for us to cook, much to my mother's chagrin!

At the end of the cottage was a slightly smaller single-storey room which we called the 'buttery'. Cool and lined with shelves, this acted as a pantry and store room. Here were found ox tongues to be cooked and pressed, joints of pork to be kept fresh in the salting crock, braces of pheasants from the local poulterer in Blackburn. The turkey was usually ordered from the neighbouring farm and my father would call round to Mr Noblett's to collect it on his way home from the office on the 23rd or 24th, resplendent at around twenty-two pounds in weight.

Surprises would sometimes also arrive in the post which had not been ordered: chests of Broken Orange Pekoe tea from our friends in Ceylon (Sri Lanka), boxes of Turkish Delight from Istanbul or hand-made Floris chocolates from our Greek friends. There were seasonal telegrams from relatives abroad who habitually left posting their cards until it was too late for them to arrive in time for Christmas and these were delivered down our long and bumpy lane by harassed post office officials. Bouquets of flowers for my mother would arrive in florists' vans, driven by slightly hysterical employees who had sometimes taken hours to find their way down our rutted and rocky track. Also, there was always a posy of real live Christmas roses from Auntie Isabel, one of my mother's oldest and dearest friends who lived in the Lake District.

Now here in North Wales we have gifts of parcels and flowers arriving from the Continent and America instead. But it isn't quite as exciting as it used to be – we now live in a village with an ordinary tarmacked road to the door. No more restorative cups of tea served to the delivery girls or postmen, although I often feel like offering them one when they arrive on our doorstep soaking wet and lashed by the gales sweeping down from the mountains or in from the sea!

But I still try to get in our winter stores, any time after the beginning of October onwards. When I was a child we regularly got cut off from the rest of 'civilisation' by bad weather so my mother always bought in extra sacks of bread flour, potatoes and the flaked barley on which we fed the wild birds during the worst of the winter weather and supplemented the dogs' meals. Boxes of candles came in by the gross, extra cans of paraffin for the oil lamps and generator, a ton or two of coal piled high behind the shed, and lots of dried fruit, cans of meat, bags of rice, pasta and dried milk. Winter vegetables could always be come by from our own garden or the next-door farms and in autumn I annually scoured the woods for kindling and logs for the fires. By December, we always had a mountainous pile of wood, neatly cut and stacked.

These days I still buy in extra coal and anthracite and secrete it away at the back of our garage, while extra canned foods go into cardboard boxes along with candles, flour, loo rolls and cat food up in the loft. I keep an extra sack of potatoes in hand until spring arrives and bags of salt for the road and paths if necessary. It is an old habit to break! I have to confess that it is always something of an old pleasure if the telephone goes dead, the local mobile mast is damaged, the electricity goes off, or the road is temporarily blocked by snow or ice and we can literally and metaphorically shut the door and withdraw into our cosy home undisturbed.

COMMENT FROM JOAN: WEDNESDAY 28TH OCTOBER 1959

Yes, this afternoon the coal was delivered. I only paid the previous bill and re-ordered more yesterday afternoon. Actually I am guilty of very bad management because as from Monday last, winter prices of £1 per ton more are in force, so this fourteen bags (Grade II) and six bags of slack will cost £8. 5s. 10d. [£8. 29p] – that is about 10/- [50p] per week for coal for both kitchen and living room fires. But after all, slacked up, the kitchen fire keeps in night and day and cooks, heats the water and oven and always has a kettle for tea singing merrily on the hob – in all a really efficient bungalow-range.

Enough of coal, but even though rationing was discontinued last spring it still gives me an 'all is gathered in' feeling to see the piles of coal in the shed and to know I needn't be too careful how many pieces I burn.

Advent

Faith is like a lamp and wisdom makes the flame burn bright.
Carry this lamp always and in good time the darkness will yield
and you will abide in the Light.

DHAMMAVADAKA SUTRA, BUDDHIST BLESSING

THE CHRISTIAN CHURCH celebrates the period of Advent over the course of the last four Sundays before Christmas Day, lighting an increasing number of candles each Sunday to reflect the approaching birth of the 'great light' – in this instance, specifically the coming of Jesus, but for everyone, the rebirth of the Light of the World (the Sun) at Midwinter. Some of us will also have an Advent wreath with which to mark and celebrate the nearing of Christmas and/or Midwinter, lighting one candle on the first Sunday of Advent, two candles on the second Sunday of Advent, and so on – a literal example of the encouraging of a small light to 'grow' as we reach our furthest point from the Sun.

Advent was a major factor in my young pre-Christmas life and a time of great anticipation. On the first Sunday of Advent, my mother would take her secateurs and we would go out into the garden and cut sprigs of evergreen: dark green holly with leaves that looked like they'd been individually polished and sporting lethal thorns, and the lighter less painful mahonia and tendrils of pliant ivy. I would watch as my mother skilfully wove them all into a wreath, forming it around a circular framework made from chicken wire and fixing the candles in between. To this she then added the little woodland gnomes made from pine cones which she had made earlier in the autumn and as I grew older I would add tiny coloured glass balls. The four red candles, one for each Sunday, were wedged in amongst the greenery and wire, so that they (hopefully!) didn't fall over. But inevitably there was always *one* wobbly one!

How to Make an Advent Wreath

YOU WILL NEED:
½ metre chicken wire
Gloves
Sprigs of holly or other evergreens
4 red candles
Small coloured Christmas tree balls
Fir cone gnomes

TO MAKE:

- Wearing thick gloves, roll and lightly scrunch chicken wire into a loose tube, then bend around to form a hoop.
- Carefully open up a space through the chicken wire in four evenly positioned places around the wire hoop. Gently but firmly push a red candle into each opening, rearranging and bending the wire slightly to ensure that the candles stand straight and are held firmly.
- Placing the hoop of wire flat on the table, begin poking in or threading through small sprigs of holly, until the wire is totally obscured by leaves, but being careful not to lose the shape of the wreath; individual leaves can be trimmed off to improve shape.
- Carefully attach coloured balls to the wire or holly using lengths of green cotton.
- Lastly, sit some of your fir cone gnomes around the wreath.

PLEASE NOTE *that I am referring to an Advent wreath which is made to lie flat upon a table and accommodate lit candles, not the decorated Christmas wreath which is made to hang on a door. However, this can also be fashioned in the same way, minus the candles. If you prefer not to use wire for your base, you may instead like to make it from several strands of ivy or young pliant willow twisted and bound together. This is also more appropriate for a door hanging.*

THE FIRST SUNDAY of Advent falls during the last week in November and very occasionally right at the beginning of December. In our house there is one decoration in particular which has always symbolised the beginning of Advent – and therefore Christmas – for me, and that is the little musical tree. It stands eighteen inches high in a square red tub and is exquisitely decorated with small glass baubles, some in the shape of houses, birds and lanterns. These are suspended from branches fashioned from real goose feathers which have been dyed green. When wound up, it plays 'Silent Night' while it slowly revolves.

The musical tree is older than me, having been purchased only a few years after the end of the Second World War when such frivolous items were only just beginning to be manufactured and imported again. When I was a child it always stood in the middle of the dining table where it would daintily turn, catching and reflecting the candle, lamp and fire-light as it played its charming carol and wove an anticipatory spell all its own. It is a marvellous example of how choosing and buying wisely can work so well – something which is largely made from natural materials (paper, feathers, wood) and which has lasted so many decades and will, hopefully, go on to last many more. The tree must have been wound up and played thousands of times over the years, and I am delighted to say that it is still with us nearly seventy years later, gracing our winter cele-brations and generating its own special magic.

AN ANOMALY

No one celebrates Advent as a time of preparation – the slow 'building of the magic' – any more. Now, most people celebrate Christmas all through Advent and then find that once Christmas Day is past, there is nothing left to do, to celebrate, and that it is all over. The festivities which once lasted for weeks or months around the central celebration of Midwinter, and latterly for at least the Twelve Days of Christmas, are all condensed into what was originally a time of anticipation and preparation. This seems quite nonsensical to me. Who in their right minds would plan any other celebration – for instance, a wedding – and attempt to conduct the church service or serve the wedding breakfast whilst at the same time trying to sew the wedding dress and bake the cake?

But this is exactly what people do with Christmas – endless parties, gatherings, 'Christmas lunches', carol services, fairs and markets and get-togethers are held throughout November and December while everyone also desperately tries to do their Christmas shopping, wrapping, decorating and baking. All to have everything ready for the 'big day'. How many tantrums and arguments begin on Christmas Day after the presents have all been opened and the dinner eaten, when massive disappointment and disillusionment set in? When all the hype and excitement suddenly come to an abrupt end? Many people go away on holiday between Christmas Day and New Year these days – what else is there to do? Everything has already been done.

When was the last time you went to a Christmas party or went carol singing between 25th December and 31st December? Perhaps this year you could begin to change all that by arranging to have a party or some kind of get-together between Christmas and New Year? Spread the fun and enjoyment!

Life is a continual process of change and unfoldment. Everything should be given time to be anticipated and prepared for. After all, we often get more pleasure from anticipating something than actually experiencing it. Take your time. Dream, plan, prepare. Look forward to things. Live and work with the seasons and cycles of nature and living which are more natural and less stressful. Everything in its allotted span... everything in *good* time!

'STIR UP SUNDAY'

The last Sunday in November, which is also usually the first Sunday of Advent, is also known as 'Stir Up Sunday' when traditionally the Christmas cake is made. This gives the cake a chance to mature and moisten and really does greatly improve it. As a child I loved the process at every stage; begging lumps of butter and sugar when it was first being mixed, being given a small handful of the succulent fruit and finally scraping the bowl when the cake tins had been filled ready for baking. The kitchen seemed to be full of mounds of moist, sweet raisins, currants and sultanas, luminous ruby globes of sticky glacé cherries, creamy heaps of ground or chopped nuts, the tangy fragrance of lemon zest and the rich aroma of spices and warmed brandy.

Once the mixture was assembled, everyone in the family would take a turn to stir it, and while they did so make a wish. As my mother made cakes for Christmas and New Year, and to give to my grandmother and numerous elderly friends, the bowl was extremely large and, it seemed to me, the amount of mixture mountainous. I used to struggle just to *move* the big wooden spoon, let alone stir with it or make my wish! Interestingly, as I think back, my wishes were never for possessions, they were always for gifts involving my family and home. With hindsight I rather think that most of them were granted, too.

In my turn I also make one large Christmas cake for us and several little ones for elderly neighbours in the village. Unfortunately I am so busy these days that Stir Up Sunday has usually been and gone before I get around to baking… but I still make my wishes!

Christmas Cake

INGREDIENTS:

6 oz (170 g) butter

6 oz (170 g) brown sugar

12 oz (340 g) self-raising flour

6 eggs, beaten

4 oz (112 g) candied peel, chopped

4 oz (112 g) walnuts, chopped

4 oz (112 g) glacé cherries, rolled in a little flour (to prevent them from sinking) and cut into quarters

1 tablespoon treacle

1 lb (450 g) raisins

1 lb (450 g) sultanas

1 lb (450 g) currants

2 lemons, grated and squeezed

A dash of brandy or rum to taste

METHOD:

- Pre-heat oven to 180°C / 350°F / Gas Mark 4.
- Grease, line and flour a 10" baking tin.
- Cream butter and sugar.
- Gradually beat in the eggs (you may use a little of the flour to prevent curdling).
- Fold in remaining flour and add lemon juice and grated peel.
- Stir in the rest of the ingredients until well mixed.
- Bake in oven for half an hour before turning heat down to 170°C / 325°F / Gas Mark 3 for a further hour, maybe longer depending on your oven. If top starts to get too brown you may cover it with greaseproof paper or a butter paper. Test by inserting a skewer – if it comes out clean the cake is done, but if it comes out still sticky with mixture, return the cake for a few more minutes before testing again.

THOUGHT: *Alternatively, if you would like a change from the traditional type of Christmas cake, why not bake a cake (using either a rich fruit or slightly lighter mixture) in a ring-shaped tin? You will then have a ring of fruitcake which you can decorate as a Christmas wreath, with leaves, fruits and berries coloured and moulded from marzipan, and glacé cherries of various colours used to represent baubles. Or, if you aren't that fond of marzipan (and I know many who aren't), why not decorate your fruitcake ring with thick white icing topped with fruit and nuts – pecans, walnuts, almonds, crystallised ginger, syrupy figs, dates, apricots and cherries, for example – a real culmination of preserved winter goodies set in sweet 'snow'. Either cake makes an unusual and stunningly delicious centrepiece!* Gillian

EXCITING SHADOWS

Each Sunday of Advent my mother would make a lovely tea to eat by the fire where, as dusk fell, the family would gather round to light the appropriate number of candles. When I was a child we would stand the wreath upon the little hexagonal coffee table which my grandfather had crafted years before. The sonorous ticking of the clock, falling ash from the glowing fire, warm shadows... My favourite carols now were gentle: 'Away in a Manger', 'Silent Night', 'Once in Royal David's City'. The room would gradually darken around the little family grouped before the hearth.

If you feel really keen to observe the passage of time, or have youngsters who would like to do so, you may want to light the appropriate number of candles every day and sing a few carols while they burn. It is no different to having one of those Advent candles which are marked off into twenty-four sections, one to be burned each day.

When I was a child the singing of the carols was left to my mother and me. My father, who played the drums in a dance band, had never been known to open his mouth and sing a note in his life. On the other hand my uncle, who visited us frequently at this time, possessed a good voice but would only muster the courage to actually use it in odd noisy places, like the shed where our gargantuan Lister generated our electricity. Here he would happily bellow out all manner of songs and light operatic pieces, confident that the noise of the engine would drown out any sound that he made. But it didn't, and none of us ever plucked up the courage to tell him!

We still firmly adhere to the celebration of Advent. When my son was small we often sat together at dusk and lit the candles and sang. Now we have reverted to just celebrating the Sundays, or even the Monday afterwards if we are all out somewhere else on the actual Sunday! But Advent tea is my favourite activity at my favourite time of year. Cloths covered in holly leaves or embroidered with wintry designs in gold thread or motifs of angels, fairies, baubles and Father Christmas are spread across the table upon which is set my favourite Blue Mandalay china. Plates of home-made cakes and biscuits, German spice cakes, cheeses, pâtés and crackers jostle for space beside the silver tea tray while dishes of hot buttered crumpets keep warm on the hearth or one of us wields the toasting fork, dispatching slices of golden brown toast – and sometimes slices of a rather more charred and blackened nature if they are allowed to get too near the burning embers! – in a veritable flurry to the eagerly waiting plates. Plain toast is transformed into a delicious feast when it is made over a real fire; there is simply no comparison. If you haven't got access to an open fire, try it out the next time you are camping or have a bonfire in the garden and then you too will understand what I mean.

As the shadows deepen in the candle and firelight, voices murmur, cups chink in saucers, logs crackle, the amber stream of tea pours from the pot, someone begins to hum and the old familiar warmth draws us in to the hearth-side… the magic of Midwinter is upon us once more!

Want to know the real secret of this timeless spell? It is simply 'togetherness'.

CAROLS

One of the drawbacks to carol singing is that people often cannot remember all the words. By the time several false starts have been made which dwindle to silence after the first verse, or half an hour has been wasted hunting for 'that carol book that Auntie gave us twenty years ago', or squabbles have broken out because six people cannot all read from the same page at once, or in searching for the words online people have become distracted by other information or conversations, everyone runs the risk of feeling thoroughly fed up and has usually gone off the idea of ever trying to sing a carol again.

But in this age of computers, it is really easy. Simply go online and type in the name of a carol, download it and print it out. Buy a folder – the kind that contains individual plastic pockets – for each member of the family, and perhaps one to spare in case you have friends or guests with you. Then, when you have printed a copy of each of your favourite carols for the family, put them in the folders, in the same order and numbering the pages so that everyone can find a particular carol quickly and easily. Pages can be individually decorated to make each carol book more personal.

Any Christmas song can be included, they don't just have to be traditional carols. With an American god-daughter, a German husband and us all residing in Wales, we have quite an eclectic selection in our books, including the Welsh version of 'Oh Come All Ye Faithful', 'Tannenbaum' in German (which the men of the family frequently serenade us with), 'Patapan' and 'Do You Hear What I Hear?'

As they were encased in plastic, you can even take your song sheets out round to the houses of friends and family and still use them even if it is raining. Here in Britain, as in many other places around the world in winter, we need to be as adaptable to the weather as possible. Like everything else, there is a unique atmosphere to singing these old sacred songs out in the damp or frosty darkness. Try it and see for yourself!

There are also all the opportunities to hear carols played or sung by live musicians and choirs, and while it is uplifting to attend a professional performance it isn't necessary to splash out on tickets. There are always carol services in the later stages of Advent, and brass and silver bands playing in main streets and shopping centres for charity, or even the Christmas Eve candlelit carol service.

Our family always enjoyed attending the children's nativity service at the little church at the bottom of our road. Inside the church would be packed with excited children and doting families, lights, candles, carol sheets and extra chairs. The local silver band always played too and shiny instruments bristled from shelves and under pews while the merry congregation shuffled, nudged, tripped and insinuated themselves into the tightest corners. Such was the popularity of the event and so packed was the church that when hot mince pies and cups of coffee were served afterwards, most people had to remain where they were seated while hardworking helpers carried trays and served people where they sat. It was only a very short walk home afterwards, but lovely to stream forth from the warm building ablaze with coloured lights with the rest of the happy congregation, calling seasonal greetings into the dark night as we went.

ADVENT CALENDARS

When I was a little child, it was very difficult to obtain an Advent calendar, but if you did find some, the very best were produced in East Germany. I had one every year – as did my son, to the point where he was still pinning one up in his student digs at university! Mine were gorgeously coloured and daintily detailed pictures of snow-covered towns with Santa and his sleigh gliding over the rooftops, or the bustling inside of Father Christmas's workshop with all the elves making, painting, finishing and packing a hundred different toys in all their glorious shiny newness, or a cosy home getting ready for Christmas with the excited family happily engaged in their many tasks of preparation. The very best calendars sparkled with a heavy frosting of glitter. I felt it almost a shame to spoil the main picture by opening the small doors each day to reveal the tiny pictures of toys, angels, sweets and decorations beneath. The picture behind the door for 6th December was *always* of Saint Nicholas, and on Christmas Eve there was always a much larger double door revealing a picture of the full Nativity.

Advent Calendars begin on the first day of December and run through until Christmas Eve on 24th December. If you have close contact with any children (or even teenagers!), there is no better way of counting down the days till Christmas than with an Advent calendar. In the twenty-first century it is easy to obtain all manner of Advent calendars: paper ones which have twenty-four little doors (one for each day of Advent) with pictures hiding behind them, cardboard or wooden ones with individual chocolates secreted away behind each door, even fabric and knitted versions comprising twenty-four little Christmas sacks or stockings in which to lay a little gift... I have even seen wooden trains and chests comprising twenty-four wooden drawers in which to place pre-Christmas surprises.

Or you can make your own calendar for an adult with a short inspirational quotation for each day, or a calendar for the whole family to join in with, mixing treats, tasks, forfeits and jokes. If you have several older children, why not get them to make calendars for each other using jokes, tasks or forfeits as a theme, or get older children to make something individual for younger siblings or relatives? Why not make a calendar for your pet with little nibbles or very simple play things behind each door or in a little drawer or sack? The possibilities are manifold and the construction and filling of these sort of calendars can bring as much – if not more – joy and excitement as the opening of them.

COMMENT FROM JOAN: 28TH NOVEMBER 1948

Jim played at Highways hostel this afternoon for a tea-dance. While he was gone I took Barry* out and I collected some evergreens to make an Advent wreath. We burnt the first of the four tiny candles tonight, then afterwards we sat in candlelight and peace for a long time. The dancing beams gleamed on my blue and white pots on the dresser and the polished apples on the table. It is only right to welcome the coming Christ-child in love and contentment.

---

* My mother's black and white springer spaniel dog.

JOINT EFFORTS — DON'T GO IT ALONE!

As Advent progresses I gradually begin to bring out our decorations. When I began thinking about it I realised that all of them bear some aspect of fire or light. Because my husband is German, over the years I have increasingly added to our collection of candle pyramids and 'smokers'. Pyramids are those decorations which have lit candles powering a turntable which rotates the whole central section containing figures from the nativity. Smokers are hollowed-out wooden figures which appear to 'smoke' when a lit incense cone is placed inside them. Our figures are carved in the forms of huntsmen, toy-makers and Father Christmas, but in Germany you can buy them in absolutely any size and character you wish. We have others for the rest of the year in the forms of herb gatherers, chimney sweeps and even stoves and houses where the chimneys really smoke. I think my favourite was a tall and buxom wooden lady whom I spotted in a shop on the Krämerbrücke Bridge when visiting the city of Erfurt some years ago. She was holding a dish of the traditional German potato dumplings which appeared to steam as the smoke rose! Perhaps in this day and age figures who 'smoke' pipes might not be deemed politically correct any more, but obviously there are alternative ways to interpret the concept.

With the smokers come the scents of pine and frankincense to permeate the shadowy candlelit rooms. We have a decoration which my husband calls a *Lichterbogen* or 'flying buttress' which was made by his father. It is a large wooden half-circle with the outline of figures depicting traditional regional occupations from his part of Germany, and along the outer rim stand ten candles which, when lit, give out an amazing

amount of light and heat. We also have large wooden figures representing a miner and an angel carrying a lit candle in each hand which are
traditionally lit and placed in the window on Christmas Eve to guide and
welcome the family, especially the hard-working father, home through
the darkness. I would suggest that there is a far older meaning to this
tradition, though, as we will discover later in the book.

Overall we tend to use decorations with real candles and electric
fairy lights and other electrically illuminated decorations which emit
deep jewel colours of emerald green, ruby red and sapphire blue, and
complement the dainty candle flames – no neon coloured flashing or
strobe-effect lighting here. What we strive to engender is an atmosphere
of mystery along with that of warmth, cosiness and nurture. Rooms
become magical caves of light, shadow and sparkling beauty; corners of
unexpected glows and glinting promise fuel the anticipation and build
the excitement.

If the decorations come out gradually and everyone is involved with
constructing Midwinter/Christmas, the necessary thought and effort
diffuses the excitement so that it doesn't get too out of hand. The adren-
aline can be channelled into action to produce, to contribute to the
whole, so that everyone (from toddler to elderly relation) has a part to
play and something to offer in producing the whole, which everyone can
then feel satisfaction and pride in and justifiably enjoy. For those people
(of *any* age) who get bored and easily disappointed, I would say that they
aren't contributing enough thought, time or action – and I do not include
money here. It has to be something from *yourself*, not your bank account.
You only get out what you put in, so if you are usually fed up and discon-
tented, get on your own two feet and *do* something about it! Make the

celebration what *you* want it to be. If you haven't contributed very much (or anything at all), then you have no real right to feel satisfaction – or dissatisfaction.

Just like any celebration or activity, a successful festive period usually depends on someone taking the lead and organising it. But that does not mean that they must solely perform every task! Organising does not necessarily mean *doing*. It means making sure that various things are ready, made, completed, gathered, bought or cooked by all the people who are ultimately going to be involved. If you live within a group of people, I suggest that different individuals make the crackers, gather the greenery, decorate the tree or construct the wreath, bake the cakes and the mince pies, write the greetings cards or put up the streamers. Yes, it is also lovely to do all these things together – it is one of the big seasonal messages of this particular time of year – but often we can't all coordinate our ordinary busy working / social schedules, and it is much better to know that everyone is doing their part and all working towards a lovely joint celebration (even if you can't at first see it happening) than to have one person take on the whole lot and become totally exhausted and resentful while everyone else feels utterly disconnected from the unfolding events and wonders what all the fuss is about.

As on any day of the year, there are also supporting roles which are absolutely vital. You don't have to be a gifted craft worker or a marvellous cook or a professional singer to make a cup of tea, pour a glass of wine, wash a few pots or light a candle and put some seasonal music on to play – or even to wrap a present or two, no matter how badly; if you never do it you will never improve! When a major event is taking place it is so often the tedious very ordinary little jobs that keep all the big preparations on course and oil the wheels of everyone's actions. No contribution is too insignificant or unimportant. Everything becomes a part of the whole and is therefore valid and worthy of honour and thanks.

If you live on your own I would suggest that you don't try to do too much, but also don't decide to do *nothing*. Ask yourself what this time of year really means to you and celebrate that in the most honest and authentic way possible. Perhaps just keep it for yourself. Or make something happen for a lone elderly or sick person who might not otherwise be able to have any festivities. Or volunteer for charity work over the festive period. Don't think about yourself, bring some joy to others as your true gift of service to your community – another all-important message for this time of the year. In helping to provide for others you will discover your own gift and your own Midwinter magic.

For those who question why they should bother to contribute their efforts, tell them that if they don't, they won't be included – and stick to it. It is an extremely valuable lesson in life to come to understand that none of us are completely separate or alone and that we all ultimately rely on each other. Hopefully this knowledge can be reached via gentle caring and love, but if that approach is mistaken for softness, make the point clearly. Everyone will live in a better world if you do.

The key word here is TEAMWORK!

Evergreenery

Gilt holly, with its thorny pricks,
And yew and box, with berries small,
These deck the unused candlesticks,
and pictures hanging by the wall.

JOHN CLARE

WHEN I WAS a child it was in the week before Christmas that the decorations began to go up; the holly behind the pictures and filling every spare bowl and jug. More holly, ivy and mahonia was pinned or tied along each length of black oak beam until the rooms more closely resembled a fantastic green bower. Nodding 'woggle head' figures marched along the ledge on the stairs. Swags of ivy and red garlanding festooned the stairs and upper corridor which ran the length of the cottage.

Sugar-pink and white miniature trees stood on every bedroom

window sill. Then there were the ancient Nativity figures which my mother arranged inside and around a 'cave' constructed from flat stones out of the stream and realistically covered by trailing long tendrils of tradescantia over the top. The whole scene stood on the living-room window sill, with a large silver cardboard star pinned halfway up one of the cross-pieces of the old twelve-paned window frame.

GREEN, THE COLOUR OF LIFE

Most people decorate their homes with some form of evergreenery at Christmas, whether it be with traditional holly and ivy, winter displays purchased from a florist or a poinsettia from the supermarket or even synthetic garlands and bunches (these days often illuminated with twinkly lights) from the shops. But why? Why do we do these things? What compels us to suddenly festoon our houses with leaves?

As autumn progresses into winter, the hours of daylight dwindle and darkness prevails for most of the time; plants are rapidly dying back into the earth and trees are shedding their leaves like colourful poignant rain. All around are dry husks, sere stalks, stiff dry leaves... death and decay. It is not surprising that our early ancestors should have felt some measure of seasonal alarm. The once scorching bright Sun high in the sky was now reduced to a glowing red orb low on the horizon which brought little warmth to the land, and everywhere nature lay dull, colourless, lifeless.

The pre-Christians perceived divinity in the world of plants and nature. Most of the growing things around them – deciduous trees, plants and pastures – lost their leaves in the autumn and appeared to be dead throughout the winter months, the spirit of the plants and trees – their very life force – seemingly lost with their foliage. Green was the colour of life. Anything left lush and green, even after the wildest storms, harshest frosts and deepest snow, would resemble nothing less than a miracle, something potent and magical which, against all odds, had managed to retain its spirit, its life force – an immortal entity which must be nurtured and kept safe.

People believed that the spirit of summer, life and growth went to shelter in the evergreen bushes and trees in winter and that by cutting them and bringing them into the house they were being offered shelter until the spring. Evergreens were also looked upon as representations of the spirit of growth / growing and life as they do not 'die', no matter how long the winter lasts or how severe the weather is. Evergreens retain green indestructible life to be honoured and kept safe until the winter has finally passed.

In the natural calendar of the seasons spring begins with *Gŵyl Ffraid* (Welsh), *Imbolc* (Irish), *Là Fhèill Brìghde* (Scottish) or *Laa'l Breeshey* (Cornish) at the beginning of the month of February, and there are many old traditions about not taking down the Christmas decorations (and in the case of real greenery, returning them to the compost heap or woodland) until the spring has returned – otherwise the sheltering spirits of spring and summer would be outside in the cold again and subject to ultimate death. Only when winter had truly ended was the greenery allowed to be removed, which could mean any time after the end of January and into February. In Lancashire, only seventy or eighty years ago, my parents remembered the old folks traditionally cooking their Shrove Tuesday pancakes on a fire made from the last of the holly from Christmas. If you wish to still follow this practice but don't want to have dusty dry greenery still hanging around all that time it may be symbolically achieved by retaining just a few small pieces of greenery, to be ritually put outside and/or ritualistically burned on a fire, bearing in mind that the element of fire literally and spiritually transmutes energies from one form to another.

In a nutshell, evergreenery basically represents undying life. For our purposes in Britain, Christmas evergreens traditionally mean holly, ivy and mistletoe with perhaps some bay laurel and fir thrown in for good measure. In other parts of the world it is whatever remains green and flourishes throughout the winter months, but the principle is the same.

HOLLY AND IVY

Holly has long been sacred to our ancient ancestors. The prickly evergreen leaves were believed to house the spirit of the Earth Goddess and the red berries to embody female energy, red being the colour of blood, the essential life-giving liquid that enables the bodies of all warm-blooded creatures to maintain life. Similarly in the Roman cult of Bacchus, holly was the female counterpart to the male ivy and the doors of houses were decorated with wreaths made from both plants during Saturnalia, which would have begun on 17th December.

Later, as patriarchal influence began to hold greater sway, the holly began instead to represent the male archetype with its vigorous prickly leaves and bright bold berries. Ivy now represents the archetypal female: gentle, clinging and pliant as a young maiden. But in mediaeval times the holly and the ivy used to fight, battling for the hand of the spring maiden. Even the legendary rivalry between the robin and the wren, celebrated in the familiar nursery rhyme 'Who Killed Cock Robin', may refer back to this time, since in several traditional rhymes they are identified with holly (robin) and ivy (wren).

Then there is the legend of the Oak King and the Holly King, two brothers who, between them, rule over the year and fight a ritual battle for supremacy every Summer and Winter Solstice. The year is ruled by each brother at the time when they are most full of life; the deciduous oak in its most vigorous growing phase from the Winter Solstice through to Midsummer, and the holly as his flowers form into berries and ripen at the beginning of winter. At the Winter Solstice, the Oak King defeats his dark brother and brings back the growing season of fertile abundance to us. But at the Summer Solstice, at the very height of his potency, the Oak King willingly sacrifices himself so that his energies may flow back into the ripening crops and the earth where next year's seeds will soon fall. As our part of the planet begins to tilt away from the Sun, bringing about another winter, the Holly King rules the harvesting and the dark and dying time of the year until, at the greatest peak of his darkness, the Oak King will once more rise up at the Winter Solstice and cut his brother down, restoring the flow of light and living energy. The oak and holly are really one life energy but it makes it easier to understand the natural process if it is divided into two personae.

Then there is *Frau Holle* – or, as some might know her in English, Mother Holly. She features in the Brothers Grimm fairy tale 'Goldmary and Pitchmary', rewarding good people and punishing naughty or bad ones. When I was a child I was told that when it was snowing, Mother

Holly was shaking her great feather bed or plucking her goose for Christmas. Originally she was an ancient earth and fertility goddess of northern Europe (more about her in 'Christmas Eve', page 220). Her tree is the elder but she also has winter associations with the holly. It is still believed in some areas that to cut this sacred evergreen at any other time of the year than Midwinter is to risk incurring her wrath and bringing all manner of bad luck upon yourself and your family.

I personally concur that this might well be so. We have a large holly tree growing outside our drawing-room window. I moved it there twenty years previously when a retaining garden wall needed to be rebuilt. It was a spindly little shrub which had hardly grown in a decade and I felt sorry for it. However once transplanted, it grew seemingly overnight into a tall, bushy, vigorous shrub which began to block the light out from the front windows on that side of the house. Alarmed, I finally decided that, much against my better judgement, I must cut it down, or at least drastically reduce its mass. I had only had the chance to remove some of its side branches when all manner of unfortunate events began to take place, including discovering that the front of the house was badly infested with dry rot and some parts of it were on the point of collapse! It is of no use to keep telling myself that the dry rot must have been present long before I cut into the holly; since then I haven't dared to do more than tidy and trim her, with her express permission, of course, and our front windows remain shady and dark. But she is a great companion and protectoress, and I love her dearly.

The meaning of holly as a sacred symbol of eternal life is held within its very name, 'holly' being related to the word 'holy'. The Celtic holly day ritual was originally performed the night before the Winter Solstice, when branches of holly were collected and put up in the houses as a protection against witchcraft and sorcery, lightning and death. The term 'holy day' has evolved from this and has now become 'holiday'. It is believed that the holly was harvested deep in the forest during the hours of darkness and it was essential to shed a drop of red blood in return for its sacrifice. If you have ever cut living holly from the tree even in daylight and tried to carry it home you will know how tremendously prickly it is, how savagely those thorns can stab and scratch and that it is not at all difficult to shed a few drops of blood!

BAY LAUREL

Also known variously as bay, sweet bay and laurel, this is an aromatic evergreen which we probably know better for its uses in the kitchen or as a celebratory crown for heroes. It is an evergreen that is quite common within the British Isles and certainly around the warmer climes of the Mediterranean. It was holy to both the ancient Greeks and Romans and dedicated to Apollo, the god of love and spiritual ecstasy. It is also known for its psychic protection, cleansing of negative influences and bringing clarity to a situation.

A VISIT TO BESSIE'S

When I was a child our main problem was the fact that none of our local holly, in or out of the garden, ever had any berries on it. My mother would buy the synthetic kind of berries – two scarlet blobs attached by easily bendable green wire – which we would artistically wind in realistic positions onto the most prominent boughs.

However, one of our neighbours further down the valley did have a huge, stately old holly tree which was usually covered in a profusion of berries. In her youth, Bessie, Farmer Sutton's wife, had once been milk girl to my mother when she lived in the middle of town. Now Bessie was very happy to let us go and gather holly from her tree.

This involved a long walk through the wood, past the waterfall, on past the lakes where swans and ducks came skimming across the water towards us for the bread that they knew we would surely bring. On past the old factory offices and gate and then up a steep rutted lane, as pitted and pot-holed as our own, to Lower Burgh Farm.

The Tudor farmhouse was one of the oldest buildings in the area. Although it had been the original Burgh Hall, it had seen infinitely better days and was now in a graceful state of slow decay and disrepair. Its ramshackle condition was a constant source of fascination to me on my rare visits.

Bessie's kitchen was a veritable Aladdin's cave. Pots, pans, food packets and kitchen utensils were liberally scattered across every surface, interspersed with a whole collection of smaller farm implements, seed packets, animal feed bills, invoices and items of post. Packets of 'worming tablets' rubbed shoulders with the milk bottle or teapot on the table as Bessie brewed us a hot drink. Tubs of rat poison stood sentinel on the shelves of a crowded and chaotic dresser. Cats, dogs, newspapers and items of clothing were summarily swept to one side (bundles so removed were carelessly deposited on top of other similar piles, forming worryingly unstable and tottering heaps) to reveal sagging chairs on which we gingerly perched to sip our scalding strong brown brew.

Bessie was one of the kindest, dearest souls, with an ever-youthful fresh and pretty face and sparkling merry eyes. As we finished our tea, she would don her old coat and tough boots and escort us out into the woods to her truly magnificent tree. In excited awe, we would gaze up at its abundant height. Thirty feet of glossy dark green leaves and glowing scarlet berries. Joyous would be our triumphal march home, proudly bearing our seasonal tokens from the true queen of the winter woods!

When I first came to North Wales I was astonished and bewildered to learn that there were no holly bushes in the valley whatsoever. I felt utterly bereft! The first Christmas we were here, I asked neighbours where I might go to find some, but none could help, until a friend informed me that there was a big old bush behind one of the many chapels in the village. Like a thief in the night, and much against my better judgement, I went with my friend, secateurs in hand, at dusk one winter teatime, and snipped off a few straggly ends which were dangling over the wall. My guilt and remorse knew no bounds. Since then I have repaid my debt many times over and in many different ways, but at the time I held my 'spirit of winter' safely until the spring, and that was what mattered to me most!

Perhaps the old chapel tree was encouraged by my attention, for since that winter some thirty years ago now, holly has spread all through the valley and proliferates everywhere. I have three self-sown trees in my garden and every time I take a walk I spot new youngsters growing in gardens and along hedges and across the lower mountain pastures. Simply amazing!

Spicy Fruit Cup

Hot, spicy, fruity or alcoholic drinks fulfil a much-needed warming and restorative purpose on days out walking and gathering in the cold. Whether you take them with you in a vacuum flask or leave ready prepared to heat up when you get back home, they are delicious and serve a very useful function! Here is an idea for a non-alcoholic version especially suitable for children, but delicious at any age.

Gillian

INGREDIENTS:

4 pints of fruit juice; mixture of apple, orange, blueberry, redcurrant, etc. – home-made elderberry or blackberry cordial is best as it also has the benefit of boosting your immune system and guarding against all the seasonal colds and flu!

15 cloves

2 teaspoons ground cinnamon or four cinnamon sticks

1 tablespoon honey

METHOD:

- Place all the ingredients in a pan and heat but do NOT boil and simmer for a few minutes.
- Strain into a heat-resistant jug or punch bowl. Apples, oranges or lemons can be sliced to float on top. Similarly, if they have remained whole, the cinnamon sticks can be re-added, so long as there is no chance of anyone accidentally swallowing a bit and choking!
- Serve hot!

MISTLETOE

The old name for mistletoe is 'all heal'. It is an extremely poisonous herb, yet in greatly diluted states and with expert knowledge and skills it is medicinally very beneficial for many serious illnesses. The application of mistletoe can bring about such benefits as the slowing and steadying of excessive heart rate, the dilation of arteries and lowering of blood pressure. It also acts quickly on the vagus nerve, reducing heart rate but strengthening the capillary walls. It has a sedative and tonic effect on the nervous system, nervous tension and nervous spasms and is also good for headaches, dizziness, irritability and energy loss.

Mistletoe has as long a history as that of the Christmas tree and other evergreens in our traditional Midwinter culture. From pre-Christian times it was the most sacred plant of the Druids, possibly in part because of the singularly unusual way in which it grows, being parasitic and taking root in the crowns of other trees. It especially favours the apple, pear and other fruit trees; also the oak, and sometimes fir trees. I have even seen it flourishing on hawthorn trees in South Wales. It develops evenly on all sides into a ball shape and keeps its small leathery green leaves all year long. Its pearly white berries emerge at the heart of Midwinter.

Some of its magic is because it appears to be born of the air, growing between the Earth and the sky, but not *of* them. Never allowed to be touched by iron or other base metals, it was traditionally harvested with a golden sickle and allowed to fall onto an outspread cloak. Maintaining its otherworldliness, it was then borne home on high to be carefully processed into medicines, incense and hung over doors (for luck), or on roofs (to appease the gods of thunder).

It is also suspended from the ceilings of living spaces where unwary pedestrians may be caught for an illicit seasonal kiss. There is an old custom that for every kiss beneath the mistletoe, a berry must be removed, and when all the berries are gone there is to be no more kissing. Token bunches were also kept until the next winter season and ceremonially burned before new bunches were hung as a symbol of continuance of the seasonal round and the joy of human procreation.

In some areas of Scandinavia and northern Europe mistletoe has long been associated with bringing good luck, protection from witches or sorcerers and promoting the conception of a child. But its deeply sacred significance is in the fact that when the opaquely white berries are crushed the juice resembles drops of human semen. Coming at the darkest time of the year when light and life are waiting to be reborn, the juice is associated with fertilising the feminine Earth to ensure the fertility of the crops for another year. The cosmic bull charges across the heavens, leaving a fertile trail to impregnate the Earth; the horned god rides the winter skies in his quest to quicken the mother goddess.

When kept for a while after cutting, the leaves and berries both turn yellow and this is perhaps why in the past it has been referred to as the golden bough, also making it a symbol of the sun and moon.

THE KISSING BOUGH

The making and hanging of a kissing bough (or kissing ball) as part of the Midwinter seasonal activities and decorations was once widespread and popular and has been making something of a comeback in recent years.

It is generally round in shape and is easiest to construct by using two hoops, one inside the other. Decades ago I saw a simple and quick version of this on the children's programme *Blue Peter* where they utilised two metal coat hangers – which also gave you a built-in hook to hang it by! I prefer to use two hoops made from twisted willow. Ask a friend or neighbour for trimmings from their garden (which is when you might find yourself constructing your hoops at Midsummer, ready to set aside until the winter!) or if they can spare you a few small branches in winter, or buy two of the largest woven wooden wreath bases you can find.

The hoops are tied together to form the quarters of an orange, covered with evergreenery – especially holly and ivy – and hung with special baubles and the best apples you can find. Ribbons of red and gold may be threaded through the greenery. Lastly, the key component is a sprig or bunch of mistletoe, carefully suspended either inside the ball or (more commonly) from underneath it.

How to Make a Kissing Ball

YOU WILL NEED:

2 metal coat hangers or 2 lengths of wire twisted together to
    form 2 hoops

2 lengths of tough string, thinner wire or coloured ribbon

Lengths of ivy and thin whippy holly branches or longer sprigs
    of holly

Strong dark cotton

Red ribbon

Coloured balls, real or synthetic fruits

Mistletoe

TO MAKE:

- Open the coat hangers out to form 2 metal hoops, or construct
  from 2 lengths of wire, twisting ends together firmly. Placing
  one hoop inside the other, to form a sphere, firmly tie at top
  and bottom where two hoops meet, using strong string, lighter
  wire or coloured ribbon. The hoops should now form a
  rigid ball.

- Begin winding round or tying young pliant branches of holly
  and ivy to the hoops until the metal is completely obscured.

- Any decorations can be used to complete the ball, but the more
  natural the better. Fruits, real or synthetic, pomanders, seed
  heads of flowers sprayed with gold or silver or as they come
  from the garden, ribbons – but always try to include some
  mistletoe!

NOTE: *you can make a kissing ball with more than 2 hoops – try using 3 or 4 hoops tied together and decorated in the same way for a really thick green ball.*

IN MY CHILDHOOD the kissing ball hung from the centre of the living-room ceiling. This held a magic of its own. Greenery was wound or tied around two hoops to form a ball and hung with specially tear-shaped glitter balls, gilded nuts and little apples. From the centre hung the most important item, a bunch of mistletoe, its plump luminescent berries each a promise of a hearty kiss, a shy peck of surreptitiously daring presumption, or at the very least a warm cuddle!

Mistletoe was the only thing that couldn't be found on our own land, much as we tried every way to propagate it, including putting it out for the birds to eat and drop the seeds in the trees, or squashing the berries ourselves into the crooks of branches on likely hosts. A frenzied search of the local markets and greengrocery shops would be made until our coveted prize had been tracked down. Our part of the north-west of England was never blessed with an abundance of mistletoe, unlike some other luckier parts of the country.

Sometimes, despite our endeavours, none could be found, and then my mother would resort to using a tiny sprig of the vastly inferior plastic variety. Apart from not looking or feeling right, one couldn't remove a berry with each kiss, denigrating an important ritual to mere licence. Mummy told me that in years gone by, if a young lady was refused this affectionate seasonal salutation, then she had to be presented with a pair of gloves instead!

HOLLY OR SLIPPER SUNDAY

When I was a child, the fourth or last Sunday of Advent was when the excitement really began to mount. In our family this day is known as either Holly Sunday or Slipper Sunday because it involves both commodities.

In the afternoon we would don our coats and boots and, bravely brandishing secateurs, my mother would lead the way to the best holly bush that year. Sometimes this was out in the woods or over the fence in Farmer Noblett's field, or even down at the bottom of our own garden path near the riverbank at the edge of our wild wood – wherever the leaves were glossiest and most profuse. We would carefully select specific branches for their intended purpose: long narrow whippy lengths with intermittent pairs of leaves for the kissing ball, bushy forms to fill jugs and vases, and smaller but equally vigorous sprigs for behind all the pictures.

Cutting and carrying holly can be quite a physically painful affair and we always wore our thickest jackets and gloves, but the holly was a tenacious adversary and we always ended up with pricked fingers, scratched faces and our hair tugged out on end. (Perhaps we too should have approached the holly under cover of darkness, but then we wouldn't have been able to see what we were picking.)

On returning to the cottage and divesting ourselves of all our outer layers, we would get back into the living room to find a cosy fire blazing up the chimney and a new pair of slippers for each of us waiting, warming on the hearth. There is something so comforting about slipping your feet into pre-warmed slippers, especially if those feet have just carried you through the frost or freezing rain! It makes a lovely day that bit more special.

Mulled Wine

An alcoholic recipe, more suited to adults who need to warm up and chill out!
NOTE: *even when made with home-made wine, this can prove to be remarkably – and insidiously – potent!*
Gillian

INGREDIENTS:

3½ pints (2 L) red wine

5 fl oz (140 ml) rum or brandy – optional

1 ½ pints (850 ml) water

2 lemons, thinly pared rind and juice

4 oz (112 g) sugar or 1–2 tablespoons honey

20 cloves

3 teaspoons cinnamon powder

2 teaspoons ginger

METHOD:

- Heat all the ingredients in a pan, but *do NOT allow to boil*.
- Simmer for ten minutes and then strain into heatproof jug or bowl.
- Slice citrus fruits to float on the top.
- Serve hot.

MIDWINTER FLOWERING

There are also various customs and beliefs around England which concern the unseasonal leafing or flowering of specific trees and bushes at Midwinter or Christmas.

The most well known of these is the Holy Thorn at Glastonbury in Somerset, which is supposed to have sprouted from the staff which Joseph of Arimathea carried when he came with his 'nephew' Jesus to the British Isles; when he stuck it in the ground one day it grew roots and its descendants always flower at Christmas.

At Stoke Edith and Kingsthorne in Herefordshire, holy thorns always blossomed at Midwinter, and in Wormsley, in the same county, a holy thorn reputedly always blossomed exactly at midnight on Twelfth Night (old Christmas Day, until the calendar was changed in the eighteenth century); in 1908, forty people reputedly bore witness to this occurrence.

There have been a whole raft of thorn-flowering instances reported in places including Quainton, Shenley and Church End in Buckinghamshire; Sutton Poyntz in Dorset; Houghton-le-Spring in Durham; Brickendon in Hertfordshire; Wormsley, Rowlstone and Dorstone in Herefordshire; Newland, Ripple and Tardebigge in Worcestershire; and West Buckland, Woolmingston and Whitestaunton in Somerset.

Of course there are many other stories and beliefs about the spirits which reside in thorn trees which pre-date the Christian religion, but it is interesting to ponder on. I wonder just how many of these thorns might still survive today? Certainly people on several occasions over the years have had a go at chopping down the Holy Thorn in Glastonbury.

I wonder why? Can individuals – or groups – really feel such animosity towards or be so threatened by a small tree?

But there may be a simple explanation to the winter flowering. It has been found that the thorn which grows in Glastonbury is a *Crataegus monogyna 'Biflora'*, which is not a native species of Britain. I wonder if all the winter flowering thorns were originally taken from the same plant? DNA of all known descendants matches and experts at Kew have identified it as the Levantine/Palestine Hawthorn. Perhaps Joseph of Arimathea really did bring it? It would certainly appear that *someone* imported it from the Middle East... and a very long time ago.

THE GREEN MAN

The Green Man or Green King appears in many stories, such as the one about King Arthur, and his likeness is carved into the stones and woodwork of many of the old Norman churches and cathedrals. If you look carefully you can find the head of a man mysteriously emerging from the leaves with foliage sprouting from his mouth and covering his face. The mediaeval masons and master wood carvers were still paying homage to the wild natural energies of the places the churches stood in and the raw living materials of their trade. These foliate heads were given the name 'Green Man' by folklorist Lady Raglan in 1939. He is the virtual embodiment of the life force that runs rampant through every green and growing thing, which is why he particularly predominates at the spring and early summer festivals such as May day. But as the representation of green life he has his place at Midwinter too, the male aspect of the feminine Earth goddess and all growing and flowering life.

Over the centuries the Christian church has variously demonised and embraced the use of living green decoration at Christmas. When the church was trying to eradicate earlier pagan practices the decoration of churches was strictly forbidden, but it was soon found to be futile; the much older practices were so deeply engrained into the human psyche that, try what they would, the church couldn't part the congregation from their earlier beliefs. So a modicum of leeway was exercised and holly and ivy were allowed in – we even have the Christmas carol 'The Holly and the Ivy' with reference to the holly wearing the 'crown'… now what exactly might that have to do with the birth of Jesus? Mistletoe has never officially been allowed as a church decoration; Druidic belief stretches out from the mists of time and still touches us!

COMMENT FROM JOAN: TOASTING BY THE FIRE, 1961
At present I am sitting on the fender-stool with my back to the fire and my, how warm it feels. Reminds me of what people used to say to me when a child: 'If you sit so close to the fire you'll melt the marrow in your backbone.' Why backbone I don't know, but I sort of remember that I read somewhere that there was more than a grain of truth in it.

WINTER GARDENS TO VISIT

Winter gardens – gardens which are planned and planted specifically to give interest and pleasure during the winter – are becoming increasingly popular as a way of extending the season to visitors all the year round in parks, pleasure gardens and particularly large country houses and stately homes. They provide beauty and inspiration and a jolly good reason to get out and get some fresh air and have a good walk and enjoy an aspect of nature which we all too often ignore. It is also one way of seeing what some evergreens look like when they are growing, rather than just look-ing at them on the computer screen or in a picture. Below are just a few suggestions of places you might like to visit, but I strongly recommend that you make enquiries in your own area and see what gems you can find!

The Winter Garden at the Cambridge University Botanic Gardens

Anglesey Abbey, Gardens and Lode Mill, Cambridgeshire

Bodnant Garden, Conwy, North Wales

Dunham Massey, Cheshire: 700 plant species and 1,600 shrubs on a seven-acre site, the largest garden of its kind within the UK

Mottisfont, Hampshire

The gardens at Kew, Alnwick in Northumberland and the Lost Garden of Heligan in Cornwall also usually have lantern-lit walks and trails, opening specially at dusk into the early evening – perhaps a visit to one of these might be one of your special pre-Christmas treats?

And if you have small children – or are simply that way inclined! – why not decorate your own garden for Midwinter? Not with the garish neon-coloured lights which festoon the fronts of buildings but with softer, more subtle lights and lanterns hung or hidden in the trees and along the paths or around your flower beds. Let your fancy take flight and your imagination explore. You might like to bear in mind an old belief that whoever brings in the greenery for Midwinter metaphorically wears the trousers for the following year!

GROWING YOUR OWN EVERGREENERY

Growing evergreens in your own garden or even wild planting them onto waste ground, woodlands and hedgerows can be extremely rewarding. You can choose the right kind of bush which will hopefully fertilise others around it. It will help to provide you with your own Midwinter decoration. From an ecological point of view it also provides the bird population with much-needed shelter from the elements, and when the nesting season arrives, plenty of sites to bring up young where predators cannot reach them. Evergreens like holly are also good for bees and caterpillars and provide safe sheltered spots for small mammals – like the hedgehog – to hibernate in the deep leaf litter which accumulates beneath their low growing branches.

There is something that you need to know about holly first though. Holly is dioecious, meaning you require separate male and female plants in order for pollination – and the necessary berries – to occur. Females produce berries, males do not. Male and female flowers appear on separate shrubs and for a female bush to produce berries it must therefore be pollinated by a male growing nearby – anywhere up to forty feet away.

Holly flowers, which are tiny and creamy white, appear in May or June and are located between the leaf and branch joint. The small clusters of flowers look similar but the males have more prominent stamens.

The *Ilex* genus contains more than 780 evergreen and thirty deciduous species of trees and shrubs native to North and South America, Europe, Asia, Africa and Australia, so you can see that it grows pretty much worldwide. Holly will flourish in most soils and copes well in full sun or shade, but does not like it too wet or boggy.

If you decide to buy a named cultivar for your garden they are usually to be found in both male and female varieties; for example, Blue Prince and Blue Princess, China Boy and China Girl and Blue Stallion and Blue Maid. But this rule does not always apply; in variegated golden hollies such as Golden King and Golden Queen genders are reversed. Better to enquire first and just check that you are getting what you think you are buying!

If you feel so inspired it is easy to go online these days and look up propagation, varieties and availability for your part of the world, but here are just a few suggestions to get you started.

HOLLIES

Ilex aquifolium, English Holly: the most common within the British Isles; glossy dark green spiky leaves and bright red berries.

Ilex aquifolium, 'Madame Briot': large spiny variegated leaves of dark green and bright yellow with slightly orange-tinted berries.

Ilex aquifolium, 'Argentea Marginata': broad foliage with creamy white margin surrounding olive green centre with clusters of bright red berries.

Ilex x altaclerensis, 'Lawsoniana': bright yellow and pale green leaves, brownish red berries in clusters and almost spine free foliage.

Ilex cornuta, Chinese Holly: one of the few types of holly that can actually produce berries without male pollination. The berries may vary in colour from red through dark orange to yellow.

Ilex x meserveae, 'Blue Holly': produces attractive bluish-green foliage with purple stems and red berries.

IVIES

Hedera helix, 'Parsley Crested': brightly coloured leaves with tightly waved leaf margins; the surface of the leaf may also be puckered or waved and results in an attractive and intriguing plant which produces long 'trails' and is ideal for cutting, for arrangements or to grow in hanging baskets.

Hedera helix, 'Ivalace': habit of producing long trailing stems which are excellent for floral arrangements. Glossy, boldly lobed, bright green leaves accentuated with pale veins and which feature crimped almost rippled edges. Makes a good 'standard' and is ideal for cascading over balustrades or as ground cover.

OTHER EVERGREENS

Mahonia aquifolium, 'Apollo': evergreen shrub with leathery pinnate leaves which are often spine-toothed with fragrant yellow flowers in late winter and early spring followed by black or purple berries. (There are many kinds of *mahonia*, from miniatures in pots to full-sized shrubs, and they make a lovely alternative or accompaniment to the other more traditional evergreens with the additional benefit of flowering early and being some of the first cut flowers to be brought into the house after the Midwinter festivities.)

Laurus nobilis, otherwise known as bay, sweet bay and bay laurel: will grow in full sun or partial shade. Will also grow in containers where it can be trained and clipped to shape, but is more hardy and thrives better if planted into the open ground.

Cotoneaster: lots of red berries in winter; can be used in Midwinter decorations and arrangements, but is also excellent for the birds.

Berberis: in this genus there are more than 450 evergreen and deciduous shrubs from all around the Northern Hemisphere, northern and tropical Africa and South America. They differ widely in habit from dwarf species to large garden shrubs, some of which make good hedging plants. They have a variety of leaf and berry colour leading up to Midwinter.

Rosemary: a wonderful aromatic evergreen shrub which should not be confined to the kitchen!

Hawthorn and the rose also provide wonderful red berries for decoration and arrangements – if the birds have left you any by the time December comes around!

PLEASE NOTE: *Do not over-crop or disfigure a plant when gathering your evergreenery, rather try to open it up and improve its shape and take from several bushes rather than just one.*

Consider the birds and other wildlife which may be depending on the leaves and branches for shelter and the berries for vital midwinter food sources – do not take too much or too many from one spot.

Walk lightly upon the Earth and understand that you share it with many other – often unnoticed – beings which have an equal right to live and thrive.

The Christmas Tree

Golden blue-tipped flames in gypsy dance
Encircle scarlet caverns with their deep-throated glow,
While youthful eyes seek pictures and the glowing coals entrance,
Keep out the biting cold of frost and snow.

'WINTER FIRE', G. MONKS

I THINK THAT it is fair to say that – with the exception of water – trees are the most important things on this planet. Without them, humanity would not have survived and would never have achieved the level of population or civilisation that we have. Take a few minutes to consider.

As far as we know, trees first appeared on Earth some 390 million years ago. They are the largest, oldest, longest-living life forms on the planet, reaching over 350 feet in height and somewhere in excess of 8,000 years in age (referring to the North American coastal redwoods and the Fortingall Yew in Scotland respectively). There is not a geographical location or culture that has not been influenced in some way by trees – they have always been an integral part of humanity's existence.

Historically in this part of the Northern Hemisphere it was the birch tree that was first to colonise the wet wastelands and grassy tundra around 12,000 years ago as the last ice age retreated. Humanity largely spread northwards, following the edge of the new forests, shaping their environment with the use of wood which was used to build houses, food stores, animal shelters, fences and defences and later to construct bridges and various forms of transport such as wheels, carts and boats. Most importantly, trees have provided the fuel with which to feed our fires, enabling us to cook our food and keep ourselves warm. Trees have also provided food, furniture and medicines, the raw materials for constructing weaving looms, basketry and dyes, and more recently, items such as glue and paper. The industrial revolution would never have taken place without the charcoal and coal – made from ancient compressed wood – with which to smelt the base metals.

Even now, in the twenty-first century, we still rely heavily on trees and their products: we still use wood in our construction industry, we still have furniture which is largely made from wood. Do you have a wealth of nuts, seeds, fruits, syrups and spices or olive oil in your kitchen? They are all products of trees. Do you read newspapers, magazines or books? Do you use toiletries? They are all produced using derivatives of trees. And our modern good health relies heavily on tree products too; for herbal, homeopathy and massage treatments in the 'alternative' sector, but also in mainstream medicine – the yew tree, for example, is providing docetaxel (Taxotere) and paclitaxel (Taxol) in our fight against cancer.

Trees also keep our planet stable and habitable. They regulate the temperature of the land surface, moderating the extremes of heat and cold that affect our desert regions. They stabilise the temperature of the soil, which is vitally important for microorganisms to promote life and growth. Trees balance our water tables, absorbing large amounts of water from the surrounding land, which is why it has been suggested that, in view of recent flooding, our upland areas should be reforested. Conversely, if clear felling is allowed to take place, it can result in the water table shrinking, the land becoming barren and the regional climate changing.

Water that is exposed to direct sunlight loses its health and integrity, especially that in springs, rivers and streams which can lead to what is termed 'wild water'. This means that the current, weakened by over-heating, increasingly fails to transport sediments from the bottom of the river bed and it fills up with stones and mud. Thus the water currents, which are normally concentrated towards the centre of the river, are diverted to the outside, undermining and destroying riverbanks and allowing flooding to take place.

But more important than any of this is the fact that trees are the lungs of our planet, absorbing carbon dioxide and giving out oxygen. They also maintain and strengthen the Earth's magnetic field by constantly discharging electricity into the atmosphere. This electricity is very weak but vitally significant when multiplied billions and trillions of times and it is this which, with the magnetosphere, protects the Earth from harmful rays from the Sun and cosmos. Unfortunately, with widespread deforestation there has been a 10 per cent reduction in the magnetic field since 1838.

As Colin Tudge writes in The Secret Life of Trees: 'The index of the health of the land, and thus its inhabitants, can be measured by the health of the trees. Trees create the context in which all living systems thrive and increase.' But then think about how many of our native trees are currently under threat from disease, let alone land clearance. What does this say about our own health and future?

TREES AS SPIRITUAL GUIDES

Trees are nature's perfect example of growth, reproduction and regeneration. Humanity's physical dependence went – possibly still goes – hand in hand with our spiritual needs. To early humans trees appeared immortal due to their longevity and were also their primary source of life. Many cultures have believed in a cosmic tree, a great mythical tree that formed the centre or axis mundi of the world with its roots penetrating deep into the underworld and our primaeval beginnings while its branches carried all forms of life and reached onwards up into the heavens.

Cosmic trees were characterised as the pillar of the world, the cradle of humanity and the centre of the planet, or even the universe – the sacred link, the path on which one can pass from Earth to other and heavenly realms. They were regarded as sources of wisdom and structures of understanding, and few people held trees in such high regard as the Celts, although the worship of the oak tree or oak god appears to have been shared by all descendants of the Indo-Europeans.

The concept of the Christmas tree contains all that is already written concerning the relevance of sacred evergreenery in the previous chapter, plus a very great deal more. It is actually the northern winter representation of the World Tree, which connects all levels of existence and life. There are three parts or levels to it: the roots, or Lower World, represents death and decay but also the home of our ancestors and 'potential'. The trunk, or Middle World, represents living existence now – our day-to-day world and life. The branches, or Upper World, represent the celestial realms of higher wisdom, progress and divinity.

Divine heroes and gods have variously climbed, died or hung on the World Tree, and they have all inevitably brought back gifts when they descended from it. These include Odin, who climbed the ash tree, *Yggdrasil*, and hung there upside-down for nine days in order to gain wisdom and the knowledge of the runes, and Jesus Christ, who hung on the cross for three days and was rewarded with forgiveness for humanity and the gift of eternal life.

In particular, the oak has been venerated. In ancient Greece, Zeus was the oak god, wielding powers of rain, thunder and lightning. For the Romans it was Jupiter who held sway over the same natural occurrences. The Germanic peoples had *Donar*, Lord of Thunder, who was also dedicated to the oak. Among others the Slavic peoples had a thunder god named *Perun* whose sacred tree was the oak, and in Lithuanian society there was *Perkūnas*, who was also a deity of thunder and lightning and associated with the oak tree.

The oldest stone circles, in Britain and in other parts of the world, probably replaced earlier wooden ones. Some years ago several large Mesolithic post-holes were discovered under the car park at Stonehenge.

They had held pine posts 2' 6" in diameter and had been erected and allowed to rot in situ. They have been dated at around 8,000 years old, pre-dating the current stones erected at Stonehenge by several thousand years.

Shamans, who represent the very first flowering of spiritual activity in every time and place around the globe, traditionally climbed their tent poles, representative of the world tree, to reach other realms of the spirit world.

Trees have also always described the yearly cycles and have been nature's calendar; everyone knew when the trees first came into leaf, blossomed and fruited. Old sayings such as 'ash (in leaf) before oak, there'll be a soak; oak (in leaf) before ash, there'll be a splash' show how until very recently people looked to the trees and their activities to predict the coming weather. They defined time and contributed to the spirit of each place.

So is it any wonder that an evergreen tree carrying the spirit of new life and representing so much that was sacred and important should be revered at the pivotal time of the year when the world was drowning in darkness and the people were awaiting the rebirth of the Sun to bring back life and save them from annihilation?

It is entirely possible that historically, when the late autumn slaughter of the cattle occurred, some of the entrails were taken into the forest and hung from sacred trees as a propitious gift to the spirits of the woodland – hence why we may still decorate our Midwinter trees with red garlanding now.

THE HOLY TREE

Fir trees have always been worshipped in alpine countries, and in the forests of Europe the fir tree has always been looked upon as holy and considered the dwelling place or seat of the gods. Even in the twenty-first century there are people in northern regions who still revere certain trees, usually distinguishable by the presence of a picture of the holy Mary.

In Asia Minor, the fir tree was dedicated to the fertility goddess, Cybele. The Romans associated the closed shape of the fir cone with virginity and dedicated it to their goddess of the hunt and the forest, Diana. According to a legend of the Siberian Takuten, the souls of their shamans were born in a fir on the slopes of Mount Dzokuo. In northern shamanic cultures holy trees were not to be cut down or stolen, and anyone who did so would be punished by illness or death – or at the very least, seven years of bad luck. Fir wood was reserved for ritual purpose and implements.

Tacitus tells us that in the forests of Europe the fir had always been holy, describing the feast of Tasana where people carried fir branches in their hands. In Egypt the palm tree was sacred to the goddess Ishtar (as it also was to the goddesses Inanna, Nike and Victoria), and was used and brought into the home at the Winter Solstice as a symbol of life's triumph over death. In Judaism, the ancient Israelite goddess, Asherah, was worshipped by erecting 'Asherah poles', which were either carved wooden poles or actual trees.

The Viking saga of Erik the Red contains an account of Mother's Night (Christmas Eve) when a travelling winter seer would pay the locals an annual visit. She carried a tall decorated staff symbolising a tree. She was greeted with a feast and incantations were sung to summon the spirits of Midwinter.

In the seventh century, Saint Boniface (who was born in Crediton, Devon, England) was a Christian missionary in Bavaria. During one Winter Solstice he was horrified to discover a group of people honouring an oak tree in the forest. Enraged at what he considered to be a pagan practice he immediately had the tree felled to prevent a repetition of such blasphemy. Amazingly the tree worshippers converted to Christianity on the spot. Some sources report that Saint Boniface planted a young evergreen fir tree in place of the felled oak as a symbol of God's undying love. Other sources claim that as the oak crashed to the ground a young fir tree sprang up in its place. Over the years the newly converted Christians began to return to the forest to decorate the fir tree to celebrate Christmas instead of revering the oak in celebration of the Winter Solstice. It is suggested that the practice spread and people began decorating their homes with fir trees.

This whole scenario is contradicted by Aurelius Augustinus, who lived between the years AD 354 and 430 and who, we are told, came to the conclusion that cutting down and destroying the spiritually and culturally sacred trees of the Germanic peoples was counterproductive to the spread of the Christian teachings and that such trees should instead be dedicated / consecrated to Jesus Christ.

GROWTH IN POPULARITY

There is evidence that in Germany craftsmen's guilds began to decorate their guild halls with trees at Christmas time in the fourteenth and fifteenth centuries. The trees were often adorned with fruit and nuts which children were allowed to remove on Christmas Day. Perhaps this is how it came about that as a child I was told that there were Christmas trees in the German merchants' quarter in the city of Manchester long before Prince Albert made the custom popular in Britain – the connection being that of German artisans.

Another claim to having originated the practice of decorating a fir tree as part of the Christmas or new year celebrations comes from the bakers' guild in Freiburg im Breisgau in the year 1419. Others suggest that the city of Tallinn in Estonia was the first to do this in 1441, but the city of Riga in Latvia disputes this, claiming that they first had Christmas trees in 1510. In both later cases the trees were erected by the Brotherhood of Blackheads, which was originally an association of local unmarried merchants, ship owners and foreigners in Livonia, an old name for modern-day Latvia and Estonia.

Across many parts of northern Europe it became the custom to bring small potted cherry or hawthorn plants into the house in the hopes that they would burst into leaf or flower at Christmas time. Poorer people also made pyramids of wood decorated with paper, apples and candles and made to look like a tree.

Possibly the pyramid trees were evolved from the paradise tree which was used in mediaeval German mystery or miracle plays which were acted out in front of churches on Christmas Eve. In the early Christian church calendar, 24th December was Adam and Eve's day. The paradise tree represented the Garden of Eden and was paraded around the town before the play began, possibly as a way of attracting attention and advertising the fact that it was about to take place. Interestingly in mediaeval iconography the tree of paradise was depicted as growing from Adam's grave and it is in this era that we also see Christ as hanging on a tree rather than the cross.

In Scandinavia the Vikings had venerated evergreens as the special plants of their sun god, Balder. On the Greek island of Chios, on Christmas morning the tenant farmers used to present their landlords with a *rhamna*, a pole decorated with wreaths of olive, myrtle and bay leaves and bound with geraniums, anemones, strips of golden and coloured paper, lemons and anything else that they could find. In Circassia a festival took place just before Midwinter when a young pear tree, decorated with candles and with a cheese attached to the top, would be carried into every house in the village accompanied by much singing, drinking and general merry-making.

In the year 1605 it was first noted that at Christmas the good people of Strasbourg set up fir trees in their parlours and decorated them with coloured paper roses, apples, gold foil, wafers and sweets. A few years later a despondent Strasbourg theologian commented that he had no idea where the custom had suddenly appeared from and why it was proving so popular.

When Charlotte, daughter of the Duke of Mecklenburg-Strelitz, married King George III in 1761, she brought her family household traditions with her, including decorating a bough of yew with wax tapers and gifts each Christmas. Members of the court would gather around the decoration and everyone would sing carols and be presented with gifts from the queen. Not surprisingly it was very popular. But at Christmas in 1800, Queen Charlotte didn't just decorate a yew bough, she had an entire tree potted up and the whole thing decorated with tiny wax candles, sweets, toys and raisins wrapped in paper. The queen then threw a children's party at the Queen's Lodge in Windsor on Christmas afternoon – needless to say, children and adults alike were utterly enchanted!

After the turn of the nineteenth century the popularity of the modern Christmas tree gathered momentum. There was mention of it in 1800 in Finland and by 1830 the practice had spread across Norway and Denmark. In 1840, Queen Victoria and Prince Albert brought a Christmas tree to Balmoral, which instantly made the practice fashionable within Britain, and soon everyone was copying the idea. By 1862 it was a growing trend in Sweden and the following year it was reported in Bohemia. After that it rapidly spread across the USA, Spain, Italy and Holland. By the beginning of the twentieth century the practice of having a decorated tree as part of our festive tradition was firmly established.

The idea of the Christmas tree took a firm hold and blossomed in many countries within a comparatively short space of time. Why? Perhaps because with the growing spiritual enlightenment of the nineteenth century it struck a chord of memory within many of us which reached far back into our dim and distant past, resonating with precious beliefs and practices which had long been suppressed and forgotten. It provided something which had been lacking within us – a space which had previously been left wanting. Humanity was ready to re-establish its sacred connections with nature, and where better to begin than with our very best natural allies and supporters, the trees?

LIGHT AND FIRE

Traditionally it was always the afternoon of Christmas Eve when the big Christmas tree was brought into our living room and set upright in its paper-covered metal bucket. Out would come the venerable cardboard boxes, themselves decorated with last summer's feathery dust and cobwebs, and all of them much older than I was myself. Boxes and boxes! Boxes of huge glass balls in every deep jewel colour imaginable (my father's favourite was the royal purple), red paper garlanding and silver tinsel. Then there were the extra special decorations. The little metal bells and candle lanterns which had graced my mother's own childhood trees back in the late 1920s and early 1930s. The huge pink, white and silver ball, painted with tiny rosebuds, which I had once chosen in Woolworths store on one of our autumn expeditions. The white glittery boot with the red felt top. The large star and fairy doll (daintily dressed with delicate silver gauze wings by my mother's quick and clever fingers), which was always the last to go up on the top of the tree... apart from the heavy, shiny silver lametta, a few strands of which were carefully draped over the end of each branch. We would also have dearly loved to put real candles on our tree, but my mother had a horror of the whole thing going up in flames, so we didn't take the risk.

I have to agree that despite the fact that Midwinter is a time to celebrate light and fire, I really do not think that having living naked flames covering a dry and oil-rich tree is a very good or safe idea – more a recipe for disaster! I cannot begin to imagine how the first candles were attached to the early Christmas trees. It must have been an absolute godsend when someone invented the tiny candle holders which clip on to the ends of the branches, but the problem of candles weighting the branches down and/or tipping to drip wax everywhere – and possibly ignite the tree – remained.

It has long been debated as to who actually invented the electric light bulb: the American, Thomas Edison, or the Englishman, Sir Joseph Swan. They both produced light bulbs in the same year, 1879. But what is less well known is that Joseph Swan invented the fairy light. Swan was born in 1828 in the north-east of England in Bishopwearmouth, Sunderland. He grew up to become a very talented physicist, chemist and inventor who patented numerous inventions – over seventy of them in the field of photography alone. In 1881 he was responsible for the first public building in the world to be lit by electric light. This was the Savoy Theatre in London, which was newly opened that year and was fitted with 1,200 incandescent light bulbs.

The following year, in 1882, the owner of the Savoy Theatre, Richard D'Oyly Carte, commissioned Joseph Swan to create miniature electric lights, powered by battery packs hidden in the singers' clothing, to decorate the dresses of four of the leading fairies on the opening night of Gilbert and Sullivan's *Iolanthe*. They were an instant success, and so the term 'fairy lights' came into being.

It was Edward H. Johnson who, in December 1882, became the first person to put fairy lights on a Christmas tree. Johnson was then the vice president of the Edison Electric Light Company. He had eighty tiny hand-wired bulbs made – not especially tiny by today's standards, but reasonably small, about the size of a walnut. They were coloured a patriotic red, white and blue, and he used them to decorate a Christmas tree at his home on Fifth Avenue. They were switched on on 22nd December, and to begin with, the local newspapers took little notice, thinking that it was just some kind of commercial gimmick. But the story was taken up by a newspaper reporter from Detroit and – as the saying goes – the rest is history. A publicity stunt it might have been, but the tremendous global impact and appeal that the lights continue to have cannot be understated.

However, initially they were slow to catch on. The little bulbs became hot easily and fire was a real danger. But in 1895, US President Grover Cleveland sponsored the first electrically lit Christmas tree in the White House. In 1903, General Electric Company in America began to commercially produce the first pre-wired Christmas light kits commercially. Unfortunately, although fairy lights grew in popularity with big businesses, who used them as seasonal decorations, they remained too expensive for the ordinary consumer to buy and didn't become available to the general public until the 1930s.

Electric Christmas lights were first used outside in 1956, when fairy lights were used to decorate some trees in the grounds surrounding the McAdenville community centre in North Carolina. The magic, colour and spectacle which these particular decorations bring into our lives – predominantly at the drabbest time of the year, but also in other seasons too – cannot be disputed. They are one of the relatively recent inventions which are enjoyed by millions around the world.

The world capital for recycling Christmas lights is in Shijiao, China, where 9 million kilos of lights are shipped every year to be broken down. Fortunately, modern techniques in recycling mean that every component can be reused. But that is still an awful lot of lights, especially when you consider how many are kept from year to year, or don't manage to get into the recycling chain but end up in landfill sites.

> COMMENT FROM JOAN: CHOOSING THE TREE
>
> This afternoon, Jill and I chose the Christmas tree. Took quite a long time to find one without two feet of spindly single twig top, that also was equally bushy in all the right places. The ceiling in the living room at the cottage is only seven feet high so we haven't much space to play with. Eventually found one – little Jill almost beside herself with excitement. Jim only just managed to fit it in when he drove over from work at teatime to pick us up, so many carrier bags and parcels and then all the extra boxes of groceries from Booths.
>
> Now said tree is standing in a bucket of water out by the Potting Shed. Smells glorious! Keep making up reasons to walk up that way, even in the dark, just so I can plunge my face into its feathery greenery and inhale all the excitement of this sacred coming season.

THE WINTER TREE

Wonderful though my childhood home was, there was one drawback to it which only really impacted us at Midwinter: we didn't have electricity, which meant that if we daren't use candles on our tree, we had no lights on it at all. We had to make do with the reflected light of all the shiny colour and glittery sparkles. What a difference all the solar-powered coloured lights would have made to us then!

I love the rampant colour and blatant gaudiness of Christmas. But I also feel deeply drawn towards the living greenery and natural aspect of

Midwinter. In our house we have full-sized Christmas trees in both the living room and dining room, and they are covered in all the decorations which we have accumulated over our lifetime in a marvellously eclectic jumble of styles and colours and themes. But the drawing room I keep solely for real evergreens and natural decorations.

The first time I decided to do this I brought in several small trees from the garden – bays around four or five feet tall which my mother had propagated for me; a couple of three-foot-high pale evergreens which had been gifts the previous Christmas and a fir tree that we had brought back from Germany as a tiny six-inch seedling and which had now also reached about five feet in height. I set them around the edges of the room and decorated them very sparingly with wooden or natural decorations in the shape of fruit or birds and hid strings of lights among their small branches. I also hung a kissing ball overhead from the centre of the room and there were copper jugs of holly and a swag of evergreens across the chimney breast above the fireplace. The whole effect was like walking into a little winter forest and sitting in the midst of a magical grove.

My next idea was prompted by one of my birthday trips to the garden centre, where a part of the display was a bare winter tree reaching from floor to ceiling and draped in silver frosted strands of moss and silver, white and green baubles, birds, fairies and gnomes. I was enchanted by it and determined to have my own. Fortunately we have a large willow tree in our garden which was self-sown too near to a retaining wall and which also now casts far too much shade. I had already decided that it would have to come down – at least be reduced in height and kept at a more manageable size – and the thought struck me that we could use one of its branches for our 'tree'.

I was not to be daunted by the logistics of such an idea. Trying to calculate the size, height and shape of a branch when it is thrashing around fifteen feet above your head is not easy. Having felled the chosen limb, the next step was to trim it down a bit to further reduce its overall mass without spoiling the shape. It was still quite huge when the time came to take it in through the front door. My husband tried the more calculated approach of lifting it – almost impossible – all the while muttering his concerns and doubts. It didn't help that a few weeks previously I'd had new windows and a new front door installed and I gritted my teeth and prayed that there would be no damage as I seized the end of the trunk and charged the unforgiving aperture. There were some horrible scratching noises, lots of grunting and panting as my husband grabbed the other end of the trunk as it hurtled past him and in a shower of dry leaves and broken twigs we were through the door, across the hall and into the drawing room! (An occasion like this is a very good time to serve hot spicy mulled wine... soothes frayed nerves and warms people up if they have just spent some time wielding a saw and balanced on a ladder ten feet up in the bitter wind and perpetual gloom of a midwinter's day.)

It looked like a minor hurricane had swept through the house but in fact clearing up the debris did not take that long. After more trimming with bow saw and loppers the tree was finally up, its base clamped in the jaws of a Christmas tree stand, its topmost branch wedged up against the ceiling with an extra anchor rope around it halfway up which my husband tied to a large hook screwed into the wall... just in case it suddenly decided to topple as it dried out.

The first thing to be put on the tree was a couple of lengths of lights – these bridge the best of both worlds as they are electric but made in the shape of three-inch-high candles. I wound lengths of fresh ivy up the trunk and added a garland of frosted synthetic gold and bronze oak leaves. The anchor rope I also disguised with ivy. Around the base I draped a swathe of dark green velvet material, leaving a place where I could easily top up the water reservoir in the stand each day, and stood several little trees in pots on it and sat some woodland elves among them. (Another year I made a 'Midwinter Lord' figure which stands about two and a half feet high, sporting vigorous beard and hair and dressed in a long green cloak and red pointed cap – he sits enigmatically silent among the gaily wrapped gifts as they accumulate in the days before the 25th.) From the branches I hung gold, silver and green decorations – baubles, birds, icicles, snowflakes, and some of the lovely soft trailing moss similar to that which had graced the tree at the garden centre. I also included fruits in natural reds, orange and yellows. The tradition of bringing in our winter tree was born!

Admittedly our Winter Tree is not an evergreen – I always have lots of evergreenery around the house anyway – but it seems very authentic to our land, geographical area and our beliefs. For us the spirits of winter still shelter among its decorated branches and it is admired and loved by us all and stays with us until sometime in February – either until *Gŵyl Ffraid* at the beginning of that month or until Saint Valentine's day. Sometime around the middle of January I remove the obvious Christmas decorations from it, leaving just the glittering icicles and moss, so that it no longer holds the connotations of Christmas and truly becomes a tree which represents the frosty winter season.

Here in Wales we have our own patron saint of lovers, Saint Dwynwen, whose celebratory day falls on 25th January. Sometimes I add some new decorations to the Winter Tree to mark this event; other years I save the heart-shaped baubles and spring flowers until Saint Valentine's day on 14 February. The Winter Tree finally returns to the outside world soon after that – the twiggy tops to be ceremonially burned and the trunk to be cut into logs and stored away for the fire the following Midwinter. Or, as happened on one occasion, my son took the wood to turn on his lathe and make into bowls and candlesticks, preserving the now sacred wood to be used at many other Christmases / Midwinters.

As for felling the tree, we remove a large branch each year but there are many branches. Furthermore, the tree is rapidly regrowing in the places where branches have already been removed, so I don't suppose that it shall ever be truly 'felled', but it does ensure that we will have our beautiful Winter Tree for many years to come!

WHAT IS YULE?

The name 'Yule' is derived from the Saxon word *hweol*, meaning wheel, and referring to the cyclical nature of the seasons of the year; also the circular motion of the Sun, which is reborn at this time. The term 'Yule' was first recorded in the early 900s and was the twelve-day celebration of Midwinter for the Scandinavian and Germanic peoples of northern Europe. *Julblot* was a solemn feast when sacrifices were made to the gods to earn blessings on the forthcoming germinating crops and growing season. The god of Yule – or *Jol* – was *Jolner*, one of the god Odin's many names.

The yule log (which, these days, most people only think of in relation to a chocolate cake) was the largest and best log to be ceremonially brought into the house to be burned during the festival of Yule. I say 'log' but it really needed to be a whole tree trunk as, once lit, it had to last for the whole twelve days of celebration. Moreover, there had to be a portion of it left over so that it could be kept until the following Midwinter and used to light the next Yule fire. This is strongly reminiscent of the ancient sacred fires of May, October and Midwinter which were ritually kindled after all the other household fires in the community had been extinguished. Fire was then taken from the sacred bonfire and used to relight all the domestic home fires afresh.

With so many people now living in towns and cities with no recourse to finding or harvesting a real wooden tree log, let alone burning it without a hearth or open fire, there are still a few alternatives that you can try. If you wish to keep a fire burning throughout the Midwinter/Christmas period, you can always purchase one of the big, long-burning church candles. Making absolutely sure that it is on a flat, flame-retardant surface where nothing can blow it, knock it over or float down onto it, you could light and burn it for a period of time every day – rather like an Advent candle but for the Twelve Days instead, and keep the stub to relight the next year and light a new candle from.

Or you can make a yule log decoration. Look out for a nicely coloured and/or interestingly shaped log. If you have that kind of garden you might find what you want on your own property, either from something that has fallen naturally or from something that needs to be coppiced, trimmed or felled. Or you may have access to woodland – always ask permission of the owner. Perhaps you may contact someone who supplies firewood and explain what you are looking for. Most people are usually interested in something a bit different and only too glad to help. Just remember that wherever you get your log(s) from, make sure that you do not damage or deface the tree or area it is situated in... and ask permission of the tree for good measure, that ought to cover all eventualities!

I include some instructions on how to decorate and complete your yule log using dried leaves and flowers, fresh evergreenery, acorns, beech masts and gilded nuts – the fir cone gnomes look charming perched among the leaves. The possibilities are endless. A single candle(s) can be added and it makes a lovely centrepiece for the Christmas dinner or tea table, or as a decoration for the sideboard, hall table or window sill. It also makes a very good present with the added benefit that it is wholly recyclable... why not give them to all your friends and relations this year?

How to Make a Yule Log Decoration

YOU WILL NEED:

A wooden log. Oak, silver birch and beech are good but wood
    from any tree can be used. If possible, look for an interesting
    shape with a dividing branch or twigs growing from it
Greenery, e.g. ivy, holly or fir
Candles, 1" diameter, white or coloured, especially dark green
    or red
Small coloured balls, birds, etc.
Fir cone gnomes

TO MAKE:

- Decide which way up your log looks best and is most stable.
- With a 1" drill bit, make one or two holes in the top, ½" deep into which to insert candles.
- Secure candle(s) in hole(s) with a little melted wax or blu tack.
- Decorate to taste, attaching greenery with press pins, balancing a couple of fir cone gnomes among the greenery to resemble the spirits of the Midwinter evergreens.

NOTE: FIRE HAZARD! Make sure greenery doesn't stick up near candle flame(s) as it burns down. For safety, consider using small battery operated synthetic candles instead.

A wooden log makes a good basis for a flower arrangement or decoration at *any* time of the year – Easter primroses and little eggs are very effective, or autumn leaves, nuts and berries for the autumn equinox in September, or even as an adjunct to your Hallowe'en / *Calan Gaeaf* decorations, or an alternative to the Ancestor Tree, with one candle, a single photo and perhaps a couple of little tissue 'ghosts' to keep it company?

Finally, you may choose to make a Christmas chocolate log cake. You may wish to bake it mindfully and need not necessarily involve anyone else but you in knowing of its deeper significance, or it may be eaten with ritual reverence and / or raucous celebration. If you don't feel up to making the cake you can always buy a reasonably priced undecorated Swiss roll from the supermarket and still put your own individual stamp on it by the way you decorate it. But I have my mother's recipe for a particularly delicious chocolate log cake which you really might like to try as it combines the rich satisfaction of chocolate with the fresh taste and colour of mint – always a winning combination and one which isn't quite so sickly when there are so many other rich foods around.

Minty Yule Log

A chocolate cake with a difference!
Gillian

INGREDIENTS:

For the cake:

6 oz (170 g) castor sugar – plus extra for sprinkling

4 eggs, separated

1 teaspoon almond extract

4 oz (112 g) self-raising flour, plus extra for dusting

1 oz (28 g) cocoa powder

For the icing:

9 oz (250 g) softened butter

9 oz (250 g) icing sugar

1 oz (28 g) cocoa powder

Mint essence

Green food colouring

METHOD:

- Preheat the oven to 190°C / 375°F / Gas Mark 5. Grease and line a 16" × 11" / 40 × 28 cm Swiss roll tin and dust with flour.
- Reserve 2 tablespoons of the castor sugar and whisk the remainder with the egg yolks in a bowl until thick and pale.
- Stir in the almond extract. Whisk the egg whites in a separate clean bowl until soft peaks form.
- Gradually whisk in the reserved sugar until stiff and glossy.
- Sift half the flour and cocoa powder over the egg yolk mixture and fold in, then fold in one-quarter of the egg whites.
- Sift and fold in the remaining flour, followed by the remaining egg whites.
- Spoon mixture into the prepared tin, spreading it out evenly with a spatula.
- Bake in the preheated oven for 15 minutes until set and firm to the touch.
- Sprinkle castor sugar over a sheet of greaseproof paper and turn the cake out onto the paper. Roll up with paper inside it and leave to cool.
- Beat the butter and icing sugar together. Divide mixture and set one half aside.
- Add several drops of mint essence and green food colouring to half the buttercream mixture. Do this slowly – the mixture should be quite strongly minty in flavour but only a pale mint green to look at.
- Gently unroll the cool cake and remove the paper. Making sure it is evenly mixed, spread the minty green buttercream over

the cake, covering almost to the edges, and roll up again.

- Add cocoa powder to other half of buttercream and beat in well.
- Set the cake upon a decorative plate or silver board and coat all sides and both ends with the chocolate butter cream.
- Mark with a fork so that the surface resembles the bark of an oak tree.
- Can be decorated with holly and a sprinkling of icing sugar to represent snow.

WHEN the cake is cut into, the whirls of pale green icing inside make a pleasing pattern, highlighting the circular log effect, and the mint flavour lends a really fresh, unusual twist to what can otherwise sometimes be a cake which is sickly sweet.
Gillian

FIR AND SPRUCE TREES

Fir trees are a genus of more than fifty evergreen coniferous trees in the family of Pinaceae. They are found through much of North and Central America, Europe, Asia and North Africa, occurring in mountains over most of the range. They can grow up to 200 feet tall. The Black Forest of Europe got its name from the dark dense needle growth of fir trees and the densest fir forests are still found in this region.

Spruce trees are found in Europe, North America and as far east as Asia. The visible difference between fir and spruce is the position of the fir cones on the branches – fir cones point up and spruce cones point down to the ground. Fir needles are softer and run horizontally from the branches; spruce needles are pointed and grow in a circle around the branch.

SOME POPULAR VARIETIES... THE CHOICE IS YOURS

NORWAY SPRUCE, *Picea abies*: can be found growing naturally in northern and central Europe and is the traditional tree used for Christmas in many homes throughout Britain and the Continent. Half- to one-inch-long green needles; neat, conical shape and wonderful fragrance. Does require a great deal of water once cut though and is prone to shed its needles.

SCOTS PINE, *Pinus sylvestris*: native of the once extensive Caledonian Forest, it is the only timber-producing conifer native to the UK. Long, flexible, soft, blue-green needles which give the tree a soft, fluffy look. The firm branches and dense foliage are best paired with larger bold ornaments that won't get lost in the boughs. Good strong pine fragrance.

NORDMANN FIR, *Abies nordmanniana*: originally from southern Russia but becoming increasingly popular, especially in Denmark. Tends to be more expensive to buy but its soft glossy needles, fat branches and attractive bushy shape coupled with its excellent needle retention possibly make it worthwhile. Its symmetrically arranged strong branches produce the ideal pyramidal specimen for a Christmas tree.

NOBLE FIR, *Abies procera*: 'king of the Christmas trees', it holds its blue-green needles very well.

FRASER FIR, *Abies fraseri*: originating from Virginia and North Carolina in the USA, this is still quite new to the British markets. It is a compact tree so is good for small spaces. Strong upturned branches with fairly soft citrus-scented needles which it holds for a long time.

BLUE SPRUCE, *Picea pungens*: very attractive tree but not always easily available to buy.

CARE FOR YOUR TREE

A tree – and particularly a Christmas tree – is just like any other plant that you might buy. When choosing a tree always make sure that it is in good condition, fresh and green in colour and certainly not dry, brown or shedding needles. As soon as you get it home, put it somewhere sheltered but cool – a protected part of your garden where it won't get damaged or blown away by the wind, or failing that in a shed or garage. Release it from its net and plunge it into a bucket of fresh cold water – preferably rain water rather than chemically treated tap water.

If it is bare rooted, give it a good drink and then get it potted up as soon as possible, making sure that it has sufficient water without drowning it. If it is already in a pot, make sure that the soil is always moist. If the weather is damp, having it outside will be best as it will benefit from the natural rainfall and moist air. If it is a cut tree, then leave it in the water bucket until you are ready to bring it inside, but keep checking to make sure that the bucket doesn't run low or dry.

Christmas cards and pictures always show the Christmas tree standing right next to the fire, but like any other living plant it has feelings, and it is really best to place it somewhere cool – away from radiators, at the opposite end of the room from the fire or even in a cooler room or hallway. Having said that, it is a main focal point, so it should be at the heart of all the activity and celebration... just bear all this in mind and do your best!

When choosing the place to put it try not to block windows, doorways or passageways to the annoyance and detriment of the rest of the household. If you are going to decorate your tree with electric lights, make sure that the tree is within easy distance of an electrical socket, or that you have a suitable length of extension cable, unless you plan on using battery operated lights, which are remarkably effective these days and so freeing.

If you have a cut tree, saw the bottom two or three inches off the trunk before bringing it in. This will refresh its ability to suck up water. Then place it in a large enough container – either a bucket or tub or one of the purpose-made stands which hold a tree remarkably firmly and have built-in water reservoirs; they can be a bit expensive but last for many years and are a good investment. On the other hand, their water capacity isn't huge, which definitely necessitates checking/refilling them every day, so you may wish to stick with a large bucket and bricks or stones to wedge the tree in place, and then top up with water. Whatever type of tree you choose (potted, bare rooted or cut) just remember to water frequently and under no circumstances allow it to dry out. Again, just do the best you can!

Finally, decorate whatever kind of stand or tub you have put your tree in, either using material or Christmas paper or tinsel or anything else that takes your fancy. Just remember that this is a living thing and an ancient symbol of everlasting and ever-renewing life and hope.

OLD HABITS DIE HARD

For tens of thousands of years folk have gone out into the Midwinter woods to honour the wild energies of natural life. The following true story is a wonderful illustration of how the memory of ancient sacred activity remains buried deep within our psyche – our very genetic coding – and even if people have absolutely no idea why, they will still find themselves drawn to certain activities which they cannot explain but feel a compulsion to enter into.

Some years ago, my son was out walking with his dog a few days before Christmas. He had taken a less frequented path which he rarely used and was enjoying the frosty sunshine when he rounded a curve in the path and could hardly believe his eyes... indeed, to begin with he doubted his sanity! For there beside the path was a small oak tree which had gaily coloured baubles and tinsel hanging from it. Unusually for him, he had gone out without his phone and dashed back home to get it so that he could take a photo of the tree because otherwise, he reasoned, no one would ever believe him.

Just as he returned to the tree, a woman was approaching from another direction carrying more decorations, which she proceeded to add to those already hanging there. My son took his photo and asked the woman why she had done it. She replied that she had decorated a little tree somewhere in that wood for several years running and that it just seemed a nice thing to do. She added that, despite it being a popular spot for dog walkers and youngsters, her seasonal decorations were never damaged or disturbed by people – little short of miraculous in this day and age – and just another example of deep-seated instinct enhancing respect for the sacred tree of the wild woods.

Father Christmas

He was dressed all in fur, from his head to his foot,
And his clothes were all tarnished with ashes and soot;
A bundle of toys he had flung on his back,
And he looked like a pedlar just opening his pack.

'A VISIT FROM ST NICHOLAS', CLEMENT C. MOORE

ONE OF THE most widely known and best loved figures of Christmas in the twentieth and twenty-first centuries is Father Christmas (known as Santa Claus in America). He is the epitome of jollity and fun, a friendly and benign spirit just for the children who represents gift-giving and the rewards of 'being good', and he brings light, love and excitement into our lives at the darkest time of the year.

But who or what is Father Christmas? Where does he fit into the other Midwinter events of rebirth, the return of the Sun and the preservation and perpetuation of natural life and the cycle of the seasons?

There are many different theories about the origins of Santa Claus, aka Father Christmas, and the lives and actions of many historical (as well as mythical) figures are attributed to him.

NICHOLAS AND WILD PETER

In old Europe, across many countries including Germany, Austria, Switzerland, Poland, Estonia and the Netherlands, Saint Nicholas was a seasonal visitor; a stern, dour, judgemental bishop who visited homes in full episcopal attire and demeanour, his sole purpose to judge good and evil. Children anxiously prepared for his visit, revising their church lessons, praying that they would pass the ecclesiastical quiz he would set them. The children who gave the correct answers were given sweets and other little gifts.

But with Saint Nicholas came his companion Wild Peter, a hairy, horned, blackened, devilish monster. Wild Peter's job was simple: to terrify the children whilst they underwent their exam and to stuff them into his copious sack and carry them off to hell for a year if they didn't know their scripture. Of course, good Saint Nicholas always saved the 'bad' children, who would then be merely given gifts of ashes, coal or sticks. This was just as well as in earlier times Wild Peter might have beaten them or – as was widespread popular belief – torn out their stomachs.

Beginning in the nineteenth century it was proclaimed in America that Santa Claus was a more up-to-date interpretation of Saint Nicholas, the tradition having been originally brought over from Europe by the Dutch community who celebrated the saint's day back in the Netherlands. But Saint Nicholas, the amiable gift-giver, didn't appear in America until *after* Santa Claus had become an established figure. What is more, the Dutch colonists in question were members of the Dutch Reformed church and as such had no time for the celebration of saints' days as they were strongly opposed to the Catholic church and all such 'papist shenanigans'. In actual fact the legend that the Dutch brought Saint Nicholas to America was invented by Washington Irving in an 1809 satire, the fictional *Knickerbocker's History of New York*, and has no basis in fact.

It is rather to Saint Nicholas's reprobate companion, glowering from the shadows, that we must look for the origins of Santa. With his coat of hair, dishevelled beard, bag and face blackened with ashes, he isn't laughing a merry 'Ho! Ho! Ho!', but he is in fact the creature who fathered Father Christmas, not Washington Irving or even some Asian saint.

It was the German immigrants in Pennsylvania who celebrated the Yule season with one of their most notable traditions – a character called Pelznickel, which literally means 'furry Nicholas', *Pelz* in German meaning hide or fur coat – the word that has become 'pelt' in English. Pelznickel was indeed 'dressed all in fur from his head to his foot' and was known by many variations of his name, including Bellschnickle and Bellschniggle among others, following in a global spiritual belief that calling a god or deity by its real name should always be avoided at all costs.

The forms in which the Christmas visitor appeared in early Pennsylvania might have been lost to us if it hadn't been for a man called Alfred Shoemaker who wrote a book entitled *Christmas in Pennsylvania:*

A *Folk-Cultural Study*. Shoemaker tells us that early nineteenth-century Pelznickel went from house to house, whip in hand, with cookies and chestnuts, rewarding well-behaved children but frightening and whipping those who had been naughty. Pelznickel's appearance varied but he was always black-faced, bell-jingling, dressed in animal skins or patches and carrying a whip or bag. The *Philadelphia Gazette* of 19 December 1827 describes Bellschniggle as: 'Ebony in appearance, dressed in skins or old clothes, his face black, a bell, a whip and a pocket full of cakes and nuts… It is no sooner dark than Bellschniggle's bell is heard flitting from house to house… He slips down the chimney at the fairy hour of midnight, and deposits his presents quietly in the prepared stocking.'

Here, surely, it is easy to see the forerunner characteristics of our jovial but shy Santa!

THE WILD MAN

The beast-man, an awesome creature, hair-covered and hump-backed, who made the crossing to America as Pelznickel, was generally known in European folklore as the Wild Man, a demon of storm, fury and destruction, but also responsible for birth, growth and fecundity, caring for all wildlife, and intimate with the deepest secrets of the universe, his goodwill and advice to humans sought after and a precious gift if obtained.

Our Santa/Father Christmas is one of the latest descendants from a long line of dark, sooty (and before that, earth-stained), hair-covered men, the remnant of a pre-Christian god of awesome power. Our pipe-smoking 'jolly old elf' is only one offshoot of this old, old god; throughout the millennia this figure has evolved in many ways and in many lands, adapting to new roles as society changed. Today there are remnants of the Wild Man from Russia to Britain to Japan to Greece, in ballets and films, in Christian churches and shopping centres. He has shaped our core mythologies in the guise of legendary characters: Father Christmas, Adonis, Pan, Harlequin, Robin Hood, Robin Goodfellow, Peter Pan, Satan, the Pied Piper, the court fool or jester... even Merlin.

These well-known figures have a single root in one powerful being – a priest to some, a god to others, and the personification of evil to still others – in a way reflecting the very composition and psyche of humanity itself. Originally a beast god who reminded people of the cyclical nature of the world, of death and rebirth, this Wild Man was part of the fertility performances throughout Europe – consort of the Earth Goddess and regularly sacrificed to ensure the continuation of all life. The Wild Man was also the link to the unknown and uncontrollable. He was the vessel through which life flowed to the people and the land; he was the conduit of divine power, the god-humanity connection.

As a godhead he was so strong, so universally worshipped, that Christianity found him *the* major impediment to its goal of European salvation. In Europe, Christianity and the old god repeatedly clashed in anger and violence. To undermine his grip on the people, Christianity labelled his worship as evil and called his followers devilish. In the seventh century, Pope Gregory tapped the persona of the Wild Man for the physical form of evil itself, Satan.

Today, one of the most recent popular incarnations of the Wild Man is in the story of Beauty and the Beast. Even our own historic Celtic Druid priests can claim some similarities in their traditional physical attributes: long wild hair, carrying a bag, a stick (or staff) and a Silver Branch – a stick with bells attached which proclaimed their presence and authority. And shamans, who as the first initial blossoming of spiritual or religious focus have acted as our spiritual intermediaries around the world since time immemorial, strike a resoundingly similar chord with their blackened or obscured faces, raggedy appearance and bells.

THE FLIGHT-SEEKING SHAMAN

In this part of north-western Europe the evolution and interpretation of the Wild Man into Father Christmas has also drawn extensively on Nordic and Scandinavian mythology and beliefs. For instance, the archetypal pair of gods, Odin and Thor, who can also be seen as aspects of the Wild Man, have survived into modern times as the Dutch Saint Nicholas – Odin, wise and light-filled god – and Struwwelpeder or Wild Peter – Thor, bringer of thunder and retribution.

The British Father Christmas has been strongly influenced by Odin and the northern shamans of old who would once have practised their magic for all the tribes of Britain as well as the peoples further east and north. The notion of a gift-giver descending from a high place can be traced back to the shaman's habit of climbing up the World Tree (realistically his tent pole) to seek knowledge from the subtle realms, and then climbing back down with gifts of prophecy and wisdom to give to the rest of the people – Santa's bag of presents mirroring the shaman's bag of gifts and tricks – as in the little story in 'The Celebration of Midwinter', page 204.

Here the horse and reindeer, the sleigh and the red and white fly agaric mushroom are closely linked to our modern perception of Father Christmas.

The old Nordic shamanism and the shamanic beliefs and practices of the Lapps and ancient Finnish peoples are closely linked to Odin, who rode across the northern skies on his eight-legged horse, Sleipnir (notice the number of legs) with the members of his Wild Hunt around the time of the Winter Solstice, in search of the souls of brave dead warriors. Legend has it that wherever the froth from Odin's horse fell to the ground it would become impregnated and nine months later, at the time of the autumn equinox, would sprout fly agaric mushrooms. Another belief is that the fly agaric mushrooms grew from a mixture of the blood (red) and froth (white) which fell from Odin's horse as he galloped through the clouds. The possibility is also suggested that fly agaric is the food of Odin's two ravens, *Huginn* and *Muninn*, who carry his thoughts and memories during their flights – in tradition ravens also being shamanic power animals as well as Odin's messengers.

In many mythologies, the red and white fly agaric mushroom is associated with the storm and thunder gods. The Germanic thunder and fertility god, *Donar* (traditionally the name of one of the eight reindeer which pull Father Christmas's sleigh) or Thor, drives his goat cart through the air and causes thunder and lightning when he throws his hammer in the clouds.

The association of reindeer and shamanism is an ancient one, as such evidence as the Ardèche cave paintings attests. Siberian mythology describes a 'heavenly hunt' similar to the Germanic Wild Hunt while in Britain we have Herne the horned hunter and his wild band of followers.

The Siberian shamans ride on reindeer sleighs high in the sky, seeking or journeying to the World Tree where the magic reindeer live. The running deer were the totem creatures of many different tribal groups.

Traditionally the northern shamans ritually ingest the fly agaric (*Amanita muscaria*) mushroom when they wish to make their soul flights or journeys to their ancestors or to make contact with other spirit worlds. Fly agaric mushrooms are known for stimulating auditory hallucinations and perhaps such acoustic manifestations and distortions can be interpreted as messages from other realms of existence. Perhaps more importantly, consuming fly agaric also produces the sensation of flying.

There is a well-established relationship between mushrooms and the gods. Homer commented on 'mushrooms... a connection between heaven and Earth'; Porphyrius called mushrooms 'children of the gods', and poets of ancient times referred to them as 'children of the Earth'. The Greek god Zeus, the lightning-thrower, was considered father of the mushrooms. Interestingly, mushrooms in general are officially classified as neither plants nor animals; they are in a category of their own called fungi. In Europe the fly agaric mushroom has long been a symbol of good luck and commonly appears on Christmas decorations and new year and other holiday greetings cards.

Apart from the sleigh being the vehicle of choice for frozen snowy climates and the reindeer the only animal hardy enough to pull them, there is another important connection between the deer herds and the flight-seeking shamans. Ingesting fly agaric mushrooms is a very risky thing to do. They are deadly poisonous and using them ritually was extremely dangerous and could easily result in the shaman's death. But it is becoming increasingly well known that the urine of animals who have eaten fly agaric mushrooms still contains very effective – possibly improved – hallucinogenic properties, with the added advantage that it is safe for humans to take. Reindeer certainly suffer no harmful side effects from eating it and will go to endless lengths to find and graze upon it. Therefore might the legend of flying horses and reindeer have originated with animals who ate these potent mushrooms, and whose magic urine the shamans then collected and drank to provide them with similar experiences of flight?

Interestingly, next to the birch tree, the favourite host tree for the fly agaric mushroom to grow on is the fir tree – another connection between the Christmas tree and the sleigh-driving, sky-flying Father Christmas?

BELLS AND SLEIGHS

When I was young, as Christmas approached, I would sometimes hear sleigh bells just as I was getting ready for bed. Transfixed by awe and excitement, I would listen wide-eyed as they grew progressively louder, circling the house. Sometimes they would actually appear to stop right outside my window and I would freeze like a statue, amazed to think that Santa could really be just a few feet away from me on the other side of the wall or roof! Eventually, after a few spine-tingling moments, the sound of the sleigh bells would gradually fade away into the distance and my pop-eyed parents would then appear at my bedroom door.

'Did you hear that?' they'd breathlessly enquire. 'Father Christmas on a practice run!'

Once I'd heard the bells, I would begin a little nightly ritual. On my way up to bed I would go out of the front door into the porch and on the side of the stone step I would carefully place a carrot for the reindeer, and some caramel toffees for Santa's elfin helpers. Father Christmas himself would have to wait until Christmas Eve for his treats but I'm sure if he'd wanted to, he could have shared in the toffees. Whatever... whoever... carrot and sweets had always vanished when I checked the porch step the following morning.

Only when I grew older, into my teens, did I discover that the bells which had so enchanted me as a child were actually a set of real sleigh bells being vigorously but rhythmically shaken by my father as he walked around the cottage. To hear them in that context was to suddenly be plunged into a magical world.

It was only when I came to take my turn in manifesting this bit of harmless magic for my own child that I came to realise what an amazingly potent effect it had on everything. As I walked around the cottage in the darkness, shaking the circlet of bells to mimic trotting or galloping deer, I began to look about me in some trepidation – I constantly felt that I was being observed, and if one evening I had rounded the house corner and suddenly bumped into some Spirit of Christmas coming the other way, I would not have been in the least bit surprised!

The sleigh is not so far removed from more southerly use either. Until as recently as 200 years ago, sleighs were used in Britain and other places on the Continent when winters were severe and the snow and ice lay on the ground for weeks, making travel and transport almost impossible. The sleigh wasn't confined to winter use either as it was brought out again in spring and summer months when wet conditions turned the lanes and fields into seas of mud.

The shamans also used (and still use) bells sewn to their robes to announce their presence as they enter the Other World and also to scare off any unfriendly spirits who might be lying in wait for them. Remember that the Wild Man has always been accompanied by at least one bell. Journeys of any kind have always been fraught with potential dangers and perhaps it is for this reason that bells have long been attached to the harness of beasts of burden and travel, whether they be horses, camels, elephants or indeed reindeer.

From Odin's eight-legged horse we get eight reindeer pulling Father Christmas's sleigh, two of them bearing the names of the German thunder god, Donner, and Blitzen, which means lightning.

COMMENT FROM JOAN: JULY 1962

I have just been reading through some of my recipes, my goodness what straits we were reduced to during and after the war until 1954. Since coming to live at Drybones in 1959 I sent my Jackson electric cooker to Mother at Cumberland House and use my wonderful bungalow range (fire oven, hobs and open fire) or two-burner calor gas stove. The kettle is always singing on the hob, in colder weather there is always a large pan of soup, and there is nothing quite like a fire oven for bread, potato pies, etc. We keep both kitchen and living room fires in all night – they only need a shovel of slack each – so we come down to welcome warmth each morning. Of course I have more dust than my 'all electric' friends but the cost or lack of open fires may account for a measure of starkness in their homes.

THE HEARTH

Until quite recently the centre of any northern home was the hearth and the fire that burned upon it. It was the focal point where everyone gathered to cook food, to eat it, to get warm and dry, and when the daylight faded, especially in the short winter days, it was where everyone came to do whatever handiwork they could by the light of the flames – spinning, knitting, mending, carving – and where they talked and sang and told stories.

Our Celtic forebears believed that the chimney was also a sacred passageway up into the higher celestial realms. It was the gateway to the land of spirits and gods. The hearth was a special place which brought all the elements together – earth, in the form of the fuel that was burned; fire, in the flames which consumed it; air, which fanned the blaze; water, which was heated there. The preparation and cooking of food could be seen as an alchemical process. In various cultures there are guardians and goddesses of the hearth; Hestia in ancient Greece (who was actually the eldest and most revered of Zeus's children); Vesta in ancient Rome; Brighid in Ireland and Ffraid in Wales. Hearthkeepers were appointed and the fire tended day and night, only being allowed to die out on special occasions (like Yule) when it would be ceremonially rekindled.

Hopes and dreams were spoken of around the hearth, prayers whispered and supplication made, carried on the hot air and smoke up to the waiting gods and goddesses beyond the chimney tops in the starry heavens. Things that had outworn their use, including relationships and emotions, were ritually dispensed with in the flames, their energies transmuted in to something new and useful.

It is from this belief that we get the tradition of shouting up the chimney to Father Christmas and of children 'posting' their letters to him. I wish that I had realised this when my son was a little boy – trying to appear to throw the tightly folded piece of paper up into the smoke while concealing it in my hand or up my sleeve used to be incredibly stressful! In old tradition, one could simply burn the letter and know that the smoke would take its essence up to the rightful place and person. SO much easier!

A DIFFERENT POSTBOX

My mother came from an unhappy home background where her parents were always separating, then returning to each other. When she was only seventeen, she decided that she had had enough of this apart/together existence and so she left home. The Second World War was still in progress then and accommodation very difficult to come by, but friends of the family found her an empty shop right in the middle of town, and she made her new home in the living premises at the back.

Being clever with her hands and good with a needle, she eventually decided to open a toy shop selling dolls which she had dressed or made, with beautiful layettes or extra sets of clothes, night clothes and accessories to accompany them, long before such things became popular with toy manufacturers. She also produced gorgeously dressed beds and beautiful dolls' house furniture, the wooden dolls' houses, forts and garages being made by her father for her to sell in her shop, and painted and finished by her 'young man', my father-to-be. Her imaginative window displays became the talk of the town!

At Christmas, she set up a brightly decorated post box in the shop for the children to come and post their letters to Father Christmas in. What nobody else knew was that she and my father spent their December evenings answering the letters where at all possible and posting their replies back to the children. It caused quite a stir in the town. One afternoon at the local market, my grandfather heard one man telling another how his little girl had sent her letter to Father Christmas, '...and would you believe it? She actually got a reply!' he exclaimed in wonderment. This was in the days long before the Post Office and other companies made a business of writing to children if their parents paid a fee. No one ever found out who was writing the letters, and they never asked for or received any money for doing it, but then I have come to understand that the Spirit of Midwinter works in many ways, using many willing hands to perform its joyous magic!

Mince Pies

Ready to leave out for Father Christmas –
and for the rest of the family to enjoy!
Gillian

INGREDIENTS:

7 oz (198 g) plain flour

3½ oz (100 g) butter, plus extra for greasing

1 oz (28 g) icing sugar

1 egg yolk

2–3 tablespoons milk, plus extra for glazing

10 oz (280 g) mincemeat

Icing sugar for dusting

METHOD:

- Preheat oven to 180°C / 350°F / Gas Mark 4.
- Grease a 12-hole and a 6-hole tart tin with butter.
- Sift flour into a bowl and, using your fingertips, rub in the butter until the mixture resembles breadcrumbs. Stir in the sugar and egg yolk. Stir in enough milk to form a soft dough and turn out onto a lightly floured work surface. Knead lightly until smooth.
- Shape the dough into a ball and roll out to a thickness of a quarter of an inch. Use a 2¾" fluted cutter to cut out 16–18 rounds. Line holes in prepared tart tin with them. Half fill each pie with mincemeat.
- Cut out 16–18 shapes (star, holly, tree, snowflake, etc.) from the leftover dough, brush the underside with milk and place on top of each pie.
- Glaze the top surface of each pie with more milk and bake in the preheated oven for approx. 15 minutes or until the pastry is a pale golden colour. Remove from the oven, leave to rest for a couple of minutes and then take out of the tin. Dust with icing sugar before serving.

CAN be reheated but be careful not to make too dry, brown or crisp; lovely served warm with a spoonful of rum butter under each lid! *Gillian*

A TALE FOR THE CHILDREN

Sometimes my parents would brave the December crowds and take me into Preston, Wigan or Manchester to visit a Father Christmas grotto. I loved these trips. Some of my classmates at school insisted that Father Christmas wasn't real but I knew better! I believed in him and the whole spirit of Christmas with a deep and unerring passion. But as I grew older, it became increasingly harder for my parents to find a really good example of a Father Christmas to take me to.

On one particularly disenchanting outing to Wigan, we had already been to see two Father Christmases and I had greatly perplexed my mother and father by hotly declaring that neither one of them was 'real'. The first one was obviously wearing a false beard which was coming loose at one side... well that couldn't be right!... and the second one grinned at me and nearly suffocated me with alcohol fumes. Certainly not!

Desperately, my parents took me into Lowe's department store, hoping to find someone who would satisfy my exacting standards. When we arrived on the second floor the grotto was temporarily closed to allow the resident Santa to have a break for his lunch. Much to my parents' horror I marched around the painted scenery and stared at the vacant throne where Father Christmas should have been sitting and was about to plunge around the back when the man himself came out from behind a curtain and, catching site of me, sat down on his chair. Ah, this was better! He was tall and well-built, with a red, beautifully detailed fur-trimmed suit. But it was his face that struck me most. Old yet ageless, wrinkled yet handsome, with the most magnificent flowing white beard reaching to the middle of his chest and soft silver curls protruding from beneath his red hat, and clear shining eyes so bright and blue as they gazed mesmerisingly upon me.

Delighted to have obviously tracked down the 'real thing', I confidently approached the old gentleman and began conversational introductions. At this point my two harassed parents caught up with me, bursting in upon the quiet grotto with broken apologies, only to have my hero turn to them, smile and kindly shake his head. Without further ado, they subsided onto some spare chairs.

Now at home, we always had many pet cats and one of our particular favourites at that time was a massive male tabby cat called Tarni. My mother would make up stories for me about their lives and characters. She said that she was 'translating' for them, from cat language into English, so that I would understand. By way of explanation for the large black end of Tarni's tail, she used to teasingly insist that every autumn, he would go off at night to help Father Christmas's elves in their workshop – his particular task being to paint the black spots on all the wooden rocking horses, using the end of his tail. But sadly, Tarni had disappeared earlier that autumn. He had been gone for several months and we were all very upset by his loss.

So imagine my joy when, as I was about to say goodbye to this perfect personification of Father Christmas, his smile broadened and he quietly said, 'Oh yes, I have a message for you too. Tarni says not to worry about him and that he will be home in the next day or two.' I warmly thanked the Spirit of Christmas and triumphantly turned to rejoin my parents.

I found it a little hard to understand why they were both looking chalk white, stuttering and gabbling words and obviously very shocked and confused. Tarni took a little longer than Father Christmas had said, but when he arrived home nearly a week later, safe and well, we were all ecstatic, although I continued to feel surprised that my parents were obviously shocked all over again. What was wrong with them? I knew that our beloved pet was coming home... after all, Father Christmas himself had told me so.

As a child, my faith was implicit, but knowing what I do now, I am as shocked and thrilled as my parents were. So, just exactly *who* had I been talking to...?

WHAT DO I THINK?

Over thousands of years, the northern population has created and brought into being such communal icons as the Wild Man, in all his many forms. Much more recently the popular belief of billions of people has fashioned and shaped the character of Father Christmas/Santa Claus. The Christian church calls it 'faith'; Jung refers to mass consciousness; but what we do know from quantum physics is that it is possible to produce thought forms which appear real, and the more people subscribe to a certain belief, the more solidly real they can become. I do not know what is real. What is 'real' anyway? But I do know what I have experienced. I do know that there is still a great deal about this world and this life that we currently inhabit that is unexplained, unrecognised and unknown. So keep an open mind. We can't prove that something is real, but by the same token, we can't prove that it isn't. And if you don't like other people's nightmares, start making your own beautiful dreams real. Think about it.

The Celebration of Midwinter

Night's black shadows vanish, the golden sun an arc,
Winter's crystals glitter – dazzle – and banished is the dark.
'WINTER SANCTUARY', G. MONKS

HIGH ON A dark hilltop a small group of figures patiently waits and watches. Fingers, numb with cold, pluck at their fur coverings, drawing them closer about their chilled bodies. Weary eyes strain to focus on the inky black of the distant horizon. Everything is absolutely still, perfectly quiet; not a rustle of grass blade or leaf, not a snuffle of fox or badger, or the flap of an owl wing on the hunt, or smaller bird disturbed in its sleep. The star-studded firmament arches over all, winking and glittering impassionately on the dark silent world below.

Softly, imperceptibly, the impenetrable darkness thins and lightens, the heavens in the east pale, the stars flicker and vanish as the dawn breaks over a dead and icy land. Lighter and brighter it grows, while the men and women remain motionless, intent on the far eastern hills, until finally the sky begins to flush deeply, burnished gold with outer edges of deep rose pink, until at last, a tiny sliver of blazing fire appears over the distant line of hills, growing bigger, brighter.

A soft communal sigh escapes the watchers, as if they have been holding their breath for a very long time. Tears of relief roll down the cheeks of the women... grins split the tense faces of the men... cheers go up from the young bucks who begin cavorting wildly with joy. Their Sun has returned to them! There is an end in sight to the cold and dark and the animals will thrive again in the coming seasons. Hunting will be good; once more the days will become light and warm; life is assured and will go on... at least for another year!

Many thousands of years later, a similar but larger group of figures waits in the dark, clustered in and around the carefully positioned rocks, waiting for the Sun to rise and pierce the space between them, reaching deep within the belly of the Earth to bring new life to the winter world. It is the coupling of these two cosmic giants, the Sun and the Earth coming together, which will rekindle the cycle of the seasons and set the growing season in motion once more. The Sun's warmth upon the Earth will quicken her seeds and the crops will grow. The animals will have food to feed their young. There will be respite from the icy darkness for their own human young to grow and prosper.

Far to the north, across the frozen wastes, the shaman (magician and priest of his people) climbs the decorated central pole of his yak-skin-covered tent. In the choking aromatic smoke from the fire below him, he rises up with it, up and out through the smoke hole above and finds himself... not on the freezing tent top, but in a different place altogether... an 'other world'... the Other World. Here the shaman communes with his gods. Here he learns what his people need to know about the coming seasons; what the weather will bring them, where the best herds and flocks will run or fly. Here the spirits take the shaman on a journey to find the gifts of the subtle realms – the gift of fire (which he will later take back to his tribe), the gift of divination (for further useful prophecies and healing in the coming months) – and as he climbs back down the tent pole to his waiting people below, the Midwinter Sun rises and he brings them the Sun itself, reborn, renewed... the life-giver.

Across the northern skies, the great god, Odin, rides his mighty eight-legged horse, Sleipnir, harness bells jingling, as they journey to collect the souls of the recently departed warriors, to reward the brave and faithful and punish the wrong-doers on this Midwinter night of nights.

Contained within these three different scenarios we have all the main components (apart from Jesus himself) of what we today call 'Christmas'.

ANCIENT ORIGINS

The celebration of Midwinter did not simply begin two millennia ago with the birth of Jesus. Its origins, beliefs and practices go much further back into the dim mists of human history. The birth of Jesus Christ is celebrated at Christmas, which falls at Midwinter, but Midwinter is, first and foremost, a celebration of the turning of the year, when the Sun's light begins to return to the Earth and warmth and life are assured for the coming spring. For where would any of us be if the Sun suddenly disappeared? It is a far more potent point in time than, for example, the Summer Solstice in June – for then the Sun is already here with us, the nights are short and light and the days long, bright and hot. But in the cold and dark of Midwinter, our ancestors did not feel that they could truly rely on such benevolent conditions returning. Their very existence depended on it and for all our ingenuity and intelligence our existence today still relies on it just as much as ever it did, made increasingly poignant now that environmental changes are manifesting around the planet and *nothing* seems quite so sure, safe and certain as it once was.

The Solstice at Midwinter has been a special and sacred time in the annual cycle of seasons for many thousands of years. It has long been used to mark and guide activities such as the migration of herds, the mating of animals, the slaughter of animals, the sowing of crops and the monitoring of winter reserves of food which was vital to the preservation and continuance of humanity. Until relatively recently starvation in late winter and early spring (before the new crops were grown and ready for harvest) was quite common. January to April used to be known as the 'famine months'. The Midwinter festival was the last celebration before deep winter with all its storms, ice, snow and floods began in earnest, with all the difficulties and possible dangers that accompanied them.

Because there was no way in which sufficient fodder could be grown or stored to feed all the herds and flocks when there was no fresh grazing to be had during the winter, only the strongest and best animals could be kept through the lean months for breeding the next spring. Hence the necessity for culling the herds in November, usually around 11th November, the feast of Saint Martin, the month of November also being known as the 'blood month'. After the slaughter of the animals at Martinmas not all of the meat could be preserved so had to be consumed quickly or go to waste. In our twenty-first-century life we are lucky to be able to produce crops of food all year round and do not need to rely on the taking of an animal's life in order to preserve our own. But until very recently only living animals could be relied upon to survive in other than perfect conditions. When drought or plagues of insects ravaged the crops or all vegetation naturally died away in autumn, only the animals were left, and without them humanity could never have thrived and prospered as we have done until modern technology came along to cushion us from the vagaries of the seasons and the weather. We owe them a massive debt of gratitude.

Here in Wales, winter lasted from the beginning of November to the beginning of February – from the time of the slaughter of the animals at the back-end of autumn to the first true signs of spring, when the first plants came into flower, the catkins blossomed, shoots and buds of all kinds began to appear and the new lambs were born, providing much-needed fresh milk, cheese and meat. With the ending of winter came *Gwyl Ffraid / Imbolc*, the celebration of early spring.

Therefore, so soon after the November slaughter, meat was in plentiful supply. The mead and wine made back in the fruitful summer months had fermented and were ready to drink. A good amount of the crops harvested in the summer and autumn months were still available. As the weather was too dark, drear and frozen to do much outside, why not enjoy sitting by the fire, feasting on the results of all your hard labour, carousing, singing and making music, storytelling and generally celebrating one's good fortune at having a decent roof over one's head, good food to fill one's belly and dear friends and neighbours to share it with? Midwinter wasn't a single date, it was the winter season itself!

Interestingly, in *The Book of Christmas*, Jane Struthers suggests that the feast of Saint Martin on 11th November marks the beginning of a forty-day period of fasting (similar to that of the forty-day period of fasting through Lent before Easter in the spring) which the Christian church imposed and which was only broken with the celebration of Christmas. Historical adjustments to the calendar might have affected these calculations, but going by our twenty-first-century calendar it is even more interesting to discover that such a forty-day period would actually end, not on Christmas Day or even Christmas Eve, but on 20th December, the eve of the day on which the Winter Solstice generally falls.

How to Make a Pomander

YOU WILL NEED:

An orange

Orrisroot

Dried whole cloves

1 metre of narrow ribbon

TO MAKE:

- Tie a length of pretty patterned or plain ribbon around the orange, parcel-style, so that there are 4 ribbon strips around the orange, allowing enough to form a loop at the top by which to hang it up.
- Press whole cloves into the orange between the ribbons. Place them close to one another but leave a fraction of space to allow for shrinkage as the orange dries out. The more cloves you use, the stronger the spicy scent. If your fingers or thumb become sore in the process, try wearing a thimble!
- Dust with orrisroot (available in health food shops) which helps to dry and preserve the orange.
- Decorate with tassels, greenery, tinsel or other embellishments.

USING *a clove-studded orange to make a scented pomander is a lovely way to emulate the sun on this day. It will last for many months as a spicy reminder of Midwinter. They also make wonderful gifts.*

MIDWINTER DEITIES

We must be careful not to lose sight of the most important central event of the season – the culmination of the darkest day and the apparent 'return' of the Sun. Because this event was viewed as the reversal of the Sun's ebbing presence in the sky, concepts of birth and rebirth, of divine beings, deities and gods became common. Even today, we are still familiar with some of these divine beings who share their 'birthday' or festivals with the return of the Sun. Here are a small selection, but there are many others originating from all around the world.

OSIRIS: In Ancient Egypt, he was a much-beloved, golden and benign solar being. After being murdered by his brother, Set, Osiris was restored to life by his sister, Isis, on 25th December. His death and resurrection came to be seen as a representation of the rising and setting of the Sun, but the fact that he was brought back to life on 25th December directly correlates with the concept that the Sun is then reborn.

MITHRAS: He was a solar deity who grew out of the original concept of Mitra, found in the Indian Vedic religion dating back at least 3,500 years, and Mithra of Zoroastrianism, the state religion of the pre-Islamic Iranian and Persian empires and one of the oldest belief systems in the world, dating back nearly 3,000 years. In ancient Indian belief he was a solar deity representing the 'friendly' aspect of the Sun and as the Persian Mithra he represented the light and power behind the Sun, a benevolent god and bestower of health, wealth and food. Mithras was an angelic divinity reputedly born on 25th December.

The story of his birth and life shares many other similarities with that of Jesus, including that when he was born (to a virgin mother, Anahita), he was wrapped in swaddling clothes and laid in a manger and attended by shepherds; that he was considered a great travelling teacher and master; that he had twelve companions or disciples, performed miracles, sacrificed himself for world peace and ascended into heaven. He has been variously referred to as 'the way, the truth and the light', the redeemer, the saviour, the messiah and the good shepherd. This last might possibly be because he was born in the astrological era of Aries, the ram.

The cult of Mithras also involved the god fighting and sacrificing a bull at Midwinter. Interestingly, there was still traditional bull baiting at Christmas in a village in the south of England as late as 1820, which just goes to show that old traditions and habits die hard indeed and are firmly entrenched in our very fibre and being!

SOL INVICTUS: The cult of Sol is possibly rooted in the Etruscan civilisation, therefore pre-dating the Roman civilisation by several hundred years. The 'Unconquered Sun', originally a Syrian god, was later adopted as chief god of the Roman Empire under the Emperor Aurelian and he was traditionally celebrated on 25th December. After the prominence of both Mithras and Sol Invictus, perhaps it is not so surprising that the Roman Empire should so readily adopt a third deity, also to be celebrated on the same day of December, this one known by the name of Jesus.

APOLLO: The Greek god of fertility and love; also reputedly born on 25th December.

THE MABON: The Welsh god of divine youth and, possibly like the Greek god, Apollo, also of love. *Mabon* was the son of *Modron*, the Welsh mother goddess of fertility.

JESUS: It took nearly 400 years after the birth of Jesus for the date of 25th December to be set as the date of his birth. There are no exact references as to the real date of his birth. Some astrologers believe that it actually took place in March, others that he was conceived in March and therefore born nine months later in December. But there is a strong connection between Jesus and the sign of the fish; after all, his birth ushered in the age of Pisces, and he was described as 'a fisher of men'. However, the church leaders of the day may have borrowed the festival of the great Midwinter event for the birth of the Son of God, like so many others before him, or else he was born on that date for a definite purpose, which was no mere coincidence.

Now, all these deities have several things in common. They are all protectors of the world – of Life. They were all sent into the world at the darkest time of the year. They were all reputedly born in caves and came out into the world, mimicking the rising or re-entrance of the Sun, not just of any morning, but of *that* particular morning... the morning of 25th December.

THE WINTER SOLSTICE

You may have noticed a distinct discrepancy between the Winter Solstice (which usually falls around 21st December, although very occasionally it can fall on 20th December instead) and the birth date of all these divine beings, which falls on 25th December. Why is this?

During the course of the year the Earth completes one orbit around the Sun. The Earth's axis of rotation tilts at 23.5 degrees. Therefore, here in the Northern Hemisphere, for half the year we are tilted nearer to the Sun, making it hotter for us and giving us our summer; and for the other half of the year we are tilted further away from the Sun, making it colder and giving us our winter. It works exactly the same in the Southern Hemisphere only the opposite way around; when we tilt towards the Sun and have our summer, they automatically tilt away and have their winter, and vice versa.

The word 'solstice' comes from the Latin *solstitium* meaning 'sun stands still', because the apparent movement of the Sun's path north or south seems to stop briefly for a few days before changing direction again. Of course, neither the Sun nor the Earth really stand still, they just *appear* to.

The day of the Solstice is the date when here in the Northern Hemisphere we experience the 'shortest day' – the least amount of daylight and the greatest amount of darkness or longest night. But the crucial point I wish to make is that it takes several days – until the morning of 25th December, in fact – for the daylight to be *perceptibly* longer than on 21st December (and even then, it is only by a matter of just over a minute). In practice we enter the darkest days of winter on 21st December and only begin to come back into the daylight on the morning of 25th December. Therefore the Sun is not 'reborn' on the morning of 21st or even 22nd December but on the morning of the 25th.

At Midwinter there is an ancient interplay between darkness and light and the natural and human worlds. Traditionally bonfires would be lit to emulate the heat and light of the Sun and encourage its return. To keep one's fire well supplied and burning might mean the difference between life and death, reflecting the nature of fire and the Sun and underlying the fact that all life depends on its continuance. Life on this planet could not exist without the heat and light provided by the fire of the Sun, or the smaller 'suns' which we light as bonfires, candles, lamps and more recently, electric lights, heating and cooking appliances. By placing candles in our windows (even if they are now electric), we are not only remembering the older practice of venerating light and warmth at the darkest time of the year, but are also showing that we welcome the Midwinter spirits of the season.

COMMENT FROM JOAN: LATE AUTUMN, 1962

6.15 p.m. What a difference it makes not having Jim home for tea – and usually how lonely – but it does give me more time. He is banding with Fred Jones tonight, until 1 a.m., at the Bowling Green, Charnock Richard. I'm glad I chased after him with that jam sponge cake as he was leaving after lunch, otherwise he probably wouldn't bother with much tea to eat.
I have the electric standard lamp lit – also a candle ('cos I like them), but I'm thinking that the batteries need charging because the light doesn't seem very good. Anyway, Ricky can start the generator when he comes, though as he is working over-time he said he couldn't be here before 8 p.m.

Solstice Sun Biscuits

These sun-shaped biscuits are lovely to make and enjoy as part of your Winter Solstice celebrations.

Gillian

INGREDIENTS:

12 oz (340 g) plain flour

7 oz (198 g) butter

7 oz (198 g) castor sugar

1 egg white

Lemon and orange jelly slices, to decorate

METHOD:

- Rub butter into flour.
- Add half the sugar and knead in with your hands.
- Add other half of sugar and work in well with your hands.
- Roll out to desired thickness – ¼" is good – and cut out with sun-shaped cutter, or a plain circular cutter if you don't possess one.
- Paint with beaten white of egg and decorate with 'eyes' and smiling 'mouths' cut from lemon and orange jelly slices. Dust with castor sugar.
- Bake on greased tray in a moderately hot oven (190°C, 375°F or Gas Mark 5) for 10–12 minutes until golden.
- Lift off and cool on wire cooling rack.

A MODERN SOLSTICE CELEBRATION

We go out into the woods to be present with the sleeping Earth at this darkest time. We take seasonal refreshments of yule log cake and flasks of hot mulled wine – alcohol or fruit juices which have usually been made in the warmth of the young summer from fresh new oak leaves or may-blossom, sun-kissed blackcurrants or strawberries. Around a campfire we gather to sit and to share our Midwinter memories and dreams for the coming year. There is laughter and story-telling and jokes and the singing of carols, and silence and stillness as we watch, wait and listen with all earthly life for the pivotal moment when the Sun is furthest from us, before it swings back in our direction again.

Last Winter Solstice my family and I waited until mid-afternoon before donning our warmest coats, hats, scarves and gloves and climbing up the valley side above our home. On reaching a more sheltered spot we stopped and looked up at Mount Snowdon curled dreaming at the head of the valley with all the misty grey mountain ridges rippling around it. The short winter's afternoon soon came to an end and we silently watched the daylight dwindle. As the detail of crag, ravine, precipice and pasture faded into twilight, house lights and street lamps flickered into being. There in the dusk we bore witness to the dying of the Light as the Sun's dim rays left us to enter this darkest time of the year alone.

With chilled fingers we kindled our own little fire of holly logs, a pin-prick of dancing flames bravely blazing out in the celestial darkness, and we called from our hearts to the memory of all our ancestors who have trod this path before us and who have also stood and watched the Light die. We would endeavour to hold the Light until the Sun returned to us. The freshening breeze bit icily through our clothes and black shadows wrapped themselves around the tiny glow from our fire as we poured steaming spiced elderberry juice into cups and toasted the land, the blessed darkness and absent Sun. Out came the buttery sugar Solstice biscuits which I had baked that morning, formed in the shape of fiery suns, and we munched contentedly. One doesn't have to actually do very much – it is enough to simply be.

Later, we walked back down into the valley, tripping and stumbling in the darkness, sloshing through puddles and lane ruts turned to streams. The dogs trotted energetically besides us, glad to be away from the smoke and flames – neither of our Labrador dogs enjoy fire at all, unless it is safely confined within a grate and they can stretch out comfortably in front of it! Below us lay the peaceful village, twinkling with coloured lights and decorations, giving no clue as to the likely ferment of preparations and celebrations that were taking place within each illuminated home.

The house greeted us, warm with glowing shadows from our own sparkly lights, while mouth-watering savoury scents tantalised us from the depths of the old Aga. Now hungry and tired, we were content to gather around the table and share the hot casserole that I had left cooking and talk about our plans for the darkest days come upon us.

Christmas Eve

Shut in from all the world without,
We sat the clean-winged hearth about,
Content to let the north-wind roar
In baffled rage at pane and door.

'A NEW ENGLAND HOME IN WINTER',
JOHN GREENLEAF WHITTIER

THINKING BACK TO my childhood, amidst all the industry of Christmas Eve – decorating the Christmas tree and all the hundred and one other little tasks to be seen to – there were hot mince pies to eat and steaming mugs of tea and cocoa to fortify us as my mother dashed between decorating in the living room and last-minute baking and preparations in the kitchen, the radio playing the 'Nine Lessons and Carols' from King's College, Cambridge all the while.

As the light of the short winter afternoon faded, everything was tidied away. Pine needles and fragments of tinsel and lametta were carefully eradicated from the deep pile of the Turkish carpet. Peace was restored. (Except in the kitchen, where activity had by now reached manic proportions!) At that time, my mother's problem was that she was trying to achieve the perfect Christmas single-handedly, my father being too busy working and me being an only child and too young to be of much help, which is why I repeatedly stress the importance of asking for (and receiving) help from others.

My father played the drums in a local amateur dance band – an extremely *good* dance band it was too, and they were always in great demand, especially in the run-up to Christmas. So Daddy was out 'banding' (as we called it) a very great deal; every Friday and Saturday night and sometimes other evenings during the week as well, and *always* on Christmas Eve – unless it happened to fall on a Sunday as dances were never held on the Sabbath in those days! There was always a rush to eat and get him out of the house extra early. I remember him from those times, smartly dressed in black evening suit and bow tie, crisp white shirt, soft of cheek from being newly shaven and smelling divinely of his favourite aftershave, Old Spice. By the time he had departed for whichever big local hotel or club the band had been engaged to play in, a long evening stretched before us and I myself had little left to do.

Carefully, I would place the icing sugar-sprinkled mince pies on a plate and Mummy would pour a glass of home-made raspberry wine for me to leave out for Father Christmas to enjoy. They were always placed on the little hexagonal coffee table by the tree in the living room.

If it was *very* cold, as a special treat, I was allowed to undress and wash in a big bowl downstairs, in front of the glowing kitchen fire. It was gorgeously warm, but with the added sensation of having that half of one's body which was turned away from the fire apparently 'freezing', while the other half that was exposed to the fire 'roasted'. One had to keep revolving, like a human kebab, to avoid getting too overdone on one side! But oh, the joy of finally slipping into a soft flannelette nightie, warm from hanging over one end of the old nursery fireguard which sometimes still stood on the hearth in front of the range.

The last thing to be done before finally going up to bed was to go to my mother to get the stocking which I would reverently lay out across the bottom of my bed. I always used one of my grandfather's old knee socks which he used to wear with his riding breeches or Norfolk suits. They had the advantage of being extremely long – about eighteen inches – even before they were stretched in the filling, and could contain an amazingly large amount of small items!

When I was a small girl, my bedtime was at 7.30 p.m. But as I reached eight or nine years old it moved to 8.30 p.m. And then to nine o'clock. It mattered little when I went to bed though, I could *never* sleep on Christmas Eve and the night would stretch interminably before me. The Lord Chancellor in Gilbert and Sullivan's *Iolanthe* enjoyed a peaceful night's rest compared to my vain attempts to find sleep on that 'night of nights', made even more frantic by the thought that if Father Christmas came and found me still awake, he would go away again without leaving anything for me! Beginning the night snug, warm and comfortable, I would quickly become too hot, tossing blankets, pillows and hot water bottle in all directions in my frenzied attempts to get comfortable enough to drop off.

Periodically, my mother would go past my bedroom door and gently whisper, 'Are you asleep?' My feigned sleepy replies would start with 'Not yet', becoming 'Not quite', and ending up with a 'Nearly'! But sometimes I would hear my father retuning from the dance sometime after 1 a.m. before I finally fell asleep without realising it.

> COMMENT FROM JOAN: 24TH AND 25TH DECEMBER 1951
> *Terribly busy in shop, Ricky still serving till 11.39 p.m. – seem to have done quite well. Washed my hair, bath and bed 2 a.m. Gosh! Am I tired. Christmas morning Eileen* woke early. All to church then opened presents – lovely! Eileen quite stupefied… silver bracelet from Jim, perfume, hankies, games. Then packing and at 1.15 p.m. ready for journey.*

IN THE HERE AND NOW

These days, Christmas Eve is a very different affair. We long ago bowed to the modern trend of putting our trees up before Christmas Eve, although usually only a week or so beforehand, so that they are in place in good time for the fourth Sunday of Advent and the Winter Solstice. The rest of the decorations start to come out from the first Sunday of Advent onwards.

---

* Eileen was a little eleven-year-old girl whom my parents gave a home to. My mother couldn't formally adopt Eileen because there wasn't a twelve-year gap in their respective ages (my mother being only twenty-two at the time Eileen first went to live with her), so she became her legal ward instead.

I really enjoy the last ten days or so before the 25th and try to keep my diary reasonably free for that period. This is when I do most of my baking, decorating and wrapping of presents – even some last-minute cleaning and polishing – and I thoroughly enjoy it all, as it's done in a spirit of love, excitement and enjoyment. Yes, I am very busy and yes, it is hard work, but it is without a lot of the stress and pressure which so often drives people on these days. It is my time to work for and give to my family. I listen to wall-to-wall carols and Christmas music on the radio or CD player and revel in the alchemy of creating and enjoying our Midwinter celebration. After all, a lot of the tasks are pleasant ones if you aren't struggling to do too much at once... and don't forget what I said about asking for help and making sure that you get it!

The celebration of the Winter Solstice falls within this wonderful period, and then we enter the darkest days when within the house everything sparkles and shines and is filled with the warmth of fresh baking and cooking and the scents of incense cones burning in all the little carved wooden figures.

Then comes Christmas Eve, my most favourite day of the Midwinter period. As little actual work is done on this day as possible. The morning might even be spent in the kitchen doing last-minute preparations for the afternoon and evening meals and a bit of forward planning for the next day too. After lunch is when we deliver cards and little token gifts to our friends and neighbours locally around the village. Being the time of year that it is I usually give tokens of light – candles or simple lanterns – but pots of rum butter make a welcome gift, and some time in the previous week I will have beaten up a huge bowlful and divided most of it into smaller pots which I collect throughout the year. A self-adhesive Christmas gift tag for a label and some pretty Christmas material or gift wrapping tied around the lid make an attractive item, as do bags of home-made Christmas biscuits, cut in the shapes of Christmas trees, holly leaves, stars, snowflakes – whatever – and parcelled in plastic bags (there are seasonally printed ones if you look around) and tied tightly with festive ribbon. My husband and son carry the heavily bountiful baskets for me as we tramp the village lanes distributing greetings and hugs along the way.

I remember one very hard winter a few years ago when the country had a heavy snowfall around 18th December which then froze hard. The lower halves of many people's cars were encased in blocks of ice, and most roads – except for the main routes – were largely impassable except by tractor or the sturdiest 4×4, and as a result, everyone was suddenly reduced to walking to bus routes. I saw more neighbours and enjoyed more laughter-filled conversations at our front gate than at any other time, before or since. On foot and up against the elements everyone was more talkative. People were getting in shopping or giving lifts to others. Many carol-singing events and parties had to be cancelled and impromptu celebrations were hastily arranged locally. We were not the only ones walking around the village delivering cards and presents by hand that year! The community came together and it brought to my mind that this is how it always must have been for rural communities before everyone had transport. Of course it is marvellous to have the ease and convenience of one's own transport, and many other modern machines and labour-saving devices too; times have to change and life moves on, but perhaps we should also consciously and actively strive not to lose sight of what is really important: friendship and a commitment to community.

Imitation Jugged Hare

Particularly good to come in to on a cold, frosty afternoon or evening after delivering presents, walking or carol singing.

Gillian

INGREDIENTS:

Thick piece of stewing or shin beef

1 or 2 bay leaves

Peeled onion stuck with 6 cloves

Strips of lemon rind (this is a must)

¼ pint (250 ml) stock or water

2 teaspoons of dried herbs – I use mint, parsley, sage and thyme (recently I sent six-year-old Gill out to bring in fresh mint, parsley, etc. and she brought lavender leaves as well!)

METHOD:

- Either leave meat in one piece or cut into slices about the size of joints of a hare (like chicken-portion size).
- Flour well and fry until just brown in a little dripping.
- Place all ingredients in a casserole (I use my old Gourmet

Earthenware Cooker[*] – the best yet) and cook slowly for 3 hours or as long as you like, adding a very little more liquid if necessary.

- When cooking is finished, strain the gravy and thicken it with a little flour.
- Put meat on a hot dish and pour gravy over. If served with redcurrant jelly[†], forcemeat balls[‡] and creamed potatoes it is very satisfying.

I HAVE BEEN known to hold 'open house' on Christmas Eve afternoon, with a table spread with seasonal delicacies, both savoury and sweet, and the kettle never off the Aga as relays of fresh pots of tea were brewed and jugs of mulled wine were ferried out. But more often it is just the family who come together around the dining-room fire as the daylight starts to fade and the cold outdoor world begins to take on that shade of magical winter blue which presages dusk and darkness. We have afternoon tea with the china holly cups and plates set out on the silver tray

---

[*] My mother knew that her Gourmet Cooker was old, but imagine our amazement when we visited the Brighton Pavilion in 1994 to enter the magnificent kitchens there and find a whole row of Gourmet Cookers on a top shelf – they were numbered and rose in size from a single small portion to around a gallon and a half! It was all I could do to restrain my mother from asking to take a couple home with her. The actual shape of a dish and the material it is made from makes a huge difference to how the food inside it cooks (hence the current popularity of the tagine), and whoever produced the Gourmet Cookers had got it just right!

[†] Cranberry sauce or jelly may be substituted for redcurrant jelly.

[‡] Forcemeat Balls: Mix 2 tablespoons breadcrumbs, ½ oz (14 g) butter, ½ teaspoon mixed herbs, ¼ teaspoon grated lemon rind, seasoning and 1 beaten egg to bind. Roll into balls and 'poach' in boiling water for 10 minutes (can also be deep fried in oil, but they are much more wholesome poached than fried) and lay them around the dish of meat and gravy to serve.

and plates piled high with spice cakes, chocolate biscuits, mince pies, home-made shortbreads and the chocolate yule log cake.

Here we gaze into the fire, toast crumpets and chestnuts and marshmallows, share the news of the day and reminisce and, if not already done the day before, we bring in the post box and open all the letters and messages from our friends and relatives far and wide. Later we open all the parcels and packages which have been arriving through the post from Germany from my husband's family and which have been patiently waiting under the dining-room Christmas tree. This is when we also open gifts from friends. The quiet, orderly peace of dusk dissolves into mayhem as conversation becomes loud with excited exclamations and laughter and the carpet disappears beneath a frothy sea of paper – our cats adding to the chaos by leaping into and burrowing under it all – and the room rapidly turns into a furnace, heated by the forty or so candles lit in all the sticks, buttresses and pyramids.

Later still we tidy up and I pin up the cards in the hall to make our 'bower of messages' and then we sit down around the table to a hot or cold supper. In the past, when my son was a child and I was busy running two businesses, this was the time when I often ended up wrapping his Christmas presents after he had gone up to bed. Quite late into the evening now, with everyone gone off to do their own last-minute preparations, I sit once more before the fire, glass of wine in hand while the deep calm and peace of the evening descends around me like a palpable cloak. This is often the time when I pick up my laptop and compose a heartfelt seasonal message to all my cyber-friends and contacts and to all my friends and relatives around the world. Despite the fact that I have already sent them cards and letters, I want to reach out and feel a contact with them and share this wonderful time with them in the actual moment. For as a mother myself, this is *my* time: this is Mother's Night...

MOTHER'S NIGHT

Where birth is concerned, there must surely also be a mother, whether it be the mother of Apollo, Mithras, Attis, Osiris or anyone else. In Christian belief, Mary gave birth to Jesus. A celestial Mother gives birth to the Sun, and what more appropriate time to celebrate motherhood than on the night before the Sun / Son is born / reborn?

The evening of 24th December has been known and celebrated as 'Mother's Night' throughout Europe and Scandinavia for many centuries. Historically many of the inscriptions relating to it are Germanic, half are Celtic. *Mōdraniht* is the old English for 'Mother's Night' or 'Night of the Mothers' which was celebrated on Christmas Eve by the Anglo-Saxons. This practice is possibly connected to the Germanic Matres or Matrones, female beings who nearly always appeared in threes.

Stretching back at least 6,000 years there are references all across Europe to three all-powerful female goddesses called the mothers who were often associated with rivers, mountains, springs and trees, usually depicted in groups of three and shown holding babies, baskets of fruit and grain or the cornucopia, a symbol of fertility and the bounty of the Earth. Scholars continue to debate whether the 'cult' of the mothers was a remnant of the earlier goddess-worshipping peoples and represented the feminine principle both within humanity and the natural world. This 'cult of the mothers' was at one time widespread throughout northern Europe, but the festival had nothing to do with the Christian mother of God – or her son – and everything to do with the plurality of mothers who gave birth to the Midwinter Sun.

In Italy they celebrate Santa Lucia on 13th December. She wears a crown of lit candles (marking the approach of the rebirth of Light) and is often depicted carrying a sheaf of corn. There are many similar representations of her bringing ships of grain to relieve a starving population which indicates her ancient origins as a grain and earth goddess, succouring her people.

In Germany they have Christkind, the literal translation of which is 'Christ child', who is depicted as a grown woman wearing a white dress and gold cloak and an ornate golden crown on her fair hair. In Russia we find Snegurochka or 'snow girl', a goddess of winter reinterpreted or reinvented as the granddaughter or young travelling companion of Ded Moroz, a Russian equivalent of Father Christmas. And in Germany, Austria, the Netherlands, Switzerland, Poland, the Czech Republic and the Alsatian part of France we find Frau Holle, already mentioned as the British Mother Holly, but in reality possibly the wife of the god Odin, a goddess in her own right, complementing her husband's soul-seeking Midwinter journeys with her own sacred work, birthing souls into life on Earth and birthing souls back out of earthly life onto a higher plain.

Here in Wales we have the Welsh goddess Modron (the Latin version of which is matron), meaning 'mother', possibly analogous with the Welsh goddess Rhiannon, who we are told in the tales of the Mabinogi gave birth to her son, Pryderi, on the night of 24th December. In Welsh mythology he is the child god who carries within him the promise of youth and the energy of the Sun, born at the time of greatest darkness at Midwinter, bringer of the light.

In Wales we also have *Bendith y Mamau*, the blessing of the mothers, which were prayers or blessings said over the heads of children on Christmas Eve. These echo the archetypal 'mothers', originally the triple mother goddess or threefold mothering spirit. Her/their associations are fate foretelling, blessings at birth and on children, weaving/cloth/clothing, cleanliness, fruits and harvest, horses, snakes, birds – especially swans, owls and ravens – and perhaps most importantly, the great sow. In both Germanic and Celtic myths she is the mate for the great boar who is killed and eaten at the Winter Solstice.

She is also magic and mystery, both the beautiful fairy queen and the skeletal crone. She is Earth and Moon, twilight, night and dawn. She is a huntress – taking life to give life, giving life to take life. She is a guardian between the realms of life and death, born and unborn, seen and unseen. She is the gatekeeper for the new year, the Sun's return. She is the mother, midwife and grandmother. She is the Hearthkeeper, the guardian of souls and ancestral spirits too. In that sense she is a shaman, a walker between the worlds. As is said of Rhiannon, she can sing the living to sleep and the dead to life. She is the balance point between yin and yang, light and darkness, between this world and the Other World, or this world and the Underworld of the dead, the spirits, the ancestors, the dark deep cavernous Earth. This is also why she is associated with justice, with the reversal of roles, with tricks and the veiling and unveiling of truth. She releases social roles that have been bound and binds up the roles that have been prevalent for the rest of the year. She is also the goddess of sovereignty in all her forms, dealing with issues of power versus weakness, self-control versus licentiousness, fruitfulness versus bareness, addiction versus freedom, ignorance versus enlightenment. She is Lady Luck. She is fortune/misfortune. She is the bountiful harvest or the deadly famine.

She is cosmic order. She is karma. This is why the smooring (damping down for the night) of the house fires was so important in Celtic lands – because the hearth represented a microcosm where ashes were divided into the four directions and blessed. But within cosmic order, in the greatest sense, you have the threefold concept of the 'cosmic egg', 'cosmic order' and 'cosmic disorder'. This great cosmic goddess is in fact what science calls the three laws of thermodynamics (thermo as in heat/fire). Thermodynamics is about where energy comes from, how it perpetuates and how it eventually falls apart into entropy. There you have the three mothers in scientific form.

She is known by many names in many countries: the great goddess, the white goddess, Brighid, the Morrigan, Cerridwen, Maeve, sheela-na-gig, the Norns, Epona, the Fates, Hecate, the Valkyries, the Furies, Vesta, Diana, Isis, Maat, Shakti, Kali, Arianrhod – the list is endless!

Of course they are not all the same as each other, but she is the archetype from which they are each drawn and descend. So on Mother's Night, when we celebrate Christmas Eve, we are also unconsciously – and maybe now consciously – celebrating all these forms and feminine deities connected to the three mothers. We are celebrating not just the rebirth of the Sun, but the re-establishment of cosmic order.

But this feminine archetype has yet another name, another persona, which is particularly relevant to Midwinter and the Northern Hemisphere...

THE DEER GODDESS

In an area which stretched from the British Isles, across northern Europe and Scandinavia, Russia and Siberia and over the Bering Strait into the Americas, the Deer Mother was venerated as a life-giving mother and facilitator of fertility. This was a reindeer-mother-goddess cult dating from prehistoric times, when the Earth was colder and herds of reindeer more widespread. Images have been found of deer in rock carvings, paintings and on monolithic stelae from the Neolithic period down to the early Iron Age – traces of a deer-goddess religion revolving around female wise women and the deer goddess, the antlered doe.

Her horns have adorned altars and heads of shamanic priestesses; they have been etched into standing stones, woven in to ceremonial cloth and clothing, cast into jewellery and painted on drums. She is usually depicted as leaping or flying with neck outstretched and legs flung out in front and behind. She is often pictured as carrying the cosmos, the Sun, Moon and stars, in her horns, her antlers depicted as the Tree of Life, representing the lower, middle and upper worlds. She is also represented as a seated woman / goddess, wearing a horned headdress into which is woven the Tree of Life and a bird – the latter being an emblem of shamanic flight. The trio of symbols is often repeated in Winter Solstice imagery and Christmas folk art, and although original meanings and definitions are now largely forgotten, how many birds in trees and bushes and how many antlered stags do we find on our Christmas cards?

Much of the information about her has been obliterated by the later bias towards masculine depictions – male shamans eating red and white mushrooms and dressed in red and white garb. In Siberia, shamanic

practitioners are constantly referred to as 'he', but red and white ceremonial clothing was also worn by the earliest shamans of the northern
regions, and these have always been *female*. The current leader of the
Mongolian Dukha reindeer people is a ninety-six-year-old woman called
Tsuyan.

It was the assumption of a more recent patriarchal society that the
horned images that were found must automatically be depicting a stag.
In Celtic society, the antlered god, *Cernunnos*, was well known in eastern Gaul, but feminine counterparts have also been found at many sites
such as Clermont-Ferrand (Puy-de-Dome) and at Besançon (Doubs),
also depicting, again, the cornucopia feminine symbol associated with
fertility... the horn of plenty and the ever-productive vagina.

The Scottish historian J. G. McKay writes that there are 'an immense
number of traditions, references, notices of customs and various minor
matters which show conclusively that there formerly existed in the High-
lands of Scotland two cults – probably pre-Celtic – a deer cult and a deer
goddess cult. The latter was administered by women only.'

The sacred significance of deer in shamanic traditions is understood
to be essentially feminine. And in Siberian shamanism, the reindeer and
the Sun have a common association. Tattoos on buried shaman women
also contain deer tattoos featuring antlers embellished with small birds'
heads. The reindeer, sun and bird imagery show the priestesses' ability
to transform into the goddess herself and move from one spiritual level
to another – to 'journey' – and also to give birth and be the keeper in
charge of the rebirth of life itself – the Sun – which takes place annually
at the Winter Solstice.

Rohanitsa, the antlered winter mother goddess of the Ukraine, celebrates her feast day on the Winter Solstice. Her clothes depict her together with her daughters (or with children who may or may not be divine), with deer horns sprouting from her head or headdress. The horns are a sign that, as tales and rock carvings confirm, in ancient times the mother goddess gave birth to deer as well as children. For her feast day women wear garments embroidered with red and white and small white-iced cookies made in the shape of a deer are given as good-luck tokens and presents.

Interestingly the traditional clothes worn by the female medicine healers in Siberia are often red, white and green with fur lining and trim, a felted red peaked hat, curl-toed boots and warm mittens of reindeer hide comprise what might be seen as the feminine origins of a long line of depictions of Father Christmas. As Mary B. Kelly writes, 'Their long lineage of connection with the induction of spiritual journeys through the drum, their relationship of healing with "reindeer magic" and their ability to create potions and salves which could incite ecstatic visions or shamanic "journeys" give us a deeper look at the solstice and contemporary Christian symbol. These priestesses-of-the-antlered-ones who flew through the night to gather blessings and healing and then distributed these gifts to their tribe members must surely be considered as proto-typical.'

Beaivi, which is the Sami name for the Sun, is usually shown as a female who is associated with the fertility of plants and animals, in particular the reindeer.

Saule is a Lithuanian and Latvian goddess of flight who traditionally flew across the heavens in a sleigh pulled by horned reindeer and threw pebbles of amber (symbolising the Sun) down into the tops of chimneys.

Tacitus tells us about the Midwinter goddess *Nerthus*, synonymous with Mother Earth, who rode a sleigh-like wagon pulled by oxen which ritually processed from village to village signalling the laying down of arms and the bringing of peace to her communities, with much rejoicing and merrymaking following in every place she condescended to visit and sojourn in. During this time, no one went to war, no one took up arms, and every iron object was locked away. Then and only then would peace and quiet be known and welcomed. The wife of the old Norse god Njord, she is possibly the mythical mother of *Freya* and *Frigg*.

Women's tapestries in Scandinavia show red felt headdresses worn by the shamanic priestesses of the Altai in Siberia. A burial ship was found near Oslo in Norway laden with tapestries featuring antlered female figures wearing red clothing. Antlered goddesses were generally a common motif.

There is also a wealth of sacred and magical imagery surrounding the female deer and reindeer in Celtic mythology and belief. These often feature tales of white hinds (does) which are associated with the goddess, who often gives birth to the Sun Child in the form of a white hind.

The image of a deer with a light between its horns may be popularly accredited to the vision of Saint Hubertus, a seventh-century Christian and patron saint of hunters. But according to the Order of Bards, Ovates and Druids, this image can also be found in Hungary, Mongolia, the Russian steppes and China, where the symbol of the cosmos and the mother of the Sun was symbolised as a large horned female doe carrying the Sun in her horns.

In the natural world the leader of the reindeer herds is always a 'deer mother' which is stronger and larger than the rest. In winter she sports the largest and most impressive set of antlers – only the female reindeer have antlers in winter as the males, the bucks, annually lose them before this season. Therefore any depiction of an antlered reindeer in winter, whether it be on a cave wall or pulling a sleigh on your Christmas card, is portraying a female reindeer. Yes, all those deer with the very macho godly names that we see pulling Father Christmas's sleigh are 'sisters'!

This ancient reindeer goddess is the feminine counterpart to the Wild Man. Both are archetypes which originate tens of thousands of years ago, back in the misty dim origins of modern Western humanity. She wears red and white and flies in a sleigh pulled by female reindeer, gives birth to the Sun and holds the key to life and death, fertility and rebirth or total annihilation. This is no product of a Coca-Cola sales drive from the early twentieth century. Interestingly, in many parts of eastern Europe, the Father Christmas figure was more usually dressed in green – similar to Charles Dickens's famous portrayal of the Ghost of Christmas Present in A Christmas Carol – and far more in keeping with the true nature of the Wild Man as sacred guardian of wild unfathomable living energy.

This regal goddess of powerful feminine origin is surely co-creator of the Spirit of Christmas and an aspect of 'Mother Christmas', which brings us back to Mother Holly...

A TALE OF MOTHER HOLLY ON CHRISTMAS EVE

Mother Holly bustled about her house, her round cheeks flushed by her exertions, eyes sparkling happily in anticipation of the night to come.

Soon her husband, the Lord of Midwinter, would arrive home for his evening meal and she had much to do!

Mother Holly went into the larder and brought out the geese which needed to be plucked, and as she took the white feathers, one handful after another, some escaped and blew about her head... and on the Earth below, snow began to fall, softly covering everything with its silent icy mantle. Having cleaned, seasoned and stuffed the birds, she energetically heaved them into her big oven and shut the door with a bang.

Next, Mother Holly had to make the beds, turning the massive down-filled mattresses and plumping the feather-filled pillows. As she did so, there were always little feathers which escaped the cotton ticking and blew about her as she worked... and on the Earth below, the snow fell faster and faster; the cattle sheltered in their barns, glad to be in the warmth, their breath billowing in steamy clouds from their great wet nostrils, while out in the woods, the owls took cover – no hunting for them this evening – and the dogs slunk back into their kennels, silencing their twilight howls.

Then Mother Holly went to fetch a brush to sweep up all the little feathers that had escaped – to and fro she wielded her broom while she and the feathers danced around and around the great kitchen floor, merrily dodging and chasing each other... and on the Earth below, a great wind swept across the frozen pastures and shook and cracked the trees in the petrified woods.

The Lord of Midwinter flung open the door and strode into the room. Tall, broad and powerfully built, dressed from head to foot in thick animal furs, his silver locks curled around his shoulders and his long white beard cascaded down his chest. His eyes twinkled with merriment, sending flashes of lightning across the sky, and when he laughed (which he did often) his great belly shook like an earthquake and the sound of it boomed around the heavens and bounced from star to star.

'Well, wife!' he embraced his lady lustily as she tutted and fussed about him, setting a marvellous dinner, steaming and golden, upon the table before him. Hastily she removed her billowing snowy white apron... and on Earth below, the wind died and the snow gradually ceased to fall. She sat down at the table with her husband and they both began to eat heartily.

Eventually, when the steaming bowls of buttered vegetables were all empty and the dishes of spicy pickles and chutneys greatly depleted, and there wasn't a scrap of succulent meat left on the goose bones, the Lord of Midwinter rose to his feet.

'Have you made sure that there will be enough Light to go round for all?' the old dame asked a little anxiously.

'Don't I always?' her husband boomed back at her, smiling gently. 'Now I must be off! The darkest time of Winter is upon us. I have far to go and much to do if springtime growth and summer's bounty are to bless the Earth again, for none of this can happen without the warmth and light of the Sun!'

The old dame also had her own journey to make that night, but did not remind him of it – he knew it well enough. Both were equally needed in their different ways.

Mother Holly watched the Lord of Midwinter don his great fur coat and big fur hat and mittens and, blowing her a kiss, he strode out of the door. From the window she watched him cross the snowy yard and go into the stables, only to reappear a moment later leading Sleipnir, the largest reindeer the world has ever known: a huge beast with thick fur, antlers like a small forest, eyes like brown melting liquid pools and eight great legs like massive pistons that enabled her to gallop across the dark northern skies like a flash of green winter lightning.

Sleipnir pulled a huge sleigh, heavily laden with numerous bulging leather sacks, each tightly tied at the top with a cord, but here and there a tiny gold and blue flame licked around the bindings and the whole load pulsed with a subdued but powerful glow.

'Time waits for none!' the Lord roared out good humouredly. 'Light and warmth must be delivered to every place on Earth before the morning or else the spring shall not return.' He paused a moment and scratched his head beneath the fur rim of his hat. 'Strange how Humanity don't seem to see the Love and Warmth and Light that I leave for them for what they really are... they call my gifts "toys" and give them to their children! Ah well,' he continued to ponder, 'there surely is nowt so queer as folk... and no accounting!'

With that, the Lord jumped up onto his sleigh, gave Mother Holly a great broad beaming smile and a generous wave of his hand and cracked his whip just once. Sleipnir the reindeer sprang into the sky, pulling Lord and sleigh after him as effortlessly as so much thistledown. The myriad bells on his scarlet harness tinkled and rang out across the heavens. Joyously he galloped around overhead, over the house and stables and yard, picking up speed as he did so and then, quite without warning, Sleipnir, sleigh and Lord were gone, leaving only a trail of silver stardust falling softly to Earth in their wake.

By now, Mother Holly had donned her own great fur cloak with the soft deep hood and was also walking towards the stables. She led out a beautifully matched pair of snow-white reindeer, small and neat, but spirited and fleet of foot as a couple of moonbeams. Behind them they pulled a smaller sleigh. This one was empty, save for a mighty pile of the softest woollen blankets.

With small, neat, precise movements, Mother Holly went back into the house, only to return a moment later with her cloak billowing out around her and the sound of little sighs and giggles and even a snore or two emanating from beneath it. Stopping beside the sleigh, with infinite care, the Mother tenderly placed each child, toddler and baby safely within the sleigh, enfolded and tucked deep within the blankets.

All safely aboard, she too jumped up into the driving seat and took hold of the reins. The white reindeer leaped for the sky at such speed that, to anyone watching, all that could be seen were two shooting stars travelling across the firmament. Just then, the silver face of the moon slid out from behind a dark bank of cloud and smiled upon them.

For Mother Holly also had her deliveries to make before the next dawn and the return of the light. Mothers wishing for a child would have their babies delivered to them this night – some almost ready to be born, others no bigger than a pea, while others yet were only a thought in their parents' heads. And when all those hopeful young souls had been placed with their mothers, Mother Holly would take the rest of the children – those who had decided that this life on Earth was not quite right for them just yet and who had taken their leave of their loving families sometime within the past twelve months – and drive them Home into the new dawn light through which Life and Death could flow so freely for those few precious moments. There, on the other side of the dawn, their spiritual families would be waiting to joyously welcome them back.

Light, warmth and new beginnings... birth, death and rebirth... the cycles of Life. And each year at this time, the Lord of Midwinter and Mother Holly, the celestial couple, rode the winter skies, sacred keepers of the cycles of that life. Mother Holly chuckled deep within her enveloping furs, gave the reins an extra little flick and hurtled off towards the Midwinter dawn.

MARKING THE NIGHT

If you would like to particularly mark or celebrate Mother's Night you can do this very simply by lighting a candle – red or gold are good colours at this time, but any will do – and, sitting quietly, giving thanks for all your blessings and perhaps thinking specifically of your own mother, or other female guardians or teachers – women who have supported and guided you over the years, being thankful for the good things they did for you and trying to understand and forgive any shortcomings. You might wish to contact one of them and have a chat.

Or you might wish to think about what it has meant to you to be – or not be – a mother or father. You might like to contact your children if they are not with you at this time. If they are, you might also like to spend a little time with them – share a seasonal celebratory drink or enjoy a hug or a cuddle. Some of us may also have 'children' which we have 'adopted' – younger people who are not officially or obviously related to us but to whom we have grown close, guided, helped, supported. You might like to think about or contact them too.

It is particularly good to take some time now just for yourself. Having reached Christmas Eve, you will have been steadily busy for some time and now you need to take a metaphorical breather. It is good to meditate for a while, or if you don't usually do this, then just sit, close your eyes and breathe deeply... absorb the stillness and peace, draw it into yourself, allow it to fill you to overflowing and simply bathe in it, in this precious moment of connection to the eternal mother, and be re-energised and healed.

Finally, you might wish to walk through your house with a lighted stick of incense or a smudge stick, or even your lighted candle, and simply bless each room in turn... metaphorically wipe the slate clean, ready for the break of day, which is only a matter of a few hours away, ready for the rebirth of the Sun and a whole new era.

Christmas Day

Through the pale arch of orient the morn
Comes in a milk-white splendour newly born,
A sword of crimson cuts in twain the grey
Banner of shadow hosts, and lo, the day!

'A WINTER DAWN', L. M. MONTGOMERY

SOME TIME JUST after six o'clock in the morning, the family begins to stir, tumbling sleepily out of bed, making cups of tea, feeding cats, not much in a mood to talk except for the briefest Christmas greeting. I am to be found in the kitchen filling flasks and bagging up snacks of fruit and sweet biscuits, while my husband gathers our lanterns and torches, the dogs cavorting about us, ready to be off.

Still in darkness, we leave the house and take a short drive – only five minutes or so. Leaving the vehicle we walk down through the fields, boots crunching on frosted grass, to the edge of the lake. It is bitingly cold. Muffled in bulky coats, with scarves and hoods swathing our heads and gloves making our hands clumsy, we arrive in a little copse of trees. Flasks are set down on the ground next to a basket of sandwiches and other goodies, ready to snack upon while we wait. We each choose a tree to lean against or a log or boulder to perch upon and then, with all torches and lanterns now extinguished, we settle down quietly to wait.

For this is Christmas morning and we are here waiting for dawn to break, to witness the rebirth of the Sun. Imperceptibly the air around us brightens and black thins to grey as the early morning light gradually filters down to us. There is not a breath of wind – no movement of air at all, everything is absolutely and utterly still. The water in the lake lies like glass. The mountains around us loom massively. Mist begins to form over the water. Water fowl are waking, invisible in the wraiths of mist though we can hear cheeps and quacks and hurried scutters across the water. Gradually the mountains around us begin to take shape. Despite the extra socks and insulated gloves our hands and feet are slowly beginning to freeze and we stir a little to encourage circulation, occasionally murmuring softly to each other, mindful not to break the breathless spell of the moment.

In a valley such as ours, we have to wait another couple of hours to actually see the Sun rise from behind the craggy ridges. Even if we climb the lower slopes to where we watched the light die on the Solstice, it still takes quite a time, and more often than not, the sky is heavily overcast and no actual Sun is to be seen all day. But we know that without the Sun's presence we wouldn't have daylight, so we take the daylight itself to signify the arrival of the Sun.

As the light grows stronger I can now see how calm and peaceful the world is around me and I send out joyous thanks for such beauty and loving greetings to all those old souls born upon this morning, including the Christ Child. Prayers for peace and communal love and understanding also go out upon the ether.

Eventually, when we are certain that it is well and truly daylight, we break open the sandwiches and pour cups of soup and coffee to wrap and warm our tingling hands around. Clouds of steam billow around us as we drink and eat, talk and laugh and our celebration begins to deeply dawn upon us. Later we sit silently again, absorbing the intense serenity of the morning. I have often noticed that early Christmas morning is like no other for its complete stillness. We have been out for a couple of hours now and not a single car has driven down the valley... no voices chatting in the village, no doors banging or even dogs barking or sheep bleating... it is as if all creation has stopped to take notice of what is being played out upon the celestial stage.

Whether we actually stay to see the Sun rise above the Nantlle Ridge depends on how clear the sky is or how cold, wet or windy it might be. This morning we are lucky. The heavy bank of cloud is thinning and blue skies are becoming visible. The morning grows lighter and brighter until the snow on top of Mount Snowdon – iced around its summit like a gigantic Christmas cake – is glowing fluorescently. The sky above the mountain ridge is now so bright that the topmost rock appears starkly black, a magnificent silhouette against a palette of orange, gold, pinks and blues. Finally the Sun itself peeps over the ridge, even in its cooler winter mode still far too bright to look at properly – just a blazing mass of bright, bright light!

Our task is complete. We bore witness to the dying of the light at the Solstice and we have now borne witness to the rebirth of the Sun. Time to go home, warm up and *party*!

CHRISTMAS MORNING

Once more gathered around the Aga with yet *more* hot drinks, we now open our Christmas stockings which have been waiting for us beneath the Christmas tree in the living room. The dogs have Christmas socks as well, full of bouncy rubber balls, roasted bones and chewy things, but their greatest pleasure seems to be in tearing up all the gift wrapping that comes off everyone else's presents until the floor is completely strewn with seasonal confetti. Meanwhile, the cats enjoy an extra sumptuous breakfast and try to play with their own catnip mice as unobtrusively as possible!

There are quite a variety of times and places where you might wish to hang or leave your stocking, and also where you might want to enjoy and unpack it. Laid across the bottom of the bed, hanging from a bed knob, hanging from the mantelpiece in your living room or laid across the hearth or even beneath the Christmas tree are just some options. It partly depends on who will be opening them, what their ages are and what shape the rest of your morning might be taking. It is entirely up to you and what you do one year might change the next. Try different approaches and see what works best for you. The important point here is that, traditionally, it really must be a sock, stocking or boot. No other receptacle will do.

One December a few years ago, a friend of mine found herself talking to a young woman on the checkout at her local supermarket. The contents of her basket showed that she had obviously been Christmas shopping and the checkout girl began to tell my friend about her little two-year-old son and what she was planning to give to him at Christmas. Naturally, the topic of Christmas stockings came into the conversation as she enthused about her little boy's excitement, but then quietly commented that she still missed her own stocking now that she was grown up and a mum herself. My friend saw the same checkout girl several times more before Christmas and they good-humouredly compared notes as to how their respective preparations were progressing.

On one of the last shopping days before the holiday, my friend quietly slipped into the store and found the young mum at her checkout, gave her a small bulging sock and wished her all the compliments of the season. Bless her, apparently the young lady blushed redder than the woolly slipper sock my friend had utilised for her stocking! She was told to put the stocking under her tree or at the bottom of her bed so that she too would have something to open on Christmas morning. It only contained some pretty soap, chocolate, a notepad and pen... oh, and of course the other slipper sock to match the one acting as stocking so that she would afterwards have a pair to wear. It is a lovely thing to give surprises! Remember, service and sacrifice... and the Spirit of Christmas which works through any and all willing conduits – we all have the ability and opportunity to be 'Santa' occasionally!

Sometimes I prefer to have Christmas dinner in the middle of the day; other years we might make it for late afternoon or early evening. I have also been known to postpone this main celebratory feast until

Boxing Day or even the day after *that* – after all, there *are* officially twelve days of Christmas, so what is the hurry? And if we plan our main meal for another day it means that I can invite people who would otherwise be with their parents or grandchildren. I love nothing better than to see lots of family and friends gathered around a table spread with a sumptuous feast in a room aglow with fire and candlelight... bright, happy, smiling faces flushed by the first glass of good wine and the flow of pleasantries and jokes.

However, if we do go out before daybreak on Christmas morning and are not having a hot dinner that day, then we usually have a brunch sometime late in the morning; our favourite is scrambled egg made with cream and topped with smoked salmon and watercress, with pots of freshly ground coffee, hot home-made rolls and lashings of home-made preserves (ginger and rhubarb with sweet memories of summer is one of my husband's favourites, whilst I have developed quite a passion for the bramble and apple or raspberry), bolstered by hot mince pies and a tin of Christmas biscuits!

PURE ENCHANTMENT

When I was a child it was a doubly massive relief to me to wake up very early on Christmas morning and, firstly, realise that I had at long last been to sleep, and secondly, that Father Christmas *had* visited me with many blessings as I slept and that my stocking was indeed bulging!

I usually woke sometime after 6 a.m. and would lie awake, hugging these marvellous facts to myself as I gently explored all the knobs, corners and protuberances on my wondrously over-stuffed sock which responded with mind-bogglingly tantalising rustles and crackles. I would never unpack my stocking until my parents were awake but I usually ended up waking them so I could do so. Sometimes I bounced up straight away and raced along the corridor to their bedroom. Other times I would sit as long as I could, knowing that they were both tired, until, unable to contain my impatience any longer, I would creep into their room and agitatedly inform them in a loud stage whisper that 'Father Christmas has been! He's been!'

One year before I could even tell the time, I marched triumphantly in upon my mother and father at 5 a.m., gleefully unpacked the contents of my stocking to an accompanying chorus of less than enthusiastic grunts, and then promptly fell asleep, propped between my still-recumbent parents, surrounded by all the litter of wrapping paper and ribbon, gifts strewn across the counterpane. And what gifts they were! Crayons, paints and pencils, rubber balls, dolls (especially the elasticated wooden ones with large red wooden feet, made in Poland, which I adored), little books, kaleidoscopes, chocolate and sweeties, net bags of wooden animals or collections of houses made in former East Germany, as so many lovely Christmas-related things were then.

My father usually went downstairs first and he always reacted amazingly to what he found there. 'Has Father Christmas left anything?' I would timidly call out, doing a quick mental review of the past year to ascertain if I had been good enough to merit more than just a stocking.

My father would reply along the lines of, 'Oh, he's been all right... my word, what a pile of presents! Oh, you should just see them! My goodness, look at that... and that! I've never seen anything like it!'

I myself wasn't allowed to go downstairs until my father had made up the fire and put the kettle on to boil for a pot of tea. When I finally *did* get downstairs I could only agree with him wholeheartedly. Those first few Christmas mornings of my early childhood made an impression upon me which has stayed with me all of my life. The darkness or grey half-light of the early Midwinter's morning would be utterly dispelled by the blaze in the living-room grate and all the candles that were lit around the room. Glowing light was reflected everywhere one looked; china, copper and glass winked warmly with yellow and orange reflections, and even the green holly gave back twinkles of light from its shiny oily leaves. White hoar frost outside would give the appearance of snow.

The Christmas tree stood in prime magnificence, glowing, glittering, shimmering, the heart and spirit of the season, while beneath its bedecked branches were piled parcels and packages of every shape, colour, sort and size. My mother had many friends and business associates who would also send gifts for me, creating extra mounds and heaps across the tops of the dresser and square piano. It truly resembled Father Christmas's grotto in fairyland, but in my very own home. I would cast a glance at the supper left out for Santa the previous evening and heave a satisfied sigh of relief – the glass had been drained and only crumbs remained on the plate!

Daddy would provide tea and hot buttered toast which had to be consumed before one piece of string was unknotted or a single layer of wrapping paper removed. The glory of the room and the rampant anticipation filled my small frame with more delight and excitement than I thought it possible to contain.

Sage and Onion Stuffing

I sometimes make this fresh on Christmas morning; other years, for speed
and ease, I make it the day before.

Gillian

INGREDIENTS:

Onion

Breadcrumbs

Dried sage

Butter

Salt and pepper

METHOD:

- Peel and finely chop onion and bring to boil in a little water with
  a shake of salt and pepper.
- After simmering gently until onion is soft, add breadcrumbs,
  a goodly knob of butter and dried sage to flavour (beware of
  using too much sage as it can make a dish bitter).
- Use to stuff your fowl and / or place some of the mixture in
  a greased ovenproof dish and cook for 30 minutes.
- Serve hot or cold with roast meats such as turkey, chicken
  or pork.

NOTE: *can also be made well beforehand and stored in the fridge or frozen in the*
freezer. Gillian

THE AMOUNTS OF ingredients you use for both the bread sauce and the stuffing recipes depends entirely on how much you wish to make, but a good rule of thumb would to be to use double the amount of breadcrumbs to onion – and remember that you can use as many onions as you wish – one of my elderly distant cousins who was renowned for her sage and onion stuffing used to make a total of 25 lb of it to distribute around the family... and it has to be said that she tended to use rather more than just a knob of butter! Home-made is infinitely better than any bought preparation – try it for yourself and see!

Bread Sauce

INGREDIENTS:
Onion
Cloves
Breadcrumbs
Butter
Milk
Salt and pepper

METHOD:
- Stick 6 cloves into a peeled onion and simmer gently in water until soft.
- Remove onion from liquor, remove cloves from onion and discard, and chop/mash onion finely.
- Return onion to liquor in pan, add breadcrumbs, a goodly knob

of butter, a shake of salt and pepper and enough milk to make a soft but not too sloppy consistency; can also add a little cream.
- Stir all together and bring back to simmer for a few minutes, being careful not to let it stick.
- Serve hot or cold – particularly tasty with sausages.

NOTE: *can be made beforehand and either kept in fridge or frozen until required.*

I am saddened to see that bread sauce seems to be falling from favour with the British public but I can assure you that there is nothing more delicious than creamy white and delicately fragrant bread sauce served with sizzling, shiny brown sausages – and it is equally delicious with vegetarian sausages too! Gillian

THE DAY UNFOLDS

At some point we have a toast for absent friends... people we love who, for one reason or another, are not with us – perhaps even remembering those who have passed away since the previous Midwinter. For many years we aimed to do this at 1 p.m. But it invariably clashed with the last stages of preparing Christmas dinner, and for me, attempting to serve such a meal whilst under the influence of a glass or two of sherry was not the best of ideas! Now, with currently no children in the house, everything is far more fluid and laid back. We tend to have our toast just before the Queen's Speech at 3 p.m., which we either watch or listen to. For me it is a bit like getting a message from one's grandmother or an elderly aunt – someone else (besides myself!) to actually say how well we have done in the past year, to draw our attention to those who need our prayers, thoughts and help, and direct our thoughts to hopes and dreams for the coming new year. It sets the tone and gives us pause to reflect amidst all the hustle and bustle and excitement.

After our brunch it is a case of clearing away and, if not having our Christmas dinner that day, completing any preparation for whatever other meal(s) we shall be having. Someone walks the dogs again – no need for us all to take the traditional Christmas afternoon walk if we have already been out for several hours earlier in the day. Eventually we retire into the drawing room where the Winter Tree awaits us in all its evocative frosty glory. The rest of the day is given over to talking, playing games, singing carols, occasionally listening to the radio or watching a bit of television (but not often or much!) and opening the rest of our presents from close family which have been waiting for us under the Winter Tree. At some point the tea tray is brought in and the Christmas cake is cut. The daylight fades once more and we are left cocooned in our own little time capsule of twinkling lights, flickering flames, shadows, warmth, good food and good company.

In my young childhood, we would only just have made a start on opening presents when the postman would arrive (yes, they used to work on Christmas morning back in the late 1950s and early 1960s!) with another fistful of cards and letters, and be invited in for a glass of something warming. Later, as we sat awash in a sea of paper and gifts, neighbours would call to give us the season's greetings and be drawn into our warm, cosy, glowing world, to choose a token gift from the Christmas tree (my mother always hung several extra there), laughing, joking and in high spirits. One person who never missed his 'Christmas glass' was old Bill Green from Woodside Cottage, and he would always stoop to look at my new toys, kindly commenting but simultaneously terrifying me with his vigorously bushing eyebrows.

Lunch was sometimes a bit of a hurried affair as we often ate later than intended and guests would begin arriving before we were through with the pudding, my mother frequently holding huge parties for Christmas Day tea. The refectory table down the centre of the kitchen would be groaning with plates piled high with every goody imaginable, while I, totally oblivious to all the clamour around me, would happily play with my newly acquired treasures.

One Christmas when I was five years old, I remember wearing red and blue tartan trousers and a lovely hand-knitted jumper, and riding my shiny new red scooter round and round the tea table, as happy as a sand boy – unlike my cousin Wendy, who had arrived kitted out in a very pretty, very frilly, fancy party dress, all ribbons, lace and bows, who was made to sit decorously still beside her parents and who bawled her eyes out the entire time. A slightly cautionary tale for parents!

As I grew a little older, my mother changed her strategy and began holding her parties on Boxing Day instead, giving us all more time to fully enjoy Christmas Day and our time together as a family. Even so, my Nainie (Welsh for grandmother) would always join us for tea. This lesser meal was triumphantly crowned by an intricate chocolate yule log cake, liberally sprinkled with icing sugar 'snow', and a Christmas cake the size of a small wheel, topped by the china Father Christmas which had always stood on the family's Christmas cakes since before my mother was born and which still graces our Christmas cakes – which means that it must have seen nearly a hundred of our family Christmases by now!

BEHIND THE SCENES

I know that for many people Christmas is an extremely emotionally tur-bulent time; expectations run impossibly high which almost inevitably leads to disappointment – reality can never measure up to fantasy, and that is what many people create in their minds. People also get very stressed and in such a highly charged situation it is easy for tempers to fray and rows to erupt. But there are ways to prevent this – or at least minimise the possibility – and even purposefully factor in some damage limitation if it does.

As I wrote in an earlier chapter, remember to keep things simple. Make the very most of less. Don't expect – or allow others – to have everything at once. I hate the thought of a massive gift-opening fest. Ripping open every present that has entered the house within a matter of minutes on Christmas Day morning with little or no thought to what is being given or how much love and thought has gone into choosing or making it. Then to be followed by sitting discontentedly because all the excitement and anticipation has suddenly evaporated.

Perhaps the recent traditions of attending a church service in the morning (or rising and going outside before daybreak!), and/or going out for a walk in the afternoon, are some of the best ways to break up the overwhelming excitement – they can help to focus our attention on the deeper, more spiritual reasons for our Midwinter celebrations and put us firmly back in contact with the natural world, balancing and calming our perceptions and staggering our activity.

Also stagger the opening of gifts. We open presents from friends and German relatives on Christmas Eve in the continental way... or you could say the Celtic way, as in older times their day began at dusk the previous evening, which means that Christmas Day would actually begin at tea-time on Christmas Eve. Then we open our Christmas stockings at some stage in the morning of Christmas Day, followed by presents from close family later in the afternoon or at teatime when we gather around the fire beneath the Winter Tree and enjoy steaming cups of my favourite orange pekoe tea and slices of rich moist spicy Christmas cake.

There are other ways of spreading out the 'giving' ceremony. We have a cheerful figure, measuring about a foot tall and dressed in red fur, with a large sack which stands at his feet and is 'held up' between his chubby hands. In the family he is known as the Christmas Elf and small gifts are placed in the sack by members of the family. Sometimes we open his sack at breakfast on Christmas Day; other times he might be stood on the tea table, or even deferred to Boxing Day breakfast or tea.

When my son was very small, a friend once presented us with a beautiful model of a snowman which stood about two feet tall. It was constructed from a large cardboard cylinder (for its body), with a papier mâché head made from newspaper. The whole thing was thickly covered in white cotton wool; the head was removable and inside the main body were individually wrapped gifts for all the family. It made a marvellous decoration which we kept – even renewing its cotton wool coating when it became a bit tatty – and refilled it with little gifts which we opened on New Year's Eve. The snowman stayed with us for about ten years until it literally fell apart, but was a much-loved element of our celebrations. Get other family members to supply the contents for these extra surprises, so that it all doesn't fall to you alone.

As previously mentioned, you may wish to use crackers as a vehicle for giving everyone a lovely gift – perhaps your main present to them. But one word of warning: sometimes people will still view things and react to them in the same way, regardless of how different they may actually be. I well remember one year my mother decided to fill everyone's cracker with beautiful little pewter trinket boxes which shone like silver and were decorated with the figures of wild animals – fox, squirrel, badger, hare, etc. – sitting on the lids. Imagine her dismay when she came to clear the table after everyone had gone home, only to find that half her guests had left their boxes discarded among the litter of cracker papers, orange peel and sweet wrappers as if they were only the usual plastic rings and cars found in the cheaper mass-produced articles.

Don't forget, it is always wise to have a few extra little things put aside so that if someone drops in unexpectedly, they can also be included in the fun.

You don't have to use 'gifts' at all. If you decide to have Christmas crackers at your Christmas Day tea, you might decide to fill them with forfeits instead of gifts, which could mean an active and hilarious gathering as each person in turn attempts to fulfil their challenges and instructions. Or you might wait until another day during the Christmas celebrations and have an iced cake where you have hidden forfeits (written small and wrapped even smaller in waterproof plastic) under the icing, or in the middle of the cake with the jam. No one will know what forfeit they are getting and as the cake is gradually devoured, the activity unfolds. And don't worry if you can't bake or are too busy – buy a cake and cut it open, or ice a ready-made one. But do please remember to warn everyone before they begin eating that they have to watch out for the cake because there is something special in it that is not edible!

The same applies if you put charms in the Christmas cake or pudding. No one wants people breaking teeth or having to be rushed to A&E!

You might also have an elf with sack or snowman which contains the clues for a treasure hunt, each person having to complete a clue and co-operate with everyone else to find the hiding place of the 'treasure', which must be something that can be shared by all.

Or you might have a Christmas meal or gathering where you provide lots of old newspapers and ribbons, bows and coloured string (along with scissors, stapler, sticky tape and glue) and everyone has to make their own party hat to wear for the gathering. Or ask everyone to bring a joke written on a piece of paper and a small token gift which will fit into a cracker; provide them with the supplies and directions to make a cracker and let them construct each other's before they decorate the dinner or tea table with them.

The key word is 'inclusion'. Don't feel that you have to provide everything ready done for everyone. That way leads to boredom and almost inevitable disappointment. Give people the chance to feel an active and important part of whatever is taking place. A person's enjoyment and satisfaction is usually only commensurate with the amount of effort or participation they have contributed.

And yes, you will probably find that – literally – at the end of the day it is easier, simpler and quicker to just do all these things yourself and present everyone with a fait accompli, but how comparatively uninspiring and sterile that might be. Which is more fun: to have everyone laughing, talking and, yes, possibly struggling to make something, making a mess on the floor, possibly being outrageous and ridiculous – or sitting in composed isolation, making inane small talk, sipping some beverage daintily and wondering exactly what they are doing there? Then there are also the people who unexpectedly shine on such occasions, producing something quirky, beautiful or unusual that takes us all by surprise and earns them recognition and admiration, giving them a precious time to shine.

And did I mention the dreaded word 'mess'? Yes. I did. But again, that doesn't mean that you should be the one to clear it up at the end of the activity – minimise the damage by first laying an old sheet(s) over the floor/furniture, get everyone picking things up and sorting them out and putting them away, and ask for a volunteer to run the vacuum cleaner over the carpet when everything has been removed.

FIRESIDE FRIVOLITIES

Termed 'parlour games' in days gone by, many of these are of ancient origin and have been providing an element of hilarity and ridiculousness for generations! The time around Midwinter is especially when *everyone* of all ages should be encouraged to join in, regardless of the mess that might be made or the embarrassment engendered! This is all part of the organised chaos symbolising the deep origins of our celebrations... the temporary stripping away of barriers of occupation, age, ability and self-opinion and the complete overturning of all our personal and cultural preconceptions.

MAKE YOUR OWN PARTY HATS: Great for children and adults alike. Get everyone in the party mood by providing them with copious amounts of old newspapers, gift ties, ribbons and bows – anything shiny, appealing and easy to use! – and scissors, paperclips, glue and a stapler. Divide everyone into couples (being careful not to put partners or siblings together) and give them a certain length of time to make a hat, not for themselves, but for the other person. You will be astonished at how creative and inspired some people can be! A great icebreaker at the start of an evening.

FORFEITS: Can be played in teams or individually, with one person acting as master of ceremonies. Takes the form of a quiz, but whoever can't answer their question correctly has to perform a forfeit instead. This is usually an action. For instance, pretending to be a train going from station to station, walking like a monkey, dancing like a ballerina, miming to a piece of opera. The more unlikely the commands the funnier it will be, but the forfeits must never be too difficult or embarrassing to perform – that would be unfair. This can be made simpler for younger children or relatively difficult for adults.

PASS THE PARCEL: Beloved by children when sweets or little gifts are wrapped within the layers of a large parcel of newspaper. Music is played and each time it stops, the person holding the parcel is allowed to remove a single sheet of paper. Sometimes they will find a present within the layers of paper and sometimes they won't.

PASS THE PARCEL WITH FORFEITS: This can be made suitable for teenagers or adults – or a mixed-age party – by inserting jokes to be read out or instructions to be followed, a chocolate coin to be eaten or a forfeit to be performed. This time, everyone is possibly less keen to be found holding the parcel as no one is sure what might come next!

WHAT'S WRONG WITH MY OUTFIT? Another good icebreaker for the beginning of the evening. Everyone is previously asked to come with two things 'wrong' with what they are wearing. This might mean that someone is wearing odd socks or odd earrings, or has a jumper on inside out, or is wearing their underpants over their trousers. See how inventive everyone can be. Everyone carries two tokens (which can simply be pieces of paper or straws) and each time someone guesses what is 'wrong' with their appearance, a token is given to them and the 'fault' rectified. The person who has collected the most tokens at the end of a specified number of minutes is the winner... and obviously the most observant!

FLOUR GAME: A heap of flour is piled onto a board or wipe-clean table (or any other suitable surface) and a chocolate coin is balanced on top of it. Each player has a blunt knife or a spatula and takes it in turns to cut some of the flour away from the main pile without disturbing the chocolate coin. If the coin falls before all the flour is removed, that person is out and the game continues without them, until everyone else has been caught out and the last person remaining can claim their prize... and eat the chocolate coin! As you may imagine, this game can be extremely messy so is best played in a kitchen – or even on a sheltered patio or in a porch.

SNAPDRAGON: A handful of raisins (or anything else which isn't flammable but is edible) are floated on a bowl of water. A tiny amount of alcohol is poured onto the surface of the water and set alight. The winner is the person who can retrieve the most raisins... hopefully without burning themselves! This is an old, old game which was particularly popular in the nineteenth century. Understandably, it is not suitable for small children and these days may be considered quite politically incorrect, but is great fun all the same!

QUIZZES: Good for bringing a disparate group of characters of all interests, backgrounds and ages together and can be loosely used as a focal point for a gathering or party while the wine and hot chocolate circulates, quickly followed by dishes of nuts, tins of biscuits and boxes of chocolates. There are lots of books of quizzes on the market too – some on specialised topics and others on general knowledge. Buy one and pop it in a family member's Christmas stocking and then they can be prevailed upon to organise it all.

CONSEQUENCES: Another game from the nineteenth century and a particular favourite with my own family.

- Everyone is given a sheet of paper and a pen or pencil.
- At the top of the sheet of paper, everyone writes the name of a girl or woman. It may be someone in the room, or a friend or relative who everyone knows, or someone famous – whoever, it is wise to use someone everyone is familiar with as this makes it relevant to everyone and increases the fun. Then the sheet of paper is folded over away from you (so that the name is obscured) and passed to the person on your left.
- Then everyone writes a boy's or man's name and folds the paper

over again, away from them, so hiding what they have written,
and again passes it to the person on their left.

- This continues with where the couple met, what she said to him,
what he said to her, what the consequence was and finally what
the world might comment about it.

- Everyone passes their paper one final time and then unfolds
the sheet of paper they end up with and takes it in turns to
read it aloud.

Needless to say, some of the results are side-splittingly hilarious. If you
don't believe me, try it for yourself and see! Again, this game is for all
ages, as long as all the participants can read and write.

IMPERTINENT QUESTIONS: This is a card game – some decks can still
be found for sale on Amazon or eBay, but you can also make your own.
Write silly, awkward, rude, impertinent questions on squares of card
and some equally silly, suggestive, rude and impertinent replies on more
pieces of card. The players work in pairs, taking it in turns to draw a
random card and ask a question to which their partner draws a card and
makes a random reply. Very simple but often with excruciatingly funny
results! The questions and answers can be as simple (fit for young children to play) or as ribald (adults only!) as you wish to make them. Just
remember to keep it kind; don't allow the tone to become too hurtful or
cutting... and no fixing answers to match the questions – both questions
and answers must be drawn randomly.

LEXICON AND OTHER WORD GAMES: Lots of games involving letters
and / or words are to be found. Some involve proprietary brands of games

sold by games and toy manufacturers; others can be accomplished by simply using a pencil and a sheet of paper. Have a look online or in books of games for ideas.

EISTEDDFOD: This is where everyone contributes something to the evening's entertainment. One person might tell jokes; another might read or recite a poem; someone else might sing a song or play a musical instrument; or someone might even elect to organise an activity or game as their 'turn'. Provides opportunities for fun and laughter but also for quieter, more reflective times too and is flexible enough to allow for lots of talking, eating and drinking in between the entertainment.

LASTLY... don't forget while you are playing your games to toast the marshmallows and chestnuts, indulge in a rousing chorus of a couple of carols and finish the proceedings off with a story, either told (if you have someone among you who is gifted enough to do this) or read from a book... ghost stories are always popular!

'ME' TIME

Yes, all this forward thinking, pre-planning and organisation is hard work. But it is also enjoyable. And if you become too busy and/or tired you can at least be happy in the knowledge that you have given everyone else a romping good time!

However, make sure that 'your time' comes at some point. This might be once the coffee and mince pies have been served at the end of

Christmas Day dinner. You might decide that this is your cut-off point and that the rest of the family can take over the clearing away and washing up – and even the making of the turkey sandwiches for tea and the bringing out of that tea or supper when it is finally required. You can then go and quietly put your feet up for an hour and do something that *you* want to do... just for you alone... perhaps the first time you have had the opportunity in many days.

Or you may decide to leave the rest of the family to clear away while you go and quietly prepare the next round of activities, whether that be games or something else. One of the things to remember is that it often isn't the amount of work or preparation that something requires, but the fact that you are having to do it under stress of secrecy or shortage of time or lack of sleep. But if you have *time* to execute your plans, you may also take enjoyment from the anticipation of the fun that you are instigating.

Alternatively you might decide to carry on through Christmas Day and then take Boxing Day off altogether – stay in bed, have breakfast there, sprawl on the sofa in your pyjamas and decadently graze the Christmas goodies whilst watching TV. Refuse to even enter the kitchen that day... or at the very least to go near the sink and do any washing up! Curl up in your favourite chair (or even back in bed) and begin reading that book you've just been given or listen to the CD you've just received. Making / giving Christmas to others is a wonderful thing to do, a real act of Midwinter service and sacrifice, but no one needs to pretend that it is easy or not exhausting!

So in the summer or autumn, when you are first beginning to plan your Midwinter celebrations, don't forget to factor in some special quality time just for yourself.

COMMENT FROM JOAN: POST PARTY... 1959

Gillian told me that she didn't like the quiet when people had gone, but she was obviously extremely tired and within ten minutes was asleep in the living room.

In fact there will now be a pause while I go and brew myself a cup of tea... Have just returned with a breakfast cup of tea to have a sleepy Gill rouse and demand a cup. Back with another tea cup, Gill sits on the fender-stool to drink her tea. I reprove her for drinking noisily, she hands me back an almost empty cup saying 'Had 'nuff' and crawls back to an armchair to sleep, though now she has wakened I rather think it will only be a matter of 'coming to' and not sleep.

EVENING SHADES

Have you noticed how different your home feels when you have hosted a party or gathering of some sort? All the doors between the rooms are wide open as people relax, spread themselves, move freely about... voices and laughter erupt... there is the tinkle of glassware or chink of cups on saucers... the drift of cigar smoke... the still appetising aroma of delicious foods now consumed but lingering, wraith-like, around the disorderly debris on the dining-room table. Fires burn in every grate and everywhere is warm... but it is not the usual warmth resulting from having turned the central heating up a notch or plugged in a couple of extra radiators. It is that very special and singular warmth generated by humanity coming together in friendship and enjoying each other's company. It floods the house and is still a perceptible presence the next day. Suddenly the furniture looks fresher, the colours of the carpet and curtains revitalised, the decorations more glittery... everything glows. This is the tangible expression and experience of loving community... and you have helped to instigate and create it. What a blessing!

Laughter is the sun that drives winter from the human face.

VICTOR HUGO

Roasting Chestnuts

At one time chestnuts were far more common than they are now. Unlike most other fatty nuts they are high in carbohydrates and were sometimes known as 'bread of the mountain' as they were ground and used to make flour. In northern Italy, before the arrival of corn, chestnut flour was used to make polenta. In early nineteenth-century America, the farmers would allow their pigs to fatten up by eating the windfall chestnuts that had fallen to the forest floor.

It is possible to cook chestnuts just about any way you choose – boil, grill, microwave – but in my opinion, the nicest way to prepare them is the good old-fashioned way... roasted!

OVEN ROAST

Preheat your oven to 200°C, 400°F or Gas Mark 6.

Cut a cross or straight line into the skin of each nut by holding it between your finger and thumb, resting it on a chopping board and using a small sharp knife to make the incision. Be careful, they can be slippery – don't cut your hands.

Place the chestnuts in a roasting tin and bake until the skins begin to open and the insides are tender – approximately 30 minutes.

Tip into a clean cloth and cover for a few minutes before peeling away the hard outer shell and the inner brown skin, leaving the white flesh of the chestnut. If you find any nuts that seem discoloured or shrivelled, dispose of them in the compost – chestnuts only have a relatively short shelf life.

TRADITIONAL ROAST

On an open coal or log/wood fire within the home, or outside on the barbecue, campfire or bonfire.

Place chestnuts in the top half of a steamer with plenty of water in the bottom half. Place the lid firmly on the pan, bring to the boil and then simmer/steam for 30 minutes.

Remove from the pan and push semi-cooked chestnuts onto a toasting fork – one to each prong, if they will fit – then prop the laden fork against the bars of the grate or against some other non-inflammable object. Even though part-cooked they can still take quite a few minutes.

You might wish to turn them around once or twice while they are cooking. The chestnuts are supposed to 'pop' when they are ready... but not all do!

NOTE: *If you are cooking the chestnuts on an open fire, make sure that your fire is hot but not flaming, then rest the chestnuts two or three inches away from the heat source. Holding the toasting fork manually is not a good idea, your arms will get very tired and possibly rather burnt!*

The Twelve Days

Walls for the wind, and a roof for the rain,
And drinks beside the fire –
Laughter to cheer you, and those you love near you,
And all that your heart may desire.

IRISH BLESSING

THANKFULLY THE DAYS are long gone when the entire working population laboured until late on Christmas Eve (as described in Charles Dickens's *A Christmas Carol*) and had to be back at work early on the morning of Boxing Day – and didn't get paid for that precious day they had off. I even remember my own father working on Christmas Eve until at least early afternoon and returning to work on 27th December, and that was as recently as the early 1960s. There are still many souls who have to forgo their holiday for our sakes; people who work in the emergency services, utility providers, entertainers and many more, but at least they are, thankfully, in a relative minority.

I also wonder if there is anyone left who insists on tearing down all their decorations on Boxing Day, as many women in my early childhood used to do. It used to appal me and break my young heart to see all the Christmas trees standing starkly rejected on the pavements, bare and bereft of their winter finery and sadly waiting for the dustbin men to come and carry them away.

The celebration of winter can last from the end of October until the beginning of February, or even later, depending on what the weather is doing and how late the spring actually might be in coming. At the very least, it is a festivity which can begin with the Winter Solstice – or Christmas Eve or Day, depending on your beliefs and inclinations – and carry over the next two and a half weeks until the evening of Twelfth Night on 5th January.

In the past I have heard many people – especially parents – bewail the fact that the holidays are too long and they haven't a clue what they are going to do with their over-fed and over-stimulated offspring during all that time. Now in the early twenty-first century we find not only children but many adults also taking longer holidays over the Midwinter period, often not returning to work until some date in early January well after New Year.

Whether it is children or adults – or both – who are on holiday, there are two states to be avoided during the holidays. One is a feeling of deflation after 25th December and the other is boredom. There has usually been such a prolonged build-up to Midwinter, whether we have been working hard to bring it about or simply anticipating it, that it is difficult not to experience some measure of disappointment or let-down after it has passed. And anyway, there are only so many presents that you can open, which in itself can become banal and boring if it goes on for too long. It is perhaps best to strive to maintain a balance between surprise and enterprise, receiving and giving, being a sedentary spectator and actively creating and participating. There is a need to metaphorically keep the pot boiling so there is always something to look forward to, but with plenty of quiet time in between in which everyone can recuperate, enjoy and digest what has already been experienced, eaten and received. Aim to have activities and quiet relaxing down-time on alternate days.

Of course, if you invite people to your home, there are preparations to make, food to cook, and you need some time set aside to achieve this. Fancy-dress parties are huge fun, but perhaps you need some time after the frenzy of pre-Christmas to make or at least complete your costume.

It is a good idea to try to keep excitement levels from building too quickly or becoming too frantic, although with little children – and even some adults – this is almost impossible. But a good way of keeping a lid on things is to have spells of more mundane activity punctuating the thrills – in common parlance, doing a bit of work. There is nothing like it for bringing one down from the clouds to ground level again. There are also other aspects of the time of year to focus on. As in the weeks leading up to Midwinter, there are several saints' days and seasonal customs which fall within the twelve-day period, so let's take a look at them first for inspiration.

'SMUDGING NIGHTS'

Our Germanic ancestors called the nights between 25th December and 6th January the 'raw nights'. There are also the four 'smudging nights' when people carry lighted smudge sticks or incense around their property to psychically cleanse and protect them from evil.

Traditionally these were the nights before Saint Thomas's day, Christmas Day, New Year's Day and Epiphany. On these particular nights the veils between the worlds once more became (become?) thin and spirits were out, hunting and haunting, depending on your school of belief. These are actually the night before the Winter Solstice, when the Sun reaches its furthermost distance from us; the evening of Christmas Eve (or Mother's Night) before the Sun is reborn the following morning; New Year's Eve as the night heralding the start of a new year; and old Christmas Eve, from before the calendars were changed in 1752.

At this dark time of year the natural world is heavily influenced by elemental energies, when Odin or Herne ride with their Wild Hunt across our northern skies, searching out the souls of the recently departed, or Mother Holly goes distributing her generous gifts. Now, too, is the time when those long gone may return to visit their loved ones or descendants and in some countries places are laid at table and beds even vacated so that the invisible visitors may rest comfortably and enjoy the best of everything. Also at this time of year we mustn't forget the natural elemental spirits of the wild wood who are sheltering with us in our festive greenery. The living energies of other planes of existence are with us, or very close to us, as the barriers which normally divide the worlds once more grow thin. One wonders if this thinning is connected to the increased amount of service, sacrifice and general good which some groups of humanity engender especially at this time of year. Such altruistic motives produce higher, more spiritual vibrations which naturally resonate with higher life forms and planes of existence.

Once these were rituals to ward off the demonic influences of the darkest time of the year and help to conjure the rebirth of the Sun after the darkest day and longest night. In some parts of Scandinavia, 'smudging nights' are still taken seriously. On 6th January 2003, a newspaper reported that in the city of Nuuk in Greenland, between Christmas and New Year, an exorcist had cleansed all the government buildings of evil spirits. After the recent political debacles here in our own UK parliament, perhaps we might be wise to also try it?

How to Make a Smudge Stick

YOU WILL NEED:
Fresh herbs – rosemary, sage, juniper, mint, lavender or whatever
   you have to hand
String
Coloured ribbon, dried flowers, to decorate

TO MAKE:
- Cut 12" lengths of your herbs.
- Bring them together in a bunch and starting at the top, wrap a generous length of string around the herbs, winding as tightly as possible all along their length, and tie off tightly at the opposite end.

- Hang up to dry somewhere warm and well ventilated, and leave for a week or two.
- Trim both ends tidily.
- Decorate the 'handle' end with dried flowers and coloured ribbon.
- To burn, ignite the leafy end, allow to blaze for a few seconds and then blow out the flames. The stick will smoulder and smoke profusely, ready to cleanse.

SAINT STEPHEN'S DAY

The 26th December is commonly called Boxing Day in Great Britain due to our custom of historically giving Christmas boxes of money to servants, tradespeople and the poor at this time of year.

Legend has it that Saint Stephen was also once a servant of the biblical King Herod. One story recounts how he travelled as far as Sweden, where he established a Christian church, but was later murdered by brigands who tied Stephen's body to the back of one of his horses, an unbroken colt, which then galloped all the way back home, bringing Stephen's body with it. Stephen is acclaimed as being the first Christian martyr and is a patron saint of horses. People later believed that Stephen could cure sick horses and other suffering animals which were brought to his grave for blessing and healing. (This again brings in the aspects of death, rebirth, animals and natural life.)

These days Stephen's sacrifice may also reflect on the 'mini death' experienced by many parents, heads of families, groups and communities who, having worked incredibly hard in the service of others, take this day off to give themselves time to rest and recover.

My own mother – who worked so tirelessly for months, from late summer onwards, both to prepare a wonderful winter celebration for all her family and also whose day job in the shop involved making, painting and dressing toys for all the Christmas shoppers – eventually stopped throwing her huge Boxing Day parties and began having this day off, snuggling up in bed with a good book and a pot of tea while my father prepared a simple evening meal of cold turkey, cold sausages, sage and onion stuffing and... chips! Big sigh of relief all round! It is something that we, as a family, have perpetuated ever since. Boxing Day is a time to completely let go and relax.

'HUNTING THE WREN'

This rather curious activity was traditionally done on 26th December, or sometimes New Year's Day. The wren is one of the smallest birds that we have here in Britain. Therefore it might strike you as strange that, until relatively recently, it was referred to as 'king of the birds' and venerated in many areas across Europe. In ancient Greek mythology the annual killing of the wren symbolised the end of one year and the beginning of the next. This seemingly barbaric custom held sway here in Britain until the nineteenth century and lingered longest in Wales and the Isle of Man – and still takes place in parts of Ireland, although without any actual death or injury to any wildlife, the wren now used being merely a symbolic model.

The wren was a sacred bird of the Druids, the pre-Christian spirituality indigenous to Britain and parts of Europe. The Druids viewed these tiny birds as mystical messengers and Druid priests would keep (and sometimes tame) the little wren to help them with their divinations. There are similar root words in English, Welsh, Manx and Irish for 'wren', all meaning 'the bird of the Druids'. The wren was sacred to *Taranis*, the thunder/bull god who often inhabited oak trees (also sacred to the Druids). Anyone found disturbing or hurting the wren at any other time of the year except midwinter would be punished, or at the very least be in danger of being struck by lightning!

The scientific name for the wren is *Troglodytes troglodytes* and refers to it being a 'creeper into holes' or cave-dweller, and it is found all across the British Isles. Harsh winters can easily see the numbers of birds plummet. They will use the house martin's nests to snuggle in for warmth and shelter, one nest being capable of holding up to forty little wrens. In spring, the male wren is exceptionally busy, building up to six or seven different nests. He then invites his hen to choose the one in which she wishes to lay her six to eight eggs and rear her young. The other 'cock nests' are then used by the male as roosting places. It isn't surprising, then, that it has been suggested that the wren became a powerful symbol of the life force due to its prolific nest-building and breeding.

The hunting and slaying of the wren possibly represented the dying year-king and the survival of the annual custom of slaying a divine animal at midwinter. In this instance, the wren was slain on the year-king's behalf, for the good of the land.

In some areas, such as Pembrokeshire, the birds weren't always sacrificed but were paraded through the streets in specially constructed and decorated 'wren houses' and then later freed – if they hadn't already died of fright... wild creatures do not take kindly to such handling.

Once acquired, the dead bird(s) would be borne aloft on a pole decorated with holly, or in a cage of some sort which would also be decorated with evergreens and ribbons, and carried from house to house throughout the community. Sometimes the wren boys and accompanying guisers would sing songs. Small amounts of money would be given in exchange for blessings from the wren and a small feather might be bestowed on each household to bring luck; in seafaring communities it was considered a preventative against shipwreck and drowning.

If you would like to try marking this day in such a way, you could have your children make a little cardboard 'wren house' and decorate it with evergreen leaves and gaily coloured ribbons. Make a model bird, either from sheep's wool or spun yarn, with little stick legs and a paper beak, or formed from modelling clay, or even just a picture drawn on card or paper... in some places an effigy is now carved from a potato! Parade it around the outside of your house and/or around each room inside your home. Play percussion instruments, sing 'Please to See the King' and mull some fruit juice to toast the wren and the coming new year with, always remembering to give thanks for what has been and respectfully focus on what you might wish to bring into being for the next twelve months.

HOLY INNOCENTS OR DYZYMAS DAY

This is 28th December, sometimes known as Childermass, the day King Herod gave the order to have all male babies under the age of two years old slaughtered because he feared the prophecy of the magi that a new king of the Jews had been born in Judea.

In some countries there used to be a tradition that children were 'beaten' on this day, either to drive out evil spirits which might have taken up residence within them, or to spare them from retribution for the rest of the coming year. Mercifully this was usually symbolic and light hearted! Husbands and wives, servants and masters also exchanged token blows, which was, perhaps, a chance to symbolically express their emotions and feelings – clear the air for the coming new year – whilst remaining within the bounds of what was socially acceptable.

Perhaps this is therefore a good day to celebrate and honour childhood, either your own or your children's or grandchildren's. Share memories, make comparisons, list the best things about your childhood, compare them to what children consider the most important qualities of their own childhood now. Or begin to make a 'memory box'.

Give yourself time to meditate on the wonders of childhood. The adults we have become stem from the childhood that we had. Think back to the highlights and low points of your childhood. Give thanks for them, for good or bad, they helped to shape you. If you cannot give thanks in this way, maybe you don't actually like the person you are now. In the case of negative feelings can you identify the occurrence and resulting memory and the direct effect they are having on you now?

What might you do to change it? (This might be where the assistance of counselling, soul healing or alternative therapies is required.)

On this particular day, you might wish to focus on praising and honouring your children, or the children of relatives and friends. Plan to do something special together and dedicate lots of quality time to them particularly on this day. Or become childlike (not childish, there is a difference!) yourself and return to some of the activities which gave you joy in your childhood. Refreshing new evaluations and perspectives can be gained from doing this. One only has to consider the recent rise in popularity of the phenomenon of colouring intricate pictures and designs as a means to soothe stress, calm nerves and relax to see how personally beneficial this might be!

But remember to be mindful of what you might begin on this particular day. There are various old sayings and beliefs that whatever is begun on this day will either never be finished or will not prosper. Historically kings refused to enter into any business on this date. King Edward VI postponed his coronation when it was originally planned for this inauspicious date. So think well and carefully about what you enter into on Dyzymas day! Perhaps this marks this particular date as one of deep reflection and introspection (rather than action), or else of carefree entertainment bordering on the frivolous.

CHRISTMAS MUMMERS

The ancient tradition of mumming refers to groups of players travelling from house to house during the festive season to play out the drama of

Midwinter. Mummers' plays are still performed throughout Britain during the solstice-tide and enact the ritual slaying and rebirth of Life, of the Year and of the Sun. Every region has its own particular version to which contemporary references are frequently added to make it more relevant and more entertaining to the audience.

The mummers usually comprise a team of men: the Turkish Knight, Devil, Ruprecht or Wild Man is traditionally opposed, fought, slain or sacrificed by King George / Saint George, the vanquisher, the hero. There is also the Doctor who administers the magic medicine which brings the unhappy corpse back to life in an act of resurrection and rebirth, the renewal of hope and life itself. Sometimes the character of Father Christmas is also a member of this rowdy band. If one accepts Phyllis Siefker 's theory in her book *Santa Claus, Last of the Wild Men*, all these characters are aspects of the same untamed and extremely ancient archetype who, black of face or with animal head / mask, hairy and shaggy, unpredictable and utterly untamed, annually shambled out of the Boreal Forest tens of thousands of years ago at the beginning of each winter. Here is the original personification of the raw elemental energies of the very life force, and all these characters portray various aspects of his nature and purpose.

GUISING

Guising comes from the same root tradition as mumming when the Wild Man used to process around the villages and towns bringing with him terror, violence, joking and ribaldry in equal measure. The people participating in guising utilise animal masks and/or shaggy costumes to obscure their identity but their activities more closely resemble the larks and antics of trick-or-treaters.

PANTOMIME

This is a mainly British institution which people from other parts of the world often find a bit difficult to comprehend. Listing its main components it is not difficult to understand why. Broadly speaking it is a musical romantic comedy for all the family which includes singing, dancing and slapstick comedy, features cross-dressing actors and combines topical humour with a story loosely based on a well-known fairy story or folk tale. Definitely audience participatory, everyone is expected – and encouraged – to sing along with at least some of the songs and to shout out certain well-known phrases to the performers such as 'Behind you!' and 'Oh yes it is!' or 'Oh no it's not!', along with much hissing and booing of the villain and cheering of the hero and heroine.

Pantomime has a long theatrical history dating back to the classical theatre of ancient Greece and Rome, but more recently developing from the sixteenth-century *commedia dell'arte* tradition of Italy. It also takes some of its roots from other European and British stage traditions such as the seventeenth-century masques and more latterly the music hall. Until the late nineteenth century the harlequinade (historically a variation of the Wild Man) was also an important part of the panto.

It is yet another form of the mediaeval mystery play and has grown out of the mumming and guising activities of Midwinter; another seasonal drama which originally belonged to the clown, the joker and the Wild Man. It always has a strong storyline, with good battling against evil and ultimately triumphing; in this respect the concept varies little from the mediaeval morality play. The word pantomime itself is a derivation of the Greek *pan*, meaning 'all', and *mimos*, meaning 'initiator'.

These days the most popular storylines used are *Cinderella*, *Aladdin*, *Jack and the Beanstalk*, *Babes in the Wood* (which also usually involves Robin Hood), *Mother Goose* and *Snow White and the Seven Dwarfs*.

When I was a child we invariably went to the pantomime, usually a local amateur production; the ones performed by Saint Paul's Players in Adlington were the very best. Their productions were of a professional standard and quality but with the added bonus of the part of the 'pantomime dame' always being played by one of my father's banding cronies, Alan Bertwhistle. He was a truly funny man and always had the audience rocking with laughter until our ribs and faces positively ached. Cups of strong tea and packets of Spangles or caramels were a treat in the interval. Many of the children in the audience sat right at the front on long wooden benches from the school.

THE FEAST OF FOOLS

The 29th December: the day when the normal order of things is ceremoniously reversed, a safe way of socially letting off steam which is just as relevant today. This was the day when most social restrictions were temporarily removed, allowing everyone in the community to behave with joyful abandon. It would appear that this is a theme for new year – the

Celtic new year of *Calan Gaeaf* or *Samhain* at the end of October and the modern new year at the beginning of January.

As the new year approaches it might be a good time to assess what we consider 'foolish'. What prevents us from behaving foolishly? How deeply would it affect you to be thought of as foolish? Is it easier for us to 'act the fool' now than in earlier centuries, and if so why?

This is a good day to hold a party and enjoy a rip-roaring time! Invite everyone who is coming to wear silly or outlandish costumes or cross-dress, paint their faces or make masks. Forfeits is a really good game for this type of assembly. Let your hair down, go a bit wild. Crazy games, lots of laughter, frenetic dancing. Just remember not to offend or upset any of your guests or family or endanger them in any way in the process. Otherwise, GO FOR IT!

HOG ROAST WITH A DIFFERENCE

It is almost inevitable that, with the sacred nature of beliefs surrounding the boar or pig, at least one day over Midwinter should be devoted to the commemoration of that animal. The hog was sacred to the Celts, with such icons as the terrifying tailless black sow *Hwch Ddu Gwta*, who gathered souls to feed into the goddess *Cerridwen's* cauldron. In Scandinavia, *Frey*, the god of sunshine, rode across the sky on a golden-bristled boar called *Gulliburstin*, who possibly represented a solar deity, his golden spikes symbolising the rays of the Sun.

Despite being virtually extinct in Britain by the reign of Henry II in the mid-twelfth century, the boar continued to be held in some reverence and is still remembered today in carols like 'The Boar's Head'. In Celtic countries the pig most likely provided the main joint of meat for the Midwinter celebratory feast.

So why not have a day commemorating the animal who has sacrificed so much that humanity need not go hungry? In my dim and distant youth I actually tried preparing and cooking a pig's head in the same way that a boar's head was prepared and decorated in the past. It made one heck of a centrepiece on the dining table but was incredibly time-consuming and gruesomely hard work to achieve – not a process I wish to repeat in a hurry! But there are other ways of focusing on our porcine friends. If you are still carnivorous, you might wish to cook a really lovely meal using a nice joint of pork to its best advantage, inviting friends to help eat it.

In his book *The Winter Solstice*, John Matthews suggests making a sweet or savoury 'boar' by utilising a half pineapple turned flat side down and decorated with cocktail sticks holding a variety of fruits, cheeses or other savoury or sweet nibbles – remembering to find something curly for its tail (like stiffened string), half a small banana cut in half for the tusks, something appropriate for its snout (a marshmallow perhaps?), ears made from large bay leaves, folded over at the top, and eyes formed from black olives or red glacé cherries for the face.

Or you might like to all make piggy masks and wear them to your evening meal?

How to Make a Golden Boar Mask

YOU WILL NEED:

Pencil

Scissors and glue

Ribbon or elastic

Card – golden or any colour you wish

TO MAKE:

- Roll card into a cone shape, 3 or 4 inches in length, wider at one end than the other, and glue the join.
- At the narrow end, cut notches to create flaps to which you can glue the end of the snout – cut a circle of card for this, just slightly larger in diameter than the narrow end, and draw on the nostrils before glueing.
- Cut similar notches at the wider end of the cone – these are to glue the snout to the rest of the mask.
- Cut out the main mask shape, remembering holes for eyes.
- Cut out 2 ear shapes and fold top third of ears down. Glue ears in place on mask above eye holes.
- Glue snout into place between and just below the eye holes
- Punch holes in the sides of the mask and attach lengths of ribbon or elastic to allow the mask to be tied in place around the face.

PERHAPS the most sensitive remembrance would be to simply place the offering of an apple out in the garden or outside your back door for the spirit of the Christmas boar to take, along with our deep gratitude.

ALL THAT JAZZ

It is always good to get out for long walks at Midwinter, even if the weather is far from perfect! This is not just an activity for Christmas afternoon but for *any* time... it blows away the cobwebs, works off some of the rich food so recently consumed, and stimulates the production of 'feel-good' hormones so that you will sleep better and avoid post-Christmas blues. It also reconnects you to the land, to the Earth and our place upon it and within the entire solar system, which is the real relevance of our Midwinter celebrations.

While you are strolling through the woods this might also be a good time to reassess the chaos caused by winter storms and to collect more fir cones or to spot natural lengths of branch or twig which you can utilise in your natural decorations the following year. Only seeds, nuts and bare wood will do for this; any evergreen will wither and die long before the next winter. But items such as interestingly shaped logs to dry out and decorate as table centrepieces, or to give as gifts, contorted lengths of thin whippy branch to lay along windowsills interspersed with cones and fruit, sprays of alder masts (which look like tiny fir cones and can be sprayed gold or silver to great effect) are all worth collecting.

In many places there are displays of Morris dancing between Christmas Day and new year and re-enactments of mummers plays – always jolly occasions with lots of colour and bustle... and usually a glass or two of hot mulled wine or Glühwein. Keep a lookout in the local press or on notice boards for details.

And then there are the 'sales'. Once upon a time sales were relatively rare whereas now there seems to be a sale at some high street outlet or via mail order every week of the year. One would think that everybody would be completely shopped out by the end of December or early January, but it seems our acquisitive natures know no bounds! Usually my only reason for going out to the shops at this time is to see what I can acquire for the following year's Midwinter celebrations. Festive wrapping, cards and decorations are usually being sold off at this time and amazing savings can be made if you have somewhere to store your trove through the spring and summer months.

SPORTS

There are often games held around Christmas, especially football matches on Boxing Day. Even if you aren't playing yourself, get out and give your local team some encouragement and a cheer!

DISTAFF DAY

This is 4th January, the day when the women in pre-industrial society purportedly returned to their ordinary work. One of the major tasks that largely fell to the women was the spinning of thread, whether that be wool, flax or hemp, and this was often performed with the help of a distaff, a simple device of a long spindle which ran through the centre of a small wheel which simultaneously spun round and drew out the thread. Unlike a spinning wheel they could be carried and used anywhere and everywhere, as women watched over livestock or children or chatted to neighbours, waited for meals to cook or sat in the evening firelight. It is from this word that we get the phrase 'distaff side of the family' when referring to the mother's relations or ancestors.

The women might be returning to their work, but it was still a time of fun and frolics and the work completed that day must have been a mere token. The men of the locality went to endless lengths to disrupt the women at their work, attempting to steal or even ignite whatever had been set aside to be spun. Meanwhile, the women would retaliate with buckets of water and other such fundamental objects of defence which led to increased chaos and general hilarity.

What do you look upon as your 'work' now, inside or outside the home? In what way can you imagine celebrating it and marking the recommencement of it? Remember, everything deserves recognition and gratitude and lends itself to the celebration of many, if not ALL days.

EVE OF EPIPHANY

Falling on 5th January, ostensibly this is a celebration with traditional Christian connotations in reference to the three wise men or kings who visited Mary and Joseph in the stable, bringing royal gifts for the baby Jesus. But at this time of so much giving and receiving, regardless of what your religious practices or spiritual beliefs might be, it is a good time to look in upon yourself and reassess the whole question of 'giving'.

There is a broad difference between what you need and what you want. Make a list of your needs and wants. There are certainly things which we might *need* but do not in any way *want* just as there are many things that we might *want* but do not in any way *need*. Many of the gifts given and received at Midwinter fall into this category, and that is fine up to a point – it's lovely to provide someone with a little unnecessary luxury or something 'extra'. But do we take it too far? Then there are people who all too frequently give something – anything – regardless of how appropriate or desirable it may be. At least the recipient hasn't been left out and the giver has appeased their conscience, no matter how the recipient feels about what they receive. Is this good enough? I certainly don't think so.

Don't be surprised if a great many of your own wants and needs are things that no amount of money can buy; for instance more time, peace of mind, friendship, to be loved for who you are, recognition, appreciation, opportunities. To consider and identify our real inner needs is often a terrifying prospect which we tend to obscure by focusing instead on all the little inconsequential needs and wants in our lives. Little wonder that fulfilling these minor requirements doesn't just leave us unsatisfied but actually riles and enrages us in an ostensibly irrational manner.

As John Matthews puts it so eloquently in *The Winter Solstice*, 'Our real wants eat holes in us... they create a Christmas list that no store could supply... (the) space to give and receive love reciprocally. The grace to seek and find our spiritual joy. Freedom from the tyranny and burden of others' expectations, of what others think. Acceptance of ourselves as we truly are.' The list is potentially endless once you begin to really consider.

So make a list of the real wants and needs that you hold deep within you. How many of your wants are actually deep needs? Reconsider the whole nature of gift giving and the appropriateness of the things which you yourself have given and received this year. Then, if at all possible, make a gift to yourself of one of the things on your list of needs. Give yourself more time or space, pursue that course of learning or experience, book that place on that workshop, book that time away from work, the home, perhaps take yourself off on your own for once.

And when you next give a gift to someone, choose something that they might *really* crave, like companionship, a listening ear, company on a journey to their old childhood home or to a place they have always longed to go. So often it isn't the things that can be popped in a box and wrapped up in pretty paper that are needed or wanted. Give with real thought, care and concern. And always try to include something of yourself, whether it be something that you have made, or drawn, or painted, or even as simple as a special message you have handwritten. The personal touch and the thoughtfulness are what are really important, more than the item which is acting as a vehicle enabling you to show your care. Think about it!

TWELFTH NIGHT

The 4th, 5th or 6th January, depending on whether you begin counting the Twelve Days from Christmas Eve, Christmas Day or Boxing Day... or whether you don't count them at all and simply have a period of time in which to celebrate and enjoy! But this is another opportunity to throw a party and bring the Midwinter celebrations to a triumphant close. Traditionally there was yet more feasting, drinking and dancing on this day, with the ceremonial removal of the decorations. You might wish to take your evergreenery outside and ritually burn it.

Personally, I favour doing it all more gradually as the season evolves into early spring and the pale thin light of January grows in strength, leaving the greenery till the last (even if it is temporarily stored in the garden shed or garage). Remember that if the spirits of the wild wood are sheltering within it in your home, you will be cruelly evicting them back out into the worst of the weather if you take their temporary accommodation and put it outside again – or worse, burn it!

While we can never actually destroy any energy, only transmute it into another form, it might be more in the spirit of the season to burn your evergreenery at the end of January as part of the next celebration and the coming of spring (see 'January', page 322).

PARTY TIME!

The Twelfth Night parties that my mother hosted had to be seen to be believed. Dozens of guests crammed into the cottage. The refectory table in the kitchen was extended by the improvisation of old wooden doors supported on trestles. Thus the 'table' extended from one end of the room, with the person at the bottom end of the table practically sitting roasting in the hearth, to the other end of the room, with the top diner squashed up against the dresser. The whole was covered in a gold satin cloth, with felt table mats in the shape of little party clowns to match, all fashioned by my mother.

John Pope would sit at the top of the table, a portly, jolly fellow, gleefully sharpening the knife and wielding the fork, happily carving the hams, rounds of pork and sides of beef which my mother seemingly endlessly provided. Home-made cold pork pies and sausage rolls, crusty breads, tasty hot soups, sugary iced cakes and cavernous bowls of cream-filled trifle marched the length of the table, with crackers, mottoes and gaily coloured paper party hats. Twenty could sit down to eat at one time; usually there were two sittings, with all the children ranged up the stairs like chattering sparrows and each equipped with a heaped plate to satisfy even the most voracious appetite.

After the feasting, several of my mother's friends would move in to clear away the dirty dishes. Games and quizzes were played. More tea, coffee and hot punch were passed around. A light supper was later served. Animated discussion stretched far into the night. Long before the last revellers left, my eyelids had drooped, all sound began to resemble noises issuing from the bottom of a barrel, and I was mercifully, if reluctantly, carried off to bed. (What Farmer Noblett thought of all those vehicles roaring up the lane past his farm in the extremely early hours of the morning I can't imagine!)

Turkish Delight

INGREDIENTS:

2 oz (56 g) or 4 envelopes of Cox's gelatine

2 pints (1,100 ml) cold water

½ pint (280 ml) boiling water

1½ lb (680 g) sugar

Food colouring / essence

¼ teaspoon salt

½ pint (280 ml) fresh orange juice or rose water, OR almost
½ pint water + whatever essence and colour you like – I use
lemon, peppermint and rose water… separately of course, not
mixed all together! A little green food colouring can be added
to the peppermint and a touch of pink to the rosewater. Nuts
may also be added.

METHOD:

- Soften gelatine in 2 pints cold water.
- Mix sugar and salt in ½ pint of water, dissolve, bring to boil and
  continue boiling for five minutes. (Do not allow to boil over or
  burn and stir occasionally.)
- Add gelatine and simmer for 20 minutes.
- Remove from heat and add orange juice, rose water, or essences
  and colours.
- Rinse a tin – 9" × 5" × 3", or near enough – with cold water,
  pour in mixture and leave to set, overnight if you can.
- Cut into cubes with a warm knife and roll in icing sugar.

This recipe dates from 1969. The note attached to it reads:

Makes about 2 lb, costs about 2/6 [12½p].
To buy costs about 4/– [20p] a half pound.

COMMENT FROM JOAN: MURMURINGS, 1969

This is like the true Smyrna or 'Greek delight'; reminds me of Daddy
in Smyrna and Spyros in Athens, feeding us with every sweetmeat he could.
How we loved his Turkish delight and crystallised fruits, and Gill fascinated
by such gaiety and colour. As I write this I wonder if dear Spyros is
now imprisoned by the fascist junta government. I sigh.

There is a sweetmeat that the Greeks praise to high heaven, a sort of
tasteless Turkish delight containing chopped nuts that someone brought
me from Farsala, specially. I call it 'Farsala Goo'. In content it is like Muscat
in Ceylon, but has no flavour – now Muscat is delightful with rose water
(how I love rose water!). Maybe I was just unlucky with the
'Farsala Goo' that I tried?

TWELVE PRESENTS

It is a nice idea to have twelve little gifts to give a child – one gift for every day of Christmas. They only need to be small things, and preferably the kind which help to direct someone's thoughts and attention. So for a child you might give a little colouring book or some modelling clay, a little story book or a packet of coloured pipe cleaners with which to make models, or stickers to put in a book, or even something useful for the return to school – pencils, colouring pens, etc. It just helps to perpetuate the fun, the anticipation, the magic. We used to tie our twelve presents onto the Christmas tree and then my son could watch, anticipate and decide for himself which one he was going to choose next.

This idea can also be used for an adult loved one, even if it is only twelve tiny pledges... an early morning cup of tea, or a single chocolate biscuit. It is the thought and love that it shows which is important... and a few moments spent opening and chuckling over something inconsequential which can bring two people much closer and is a gift in itself.

OLD CHRISTMAS DAY

As well as Epiphany, 6th January is also old Christmas Day, the day it would have fallen on before the calendar was altered and the day on which the Greek Orthodox church still celebrates Christmas Day. Interestingly we have noted in the past that it frequently snows on 6th January, even if it is only a slight flurry, which is far more in keeping with everyone's image of a white Christmas!

New Year – The Time of Janus

Begin afresh, wipe clean the slate,
Let Old Year's sorrows slip away...
'MIDNIGHT', G. MONKS

ONCE UPON A time, the beginning of a new year was celebrated with wild and gay abandon. In ancient Rome, for instance, the *calends* was a riotous outpouring of fun and festival. In Celtic lands, a new year (whether in January or November) has always been celebrated with the typical return to social role reversal and chaos. Today, many people dress in their finest to attend sparkling dinners and dances and make a grand occasion of it. Some – like myself – love this particular time of year, while others cannot bear it and retire to bed extra early to avoid it.

Love it or loathe it, new year is a time for looking back and assessing some of the positive aspects of the year just ending and perhaps giving thanks, not simply for our good fortune but for having come through the more negative events as well. For some the occasion starkly brings to mind the passage of time and all their previous losses – of loved ones, of opportunities, of youth and time itself – and seems almost too much to bear. For others it is a chance to wipe the metaphorical slate clean and begin again. It is good to feel gratitude for what we have and are, just as it is good to look forward with excited anticipation, to plot and plan our next endeavours and adventures upon this newly begun span of time which suddenly stretches before us like a pristine sheet of paper, unsullied and full of potential.

However, the sheer practicalities of changing the date and moving on plunges deep into our very beings and touches our innermost essence. It stirs and enlivens us, but simultaneously rocks and terrifies us. For between nightfall on 31st December and daybreak on 1st January we pass over one of those strange liminal thresholds of time and space which are, by dint of their very nature, shrouded in uncertainty and mystery. This is one of those particular occasions when we are neither in the old year nor the new... literally neither here nor there... temporarily suspended between two dates, two years, two states of being.

If any ancient deity is specifically associated with this time of year it is the Roman god Janus. He rules gates, doorways, portals and passages and represents transition, maturation and beginnings and endings. I was half-jokingly taught as a child that the old year just coming to an end looked like a very old man but in the morning, when the year had been born anew, it would look like a baby, and Janus embodies this dual aspect of life. He is represented as having two faces, giving him the ability to look both ways at once, back into the past and forward into the future.

He is also a contender as another possible solar deity, which doubly supports his association with this time of the year. Unsurprisingly, the first month of our year still bears his name – January.

NEW BEGINNINGS AND RESOLUTIONS

With this in mind it is not then surprising that many new year customs revolve around finishing things off and leaving everything ready to begin afresh. Traditionally the house had to be cleaned from top to bottom to provide a worthy welcome to the spirit, the energies of the coming new year. But it all had to be completed well before darkness fell on New Year's Eve, and nothing must leave the house during the course of New Year's Day for fear that it would take all the luck of the household with it. Similarly, no washing was to be done on New Year's Day in case you washed someone out of the family. All debts had to be settled beforehand or else you were sure to remain in debt for the duration of that year.

This is probably the most popular time to actively decide to make a positive change in your life – although there are many other appropriate opportunities throughout the year to practise this empowering form of decision making. Many people still go through the motions of making new year resolutions... in the early twenty-first century these seem to involve diets and exercise more often than not, and just as frequently fall by the proverbial wayside after only a very few days. At least it serves to make people stop and think!

But if you are serious about your resolutions, I would suggest that you decide to make just *one*. It is easy to think of lots of things that you would like to change about yourself or in your life. But trying to do too much all at once is unrealistic and destined for failure almost before you have begun. Think about what you really want to change more than all the rest put together... what is most pressing? What is it that your consciousness is repeatedly drawn back to? Choose *that* one... and then stick to it!

You can help yourself to do this by reminding yourself constantly – devise an affirmation and keep chanting it to yourself, or write it down on pieces of card or paper and stick them up in various places where they are going to continually keep catching your eye throughout the day, at work or at home... or even in the car. At the end of every week, reassess how you feel about your resolution and whether you are succeeding in bringing it into being. Remove all your paper affirmations and put them up in similar but different places, or write different wording; we are very quick to adapt to something and will rapidly cease to really 'see' them, so keep them fresh, and good luck!

JUNIPER AND WATER

In Scotland on Hogmanay, people traditionally collected boughs of juniper and brought them into the house alongside buckets of fresh spring water. The juniper was laid near the fire to dry out. In the morning, the head of the household took the first drink from the water and then went around sprinkling everyone else with drops of water from his bucket. Then all the doors and windows in the house were shut tight and the juniper was set alight and paraded through the entire house until everything was thoroughly fumigated. This most certainly dates back to an ancient ritual which involved the burning of sacred juniper upon the open hearths of the house to ensure that the gifts of new year were properly received and celebrated.

You might like to try this for yourself as an alternative to the fourth 'smudging night'. Cleanse and bless some water by leaving it outside overnight at full moon and then store it in a clean dry bottle with an air-tight top. You can use this to sprinkle around your home. You can also ignite some dried juniper needles in an incense burner, or purchase some juniper incense, which is quite common, and carry that around your home too – or simply leave it to smoke in your main living space.

LITTLE YULE

It is interesting to learn that in Gaelic, there are names for 'big Yule' and 'little Yule'; *An Nollaig Mhor* means big Yule, or Christmas, and *An Nollaig Bheag* means little Yule, or New Year. When I was a child, my mother did not enjoy New Year's Eve so it was always made very little of but New Year's Day was quite another matter! Thinking back to my young child-hood, New Year was always a more relaxed form of Christmas. Once more my father would be out playing with the dance band and would return home even later than usual as the parties and dances would last that bit longer to facilitate seeing in the new year at midnight. Happily I was far more relaxed at New Year, even though we had a re-run of Christmas with a second bulging stocking on New Year's morning and a few extra little gifts at tea on New Year's afternoon from 'Father New Year' –

the same entity who at midnight the previous evening had miraculously become a newborn baby again.

At one end of the refectory table stood the New Year cake, brimming with succulent moist fruit like its Christmas predecessor, and always decorated as a Victorian coaching scene comprising a little forest of tiny imitation fir trees and an inn with welcomingly red windows and a snowy roof set amidst a sugar-icing snow-filled landscape. A minuscule stage-coach and horses galloped down a deeply rutted lane (courtesy of a kitchen fork dipped in gravy browning). Painted leaden porters, shock-ingly out of proportion to the rest, waited to load barrels and trunks onto the approaching vehicle. At the other end of the table stood a papier mâché model of Charles Dickens's old curiosity shop whose red tiled roof could be removed to disgorge little gifts to any family and friends who were present.

Home-made crackers were dotted about amongst the food: wedges of home-made pork pie, platters of cold meats, dishes of pâté and salads with golden pats of butter and soft shiny brown bread rolls and some-where among them a huge glass dish of trifle, glowing ruby red and topped with whipped cream... truly the ermine-clothed queen of the feast!

Gifts at New Year were and remain allied to the nature of the season and the celebration – in other words, new beginnings and the inspira-tion for that fresh start. So if you do wish to give a gift(s) at this time, items such as diaries, notebooks, new clothes and seeds or plants and the like hold particular emphasis and relevance.

As I grew into my early teens my mother temporarily overcame her horror of New Year's Eve and for a while she joined me in celebration.

Sometimes she would arrange tickets for wherever my father was playing with the band. The first time this happened I was just fourteen years of age and wore my first strapless long dress (with real whalebone stiffeners!) but spent the evening terrified that the bodice was going to fall down. However, in all other respects it was a brilliant occasion at one of the big hotels in the Lake District, with an excellent dinner, dancing and finally a fellow in full Highland dress playing the bagpipes just before midnight.

Other times, we would elect to stay quietly at home, but then at about 10 p.m. my reluctant parent would disappear into the kitchen and begin assembling a special little celebratory supper, just for the two of us. I well remember that my first taste of caviar was on one of these occasions; the wine decanter was also set upon a little table and we watched the Hogmanay programme from Scotland on TV and felt well satisfied with our evening's endeavours. Once I even remember the record player coming out and pushing back the settee and chairs while my mother taught me how to jitterbug!

COMMENT FROM JOAN: PARTY PLANS, NEW YEAR, 1960

I've been thinking that I'll wear my new cocktail dress (that I bought last week) for the first time at the party. It is a fascinating material, black shot through with bronze, but the black is not noticed, it just gives the whole the sheen of copper in the firelight; classic V-neck style but the material is all.

WIGGLE ROOM

For me, I think that spontaneity is the key to success. Have your food and drink bought and prepared, buy your tickets well in advance and send out your invitations in good time, but simultaneously always try to leave yourself a little wiggle room so that you can seize the moment, follow your sudden inclinations, deviate from what was planned and enjoy that little bit extra without missing out on anything.

One of the instances when this worked out really well was during the very cold winter of 2010–2011. We had settled for a quiet New Year's Eve at home, just the three of us, my husband, my son and myself. I had cooked a nice dinner and we had eaten quite early, lingering around the dining table afterwards, drinking coffee and nibbling on nuts and fruit. As we were clearing away afterwards, I stepped outside into the garden for a breath of fresh air and was instantly entranced! A full moon was gliding high in a cloudless sky and all the mountains around us were full of snow and frost and sparkling white. I flew back indoors and rushed through the chores, calling to the others that I was going to go out for a walk and asking if they would like to accompany me.

We wrapped up warmly as it was a bitterly cold night and set off through the village. It was like a ghost town! Not a soul around... no vehicles on the roads... no lights in any of the windows either, so I guessed that everyone had closed their curtains against the freezing weather. We walked around the lake, our feet crunching on frozen snow, sometimes bursting into song or laughing and joking and larking about, at other times simply standing in silent reverence of the moment and the view before us. It was as bright as day. The mountains were magnificent.

When we reached home again, we couldn't tear ourselves away from the glorious prospect of the Nantlle Ridge in all its winter splendour, so we got out our garden chairs and unearthed the little barbecue stove and some logs. While the fire got in and began to blaze, I went inside and made a jug of cocoa and got out the mince pies. The fire was roaring when I returned with a heavily laden tray. And then we just sat and gazed out across the valley towards our beloved peaks and ridges, now dressed in snowy sequins and draped in frosty lurex.

Midnight came and our mobile phones began to ring as friends and family called from around the world to wish us a happy New Year. They couldn't believe that we were sitting out in the garden in the middle of the night in all that snow! That evening as we sat on our frosty hillside we spoke to people in Germany, Sweden and America, as well as from all around the British Isles – all thanks to the magic and blessings that modern technology can bring us!

FIRST-FOOTING

This is another activity which reflects the focus of New Year being on thresholds and when to cross or not to cross them and what to take with you when you do. It is a tradition which can be variously found in different places but is generally identified as being Scottish in origin. It refers to the belief that whoever was first to put their foot over your threshold after midnight at New Year could bring fortune and good luck to the whole household. Unfortunately, this was reversed if the first person to enter was either a woman or fair-haired. (A memory of the ancient, fair-haired folk who originally inhabited these islands.) Ideally, the 'first-footer' should be dark-haired and a man – since the rise of patriarchal society women have frequently been outlawed from anything of relevance. To avoid the danger of incurring bad luck for the following twelve months someone in the family would leave nothing to chance by arranging beforehand for a suitable (i.e. masculine and dark) friend or neighbour to come to the house to perform the task. This person would arrive just after midnight carrying a gift, traditionally a lump of coal or a bottle of whisky as an omen of prosperity to the household.

We hedge our bets by placing salt (representing the flavour and zest for life), coal (fuel or energy), bread (food) and money (abundance) on a platter. My son – who is the darkest one among us – then brings it to the front door, banging loudly upon it and on being allowed admittance is then presented with a glass of wine with which he proposes a toast. A tray of filled glasses is passed around to the rest of the company present and we all drink to the New Year, before hugging and shaking hands and rushing back outside to listen to the church bells ringing and other people throughout the village and around the valley calling greetings and making a rumpus with horns and fireworks.

MARI LWYD

Here in Wales on New Year's Eve we have the tradition of the Mari Lwyd – Y Fari Lwyd translates as the Grey Mare or the Grey Mary or even the Venerable Mary. The skull of a horse was fixed to the top of a pole so that the jaws could be made to snap open and shut by the bearer who, along with the contraption supporting the head, was totally enveloped in a voluminous white cloth. In Celtic Britain the horse was seen as a symbol of power and fertility but also as the personification of the horse goddess, Rhiannon, Queen of the Underworld (who shares some similarities with the ancient Roman goddess, Pomona).

Customs involving animal skulls are widely known around the world. The Celts placed huge emphasis on the importance of the head, whether it be animal or human – they considered it to be the seat of the soul. Animals such as the horse were considered to have mystical abilities and to be able to cross – or fly, as in the case of the mythical winged horse, Pegasus – between the worlds. Such creatures were usually white or grey in colour, as in the case of the Welsh god, Arawn, King of the Underworld, who rode a large grey horse accompanied by his pack of dogs, the Hounds of Annwn, who were also white with the exception of their glowing red ears.

Again, this custom focused people's minds on the 'dying' of the old year and the period of transition – the threshold which had to be crossed to attain a fresh new start in a new year. Traditionally the Mari Lwyd and her entourage of followers would travel from house to house and pub to pub on New Year's Eve and attempt to gain access to each establishment by performing a series of verses or pwnco. The inhabitants were supposed to reply with their own verses and a battle to outwit the Mari Lwyd and her gang would ensue in an effort to prevent them from entering.

Eventually the Mari and her followers would be allowed in as they actually conferred good luck on the household for the coming year and scared away anything unsavoury from the previous year just about to end. Once inside, songs were sung and the group were given refreshments.

Unfortunately the Mari could also become quite mischievous, taking a fancy to any likely young woman present and chasing them around the property and generally causing mayhem!

How widespread this custom used to be is difficult to say. It was certainly upheld in Glamorgan and Gwent in South Wales, but like many other ancient practices in recent years it has seen a growing interest and resurgence of groups performing all across Wales. No one can recall in detail the original characters of the group who processed around the district with the Mari Lwyd. Reports from the early 1900s include a Leader in charge of the Mari, a Sergeant, a Merryman and a Punch and Judy, but there are also memories of a far older tradition when figures wearing rags and with blackened faces accompanied the horse. Does this sound at all familiar? Think back to the origins of Father Christmas and the Wild Man who annually came out of the woods every Midwinter!

CONCERT FROM VIENNA

It has long been a family tradition for us to rise comparatively late on New Year's morning and even then only to flop back down into comfy chairs while someone puts the kettle on and we switch on the television to watch the New Year's Day concert from Vienna, which sometimes used to have my father dancing around the living room with his little grandson! It is always a glorious occasion of colour, with hothouse flowers in full bloom, graceful dancers and exquisite music performed by some of the very best musicians in the world. Works by many other classical composers are chosen as part of the programme, but it is the members of the Strauss family who best capture that elusive sense of occasion, charm and gaiety from a bygone age, especially when it comes to the final piece, 'The Blue Danube'. As the first barely audible notes filter out into the auditorium the atmosphere is tangible, even through the television set!

There is another belief that whatever you do on New Year's Day, you will do for the rest of the year. When I was much younger I decided that this was patently untrue – there was no way that I would be allowed to stay in bed till late morning on school days... or any other days if it came to that! Nor would we normally watch television at ten o'clock in the morning, or unpack a new year stocking, or eat a full celebratory dinner in the evening. Since I have grown older (and hopefully a little wiser) I have come to understand that it means if you are happy or sad and lonely or busy or fulfilled on the first day of the new year, then you are only reflecting what kind of year you might generally look forward to for the other 364 days. Bearing this in mind, it is perhaps wise to try and be as happy or at least positive on the first day of the year as possible – there is certainly no harm in trying, and perhaps the very fact that you are aware and making a positive effort means that you are bound to have at least a reasonable time of it, just because you are focusing your intention on making it so!

THE CALENNIG

The *Calennig* is another Welsh custom, the roots of which, by its very nature, reach back into the dim and distant origins of modern humanity.

Certainly it is recorded as far back as the Middle Ages. Still practised in some parts of Wales, like so many other traditions it too is staging something of a comeback in popularity. The word itself is thought to originate from the Latin *calends*, or 'first day of the month'. In modern times, the word *Calennig* is sometimes used to describe the New Year's celebration where folk gather for fireworks or larger towns hold organised festivities.

The *Calennig* itself is traditionally an apple stuck with three wooden legs in the form of a tripod with a fourth wooden 'handle' stuck in the back of the apple by which it could be easily carried. A small candle or a sprig of evergreen was pushed into the top and the sides of the fruit were decorated with nuts and ears of dried grain from the previous harvest. In some areas, cloves and dried fruit were used. The Christian definition is that the apple signified the World, the three legs represented the Holy Trinity and the candle stood for the Light of the World (Jesus or God).

However, the more timeless interpretation, which still has deep relevance today, is that, yes, the apple represents the World – but the apple is also a very magical fruit appearing in many myths and beliefs around the world and in this case refers to the 'other world' and rebirth. The number three also appears in many places and in numerous beliefs, myths and folk tales, and it too has deeply significant and magical properties which pre-date the Christian belief. The evergreens, as you will remember, are also the symbol of nature's undying life and the promise of the return of spring, while the nuts and grain represent seeds, fertility, new life and abundance.

Where the quick-witted and boisterous tradition of the *Mari Lwyd* on New Year's Eve was for adults, this more gentle custom was one for the children. Youngsters would be out early on the first morning of the new year, and sometimes carried on until after dusk. They would travel from house to house singing traditional rhymes to 'let in' the coming year and to wish the occupants health, wealth and happiness.

How to Make a Calennig

YOU WILL NEED:

An apple

A red candle

3 cocktail sticks or wooden skewers

Ears of wheat or corn, nuts (or substitute with grass seed heads or synthetic ears)

Gold or silver (spray) paint – optional

TO MAKE:

- Make a hole in the top of the apple, slightly smaller than the candle, and gently push the candle down into it until the candle stands firmly.
- Push the 3 cocktail sticks or skewers into the apple to form a tripod of legs (my mother and I always used cocktail sticks for ease, but they can be a bit insubstantial and inadequate if the apple or candle is large!).
- Push ears of wheat or corn (or substitutes) into the flesh at the top of the apple.
- Glue selection of plain or gilded nuts between the ears of corn and around the base of the candle.

I AM SOMEWHAT bemused to hear children referring to these 'Christmas decorations' as 'Christingles'. In Wales, they have always been called a Calennig and are made a New Year for the children to carry from house to house, singing New Year carols as they go.

The apple represents the world – but it must be an apple, not an orange, as apples have vital pre-Christian significance. The candle represents the 'Light of the World'. The three legs represent the Maiden, Mother and Crone (now translated by the Christian church as the Trinity). The grains and nuts represent food and abundance.

WASSAILING

The word wassail originates from the Anglo-Saxon *waes hael*, meaning 'good health'. It is traditionally done on New Year's Day or Twelfth Night. Some people like to wassail on 17th January, which would have been Twelfth Night before the calendar changes of 1752. The purpose of wassailing is to scare away evil spirits and awaken the fruit trees, especially the apple trees, and to ensure a good harvest of fruit the following autumn.

Wassailing has traditionally been carried out in the cider-producing counties of Devon, Dorset, Herefordshire, Somerset and Gloucestershire and involves going to the orchards at dusk or after dark. Sometimes the assembled company will have just one spokesperson to make the appropriate speeches and lead the celebrations. Some communities have a king and queen to lead the ceremony. In others a child below the age of puberty is lifted into the lower boughs of the tree where it remains seated – if a little boy, he is usually referred to as 'Tom Tit' or 'Robin' in reverence of the birds which thrive on the fruit trees and keep them free of pests; if a little girl, she might represent the spirit of the tree itself, made incarnate in human form.

In Camborne, Cornwall, wassailers were accompanied by a young girl dressed in evergreens who was known as Lucy Green. She was the embodiment of natural life – of life itself – seasonally taking shelter in the never-dying evergreenery of Winter. It is interesting that they should call her Lucy… reminiscent of Saint Lucy and her festival on 13th December, the old Winter Solstice!

A king or queen tree is chosen to represent all the rest – usually the biggest and/or oldest. Speeches and toasts are made thanking the tree for its great bounty and exhorting it to renewed and redoubled efforts in the coming growing season. The tree trunk is beaten to 'enliven' it; toasted bread is dipped into the wassail beverage and hung on the branches or wedged into clefts of branches. Some of the liquor from the wassail bowl is sprinkled over the tree and on the ground around the roots. Then everyone drinks from the mighty wassail bowl, after which a great hullabaloo ensues with shouting and singing and the banging of drums, blowing of horns and crashing of pot and pan lids, finally rounded off by guns being fired into the topmost branches.

People also process around the boundaries of the land, carrying flaming torches, sprinkling a libation from the wassail bowl as they go, and making the maximum amount of rumpus as they do so – all to scare undesirable spirits away from the orchards and fields and to reawaken the land.

Historically in some areas, like eighteenth-century Devon, only the men would go out to the orchards, but when they returned to the house it would be to find that the women had locked them out and a riddle or something else had to be correctly guessed before they were allowed to re-enter. Here we again see the door or threshold as representing the boundary between this world and the Otherworld; the women are playing the role of Guardian, whose permission must be sought and won before any may enter. As such there are also many resonances with the parading of the Mari Lwyd in Wales and much longer ago the rowdy gangs of youths who accompanied the Wild Man from the forest on his village sojourns.

Wassailing can also be done to bless and stimulate the health of a community, hence many traditions of troupes of people – frequently men but, as in the case of Staffordshire and Warwickshire in the early nineteenth century, sometimes exclusively women. In these cases the wassail bowl was carried around the village or town from house to house and the properties and occupants were blessed with toasts and songs in exchange for treats, usually in the form of food and drink or a few coins. But woe betide any who would not comply and make some form of payment... in those cases properties might be vandalised or families cursed!

A form of wassailing was reportedly carried out at the court of Henry VII at the turn of the sixteenth century where it was recorded in the Collection of Ordinances of the Royal Household. In his book The Golden Bough, James Frazer records that similar customs were widespread in various parts of Europe and were generally aimed at banishing witches, perhaps ensuring that the sacred feminine deity of old returned to her own realms for another year. T. F. Thiselton-Dyer mentions a parallel custom which was prevalent in nineteenth-century Bohemia, although this was performed at Easter. And in Normandy, on the eve of Epiphany (or what would have been old Christmas Eve) lighted torches or brands were thrown at the trunks of fruit trees and small bonfires of straw lit beneath their branches.

Personally I have always associated wassailing with old Twelfth Night, which is when we have always gone out onto our land to bless and enliven it. The suggestion that the cacophony created in wassailing is one way of officially putting an end to the Midwinter festivities, or frightening the Otherworld spirits back into their own realms is perhaps a valid one, although I have always found that they very well know when it is time to depart and need no encouragement or reminders! What sits much more comfortably with me is it being a way of reawakening the Earth's energies and facilitating the first early stirrings of spring.

If you would like to try doing some wassailing for yourself it is great fun, but must be entered into whole-heartedly and with great gusto. The first year after we acquired our land down on the Llŷn Peninsula we naturally wanted to appropriately bless and enliven it, so gathered a group of friends about us and drove down to *Cae Non* with instruments to make noise, cider to spice and heat and a real willingness to fully enter into the spirit of the celebration.

We decided to walk the boundary just as dusk was falling – full darkness would have been far too dangerous as the terrain was so wild, boggy and uneven. We carried a large bowl of hot steaming cider punch, besides which all brandished drums, whistles, bells and saucepan lids and were led by my redoubtable husband lustily blowing on his great horn – even though it produces a sound reminiscent of a cow in great pain. Every so often we would stop at a particularly special or relevant spot and someone would offer a blessing or propose a toast, and the land would be sprinkled before the bowl was passed around for everyone to drink from. Then off we would go again, banging, shouting, blowing and braying like maniacs.

It just so happened that as we left the top of the field to process down to the bottom boundary which runs alongside the public road a little way, a couple of cars pulled up with a tractor and trailer and several men appeared to unload bales of hay for the sheep in the next pasture. But when they spotted us they froze in astonishment. The Welsh are not familiar with the tradition of wassailing. Not to be deterred, we kept going, no doubt looking as if we had all just escaped from bedlam to the party of Welsh farmers, who had probably just come from the chapel. In silence they watched our frenzied procession pass by. I did try to give them a little wave and a bit of a wan smile but I really didn't know whether to faint with embarrassment into the undergrowth or double up with laughter. Perhaps it is a good idea to involve your neighbours in anything you intend to do, or at least let them know about it so that everyone is spared the blushes and confusion!

The tradition of wassailing the trees and the land rapidly dwindled after the turn of the twentieth century until the millennium, when interest in it was rekindled by folk enthusiasts who began to revive the practice, which has now been taken up by community orchards and cider farms so that there are literally hundreds of wassails again around the country.

Annual wassails are held in Carhampton and Dunster in Somerset and in Whimple and Sandford in Devon on the 17th January, while in

Clevedon, North Somerset, there is a very popularly attended celebration in the Clevedon Community Orchard, combining the traditional elements of the wassail with the music and entertainment of Bristol Morris Men and their cantankerous Horse!

Look online for details of wassailing in your area.

> Good luck to the hoof and the horn
> Good luck to the flock and fleece
> Good luck to the growers of corn
> With blessings of plenty and peace
>
> MIRANDA GREEN, SOMERSET RHYME, CELTIC GODDESSES

Queen of Puddings

A lovely hot, comforting dessert to indulge in after being out in the cold — one which can turn a snack meal into a sustaining feast.

Gillian

INGREDIENTS:

½ pint (280 ml) of milk
½ pint (280 ml) of breadcrumbs
Grated rind of one lemon
1 oz (28 g) butter
1 oz (28 g) sugar
2 egg yolks
2 tablespoons raspberry or other jam

Mixture for meringue:

2 egg whites

2 oz (56 g) sugar

METHOD:

- Warm the milk and add the butter and sugar to melt it.
- Add breadcrumbs and grated lemon rind and leave for half an hour to swell.
- Beat in the egg yolks and pour into a greased ovenproof dish.
- Bake at 180°C, 350°F or Gas Mark 4 for about half an hour until set.
- Spread a thick layer of jam on the top, heating the jam if necessary so that it will spread easily.
- Whisk the egg whites very stiffly, then fold in 1½ tablespoons of sugar. Pile on top of the pudding and dredge with remaining sugar.
- Return to a cooler oven (160°C, 300°F or Gas Mark 2) for 20–30 minutes until the meringue is lightly coloured and crisp to the touch.

Serve hot on a cold evening!

SOMETHING NEW...

New year is an integral part of our Midwinter festivities, but these days it seems to amount to little more than having a party on New Year's Eve where too much is drunk, and New Year's Day, which is largely occupied in recovering from a surfeit of both food and alcohol. Oh, and with some fireworks, a quick verse of 'Auld Lang Syne' and a few handshakes thrown in for good measure. But it can be and is so very much more than that!

Again, it is a time of family and community; of coming together in co-operation and neighbourliness; of celebration; of your thought and effort as you truly give to and serve those around you; a cleansing of the old and outworn in every respect and a chance to begin again, to turn over a new leaf, a clean page, and start afresh. Rather than a belly ache or a hangover, how much better to set the tone of your new year with these aims to focus on!

Hopefully the information given here will have provided you with some ideas of how you might celebrate more inclusively with the people around you, and how you might develop very personally authentic activities of your own. Whether you decide to hold a midnight garden party (always weather depending!), construct *Calennigs* with your children, tramp around to your friends and neighbours bringing song, jollity and good wishes, or gather to wassail your garden, local orchard, farm or even town centre, make your next new year a real highlight of anticipation and celebration... have a blast!

January

Over the land freckled with snow half-thawed
The speculating rooks at their nest cawed
And saw from elm-tops, delicate as flowers of grass,
What we below could not see, Winter pass.

'THAW', EDWARD THOMAS

HOWEVER YOU CELEBRATE Midwinter/Christmas, it is true to say that after New Year's Day, the frenetic desire to celebrate wanes dramatically and the whole focus of life fundamentally shifts. From larks, sprees, excitement and holidays the stark reality of a return to work or school and a far more mundane schedule undeniably and implacably confronts us.

Yes, there are still five days of the Twelve Days of Christmas left, but their traditional celebration tends more towards events like Distaff day and Plough Monday, which are both to do with the return to traditional employment for both sexes. Schools also often return to begin the spring term before Twelfth Night. In our busy twenty-first-century life, where does this leave us? The answer is that there are still lots of things to do, look forward to and celebrate – they are just of a different, quieter, less obvious nature.

Why not celebrate your own return to work? Whether it is within the home or outside of it, you can still do something a little special to set the tone for the new year. Buy a new pot plant or bunch of flowers to brighten up your home or workplace and give it a fresh feel. Select a box of biscuits for everyone to share at coffee break, or better still, bake your own cookies. If you really feel like being extravagant, select a big box of cream cakes on your way into work and let everyone choose their own.

Privately give thanks that you have work, school, college to return to. These institutions give our lives security and opportunity. Not everyone is so lucky; there are many children and adults in the world who can only dream of what you are in danger of grousing about. Count your blessings!

PLOUGH MONDAY

In times past this was traditionally the day when work in our agricultural communities geared up several notches. It usually took place on the first Monday after New Year's Day and, if the weather was fit, saw many men out in the fields ploughing the land, ready for the frosts of January to break the newly turned earth back down into a fine tilth ready for the spring planting. In many parishes, a plough would have been brought into the church the previous Sunday, decorated and blessed.

As in the case of Distaff day, this return to labour was often accompanied by jokes and horseplay, carrying on the spirit of jovial role-reversal as boys, men and masters were all treated equally and subjected to the same tricks and ribaldry. Horses and ploughs would be decorated with evergreens, herbs or dried flowers. The women, perhaps taking pity on their menfolk, would more usually forget all the tricks and palaver that they had caused a few days previously on their own return to work and bake or cook extra treats to be taken out to the fields or enjoyed by all the family on the men's return home at dusk.

I well remember one year when I was in my early teens. Looking out of the back kitchen window one very dark, moonless Sunday evening in January I suddenly spotted a pinpoint of light. At first I wondered if someone was walking down the path beside the river towards the cottage and it was the light from their torch. But as I continued to watch, spellbound, I observed that the light was actually moving backwards and forwards through the darkness, but not getting any closer.

I called the rest of the family and we all debated what it might mean or what might be the cause of it until my uncle decided to don his wellington boots and coat and take a walk up through the woods to see for himself. None of us could have guessed the answer. Uncle Ricky returned, his face wreathed in smiles, to tell us that he had walked along the river bank until he reached the spot where it bent sharply to the right and the river flowed around three sides of a large flat field, barely discernible through the leafless trees from our cottage. There he saw the neighbouring farmer, sitting on his tractor, dragging a plough behind him. The machine's headlights were relatively dim, but tied to a pole lashed to the side of the bonnet was a bright pressure Tilley lamp.

What had driven our neighbour out into his fields at that time on a Sunday evening in the pitch dark we never discovered. Perhaps his family had driven him to distraction and he sought peace and quiet. Or perhaps subconsciously he was following the age-old practice of beginning the agricultural year? We never did find out – we felt a bit embarrassed to ask him. But it certainly stuck in my memory!

COMMENT FROM JOAN: QUIETER SOCIALISING, 1961

Mrs Pope brought Jane down to play with Gillian. They came for lunch – chicken, etc. – and Jim managed to get home too, so we had quite a merry gathering. Just as we were finishing lunch Mr Noblett from the farm – our nearest neighbour – called to enquire if we had seen his black dog. He says Mr Turner's dog (both dogs) had gone too. Of course we hadn't seen anything of either – hope they haven't gone astray, though Tom Noblett seemed to think that they might be off hunting... nice dog too.

When we had cleared the table and washed up we sat back talking in the living room, eating the ½ lb box of chocolates Mrs Pope had brought. The children decided to go for a walk in the wood and came back just as I was bringing the tea tray through from the kitchen. Although I had made a large chocolate cake, Gill wanted arrowroot biscuits with her tea, as usual!

MEMORY TIME

As I have suggested ways to make the most of the pre-Christmas and Midwinter period, I would suggest that you do exactly the same with your post-new year time. Just as you may wish to actually celebrate your return to work or school – or simply ordinary, quieter domestic chores – I feel that it is really important to make the most of the lull which comes after New Year because it is unique and very special in itself. This is the time to catch your breath (perhaps for the whole year) and to process, appreciate and store away all the gaiety, fun, activities and occurrences which have taken place in the preceding days, weeks and months – hopefully turning them into many golden happy memories.

Unfortunately, for a lot of us, with our hectic, bustling lives, our memories are sometimes not all that reliable. It is no use trying to convince yourself that you can never forget who gave you that wonderful pair of woolly socks or those particularly delicious dark chocolates or buttery biscuits; you will turn round at the beginning of January and suddenly panic. The cards and gifts, the many faces at parties, the hurried invitations to meet up in the new year as you are literally heading out the door, will all have begun to slide together into one bewildering blur, and the more you try to remember exactly who said or gave what, the less sure you will become. The answer to this problem may be to simply keep notes and *write it down*. I am hardly suggesting that you go through the Christmas season with a notebook and pen clamped to your hand, but in actual fact, that is what many people do these days as they perpetually have their mobile phones in their hands, on which you can add to address books and calendars and make all manner of notes... so actually, there are many things that you may very well be able to jot down at the time.

If this idea does not appeal – or if, like me, you do not have or use a mobile phone very often – write this information down on a piece of paper. And as odd pieces of paper are notoriously fickle and so easily go astray, I would advise that you purchase a notebook which you can make all your notes and lists in and then keep it from year to year. Use a really attractive or expensive notebook which has perhaps been a present from someone – or you may wish to use a rougher version which you don't feel bad about scribbling in, or a thick spiral-bound affair in which there is room for expansion with added receipts, business cards, notes, recipes, cuttings and some of your favourite cards and letters, so that it truly becomes an ongoing, living record of your Christmases.

People who write lists are often joked about, but believe me, it really does make life easier and pleasanter for both yourself and everyone else around you. When next autumn comes around it is so much easier to be able to simply get your notebook out and turn back the pages to see who you sent and gave what to last year so that you don't leave anyone out this year or make the social faux pas of repeating yourself.

There are certain lists, such as cards and gifts sent and received, which I find fairly imperative. But there are lots of other things you may enjoy recording, such as parties attended, with a note of place, time and guests; or the Christmas visits you made, with notes of when they took place, where, and who was present. You may also wish to note down which religious services and carol services/concerts you attended and even school plays – especially in families or groups of people where there are several children or stepchildren, possibly of mixed faiths and cultures, so that no one is left out. It's also good to remind yourself what outings you enjoyed with the date, activity and weather – keep it varied from year to year or alternatively repeat something everyone really enjoyed. Looking ahead, make notes throughout the year of any shops, mail order catalogues or craft workers / suppliers that might be particularly useful.

You may have a member of the family, such as an older child or teenager, who would like the task of being the family 'Christmas scribe', and they may like to include lots of details and even illustrate or decorate them too. You will be surprised at how useful it can be to be able to check back from year to year, and in time it can also become a treasured historical record of your family celebrations.

COMMERCIAL EXPLOITS

I find that one of the best times to do my Christmas shopping is in early January. Christmas cards, wrapping paper, tags, ties, bows and all manner of seasonal frippery (if you go for that kind of thing) are then on sale for sometimes a fraction of the cost that they were on 24th December. Similarly, if you saw something in December which you would have loved to get as a gift for someone but couldn't afford, you may find that it has been reduced in price by the end of the month – buy it now, wrap it carefully in paper (so that even outer packaging doesn't get damaged, faded or generally tired-looking) and put it away in your loft, cellar, garage or 'present box' at the bottom of your wardrobe, ready to use next Christmas. (With this in mind you may like to add another list to your Christmas record book or even at the back of your diary: Presents Already Bought!)

Buying my Christmas cards in the January sales I find I see cards then which I hadn't noticed in the busy run-up to Christmas and have more time to reflect and do my dreaming. Yes, this necessitates storing them for nearly a whole year before they can be used and yes, I don't have such a tidy house as some of the people I know! But I keep a sturdy cardboard box – about twice the size of a shoe box – pack the cards carefully away and tie up the box with pretty Christmas ribbon and store it at the back of a big cupboard. Whenever I feel like beginning to write my cards, there they are, ready and waiting for me to begin – no fuss, no panic, no mad last-minute dashes.

BUDGETING

I have to admit that I am not a great fan of budgeting. In the past, every time I have attempted it I have found that I apparently can't afford anything, or at least very little. But there are several ways you can go about this knotty problem with varying degrees of ease and success. One suggestion I have heard is that you keep all your receipts from the previous Christmas (for food, gifts, cards, postage, seasonal tickets and treats, etc.), add them all up and divide the resulting total by twelve, then put that sum of money to one side each month so that by Christmas you have it all to hand. A good idea in a household that has plenty of money to spare at the end of each week or month but more difficult for the family that hasn't such a ready surplus. Or you might like to set aside even a small amount – whatever you can spare that won't be missed – which will provide an extra little nest-egg for treats when it is taken out and counted the following winter.

Whatever you do, do try not to overspend. There is nothing worse than reaching the new year with a load of debt or your credit cards maxed out! Try to be honest with yourself – and the rest of the family too – if your bank balance isn't so flush. Buy only what you really can't make or do without, or items that you can then make or bake into something yourself.

One of the important things to consider is that doing a little wise buying and preparation now, at the beginning of – or throughout – the year, means that come December you aren't panicking at the last minute. For many of us this is the time when too much money is spent or wasted, when we are rushed and feel forced to grab inappropriate items at vastly inflated prices, simply because we feel we have to have *something* rather than *nothing*, because we have left it too late for any alternative.

A DIFFERENT KIND OF CHAOS

Then there is recycling.

If you train your family to open their gifts with care (as opposed to ripping all the packaging to smithereens in their frantic attempts to get at the contents) then you can save the largest, nicest pieces of wrapping paper, possibly trim them, smooth them out, roll them around a cardboard tube or fold them and keep them flat in a carrier bag or a cardboard box. Not to be used for people outside the family but certainly good for the children, especially where larger pieces can be cut up and utilised to wrap all the stocking contents the following year.

Christmas cards can be cut down and trimmed, a hole punched in one corner and coloured thread tied through to make gift tags for next season. Small sturdy (but plain) boxes can be recovered in pretty paper – perhaps even some of the reclaimed Christmas paper – and put to one side for gifts next season. Yes, there are a myriad of bags and boxes on sale each year, but at what cost to your pocket and the planetary resources? And if you – or your children – do it yourselves, it is unique and has absorbed all your thought and care, contributing so much more to the whole experience of giving and receiving.

Save any viable decorations from your Christmas crackers (pictures, fancy ties, etc.) and reuse them when making crackers of your own. Actually, this is a good time to make your Christmas crackers, when you possibly have a lot more time in the quiet, dull days after all the festive celebration. Or have a go at making some of your own cards and gifts to put away. The whole impulse and habit of gift-giving is still very much with us at this time, so it is easier to focus, and it can give you a lot of genuine pleasure and anticipation.

You don't have to take time out to do these things during your celebrations, unless you want to, of course. Things like wrapping-paper and cracker detritus can be bundled into plastic carriers or bin bags and stowed temporarily in the spare room, under the stairs or back in the loft or present cupboard... or stuffed in the Christmas decorations boxes so that you are reminded to sort them out when you come to put the decorations away. There is nothing worse than being presented with an avalanche of dusty bags filled to overflowing with crumpled paper when you are rushing to get the tree set up on Christmas Eve!

Some of these activities are also very good for children. It gives them something to do at the end of the holidays which is meaningful, useful, and while still being focused on Christmas, also helps to underline the important relevance of *giving*, and thought for others. It can be equally exciting to plan treats and surprises for others as it is to receive them yourself – often more so – and the sooner such ideas are imparted to our little ones the better.

I have heard of people who throw all their decorations away in January and simply buy new ones the following December. What an unutterable waste! The odd length of tinsel may have become a bit bald or a synthetic tree may have lost too many branches over the years... decorations (especially the much beloved) can become frightfully tatty and we may eventually decide to replace them, but that is quite different. There are also always a number of breakages to factor in. But by and large, choose decorations which you can add to or use in various ways and keep them. This is a good way to help to begin to save money or budget. It is also far more environmentally friendly. If you *do* decide that something has to go, as long as it is reasonably decent please do consider donating it to a charity shop so that some less fortunate family can make good use of it. The dustbin is the absolute *last* resort for anything... pass it on, reuse, recycle!

While you are thinking about bargains, recycling and generally organising yourself, don't forget that you will soon be taking down all your winter decorations. Again, my main message here is to try and do it in as orderly and organised a way as possible for it will make your life immeasurably easier come next November/December if you do or, conversely, aggravatingly difficult if you don't!

While you are sorting out all the wrapping and boxes from Christmas, keep a lookout for any which may be good to pack things in, or utilise torn gift paper as extra padding for delicate items. Perhaps you might pick up some extra plastic storage boxes in the new year sales. On the other hand, good sturdy cardboard boxes from the supermarket checkout area will do just as well; these can last for many years and are absolutely free, which is good for your budgeting as well as the environment.

Wrapping lengths of tinsel and strings of fairy lights around a piece of card and then slipping them into bags or standing them up in cardboard boxes is a good way to prevent them from tangling and becoming damaged while they are in storage.

Don't put all your tinsel in one bag and all your fairy lights in another and all your baubles in yet a third container. Pack them away room by room, clearly labelled, so that if you want to have the same decorations in the same place again next year, you have everything to hand and sorted. Or if you have help to put them up you can simply present your volunteers with the right boxes and let them get on with it. If you decide to change your mind and create a different effect, that is fine, but at least you know where you are starting from.

TO RECAP:

- Work on one room at a time.
- Take everything down, dusting, wiping or gently shaking it as you go.
- Pack decorations away as carefully as possible.

- Keep everything together in boxes.
- Above all, use a thick marker pen to label the outside of everything – you might think that you will remember but trust me, you won't!

Carrot and Ginger Soup

The following hearty recipe is excellent for serving after a few hours of un-decorating your house, or to come in to on a raw January afternoon or evening. Serve with a swirl of yoghurt and a sprinkle of chopped parsley in each bowl and a basket of good crusty bread.

Gillian

INGREDIENTS:

1 onion, peeled and chopped

2–3 cloves garlic, peeled and chopped

1 tablespoon of olive oil

2 sticks celery, chopped

1 red or green pepper, chopped – leave the seeds in as they add nutrients and taste

2 lb (900 g) carrots, peeled and sliced thinly or diced if you prefer

2 oz (56 g) flaked barley

8–10 slices of fresh root ginger

Powdered ginger to taste – I suggest 2–3 teaspoons

Salt and freshly ground black pepper to taste

Vegetable stock

METHOD:

- Gently steam-fry onion and garlic in a large pan in olive oil and a drop of water for a few minutes.
- Add rest of ingredients, bring to boil and allow to simmer until all vegetables are soft, stirring occasionally to prevent sticking.
- Can be served as it is but is much improved if pureed. Add a blob of live Greek yoghurt and some chopped fresh parsley to the top of each dish and serve with crusty bread.

SAINT DWYNWEN'S DAY

Here in Wales, on 25th January, we celebrate Saint Dwynwen (pronounced d-oo-u-n-wen). This is our Welsh equivalent of Saint Valentine's day. The popularity and celebration of Saint Dwynwen's day has increased considerably in recent years, with special events such as concerts and parties being held, and yes, even greetings cards printed. Historically this was the time for young men to present their sweethearts with a 'love spoon' which they would have spent many hours carving through the long dark winter evenings. Also, nearing the end of January we are on the very brink of early spring, the seasons are turning and – just like the birds and the bees and all the rest of nature – thoughts are beginning to run to romance, pairing up, and beginning a family of one's own. Whatever, we never need a specific reason to let our loved ones know how much we care for them! But who exactly was Saint Dwynwen, and what relevance does she have for young lovers?

THE STORY OF SAINT DWYNWEN

Many hundreds of years ago, back in the fifth century, *Brychan Brycheiniog* was a son of Prince *Anlach* of Ireland. But his mother, *Marchel*, was from Wales and through her, *Brychan* inherited the Welsh kingdom of *Garth Madrun* in the area now known as the Brecon Beacons. When his father died, the young man decided to cross the sea from Ireland to South Wales and claim his inheritance, changing its name to *Brycheiniog* to match his own.

Here *Brychan* prospered. It is believed that he married three times during the course of his life and that he fathered between twelve and sixty-three children, although the most popular number is twenty-four. But perhaps legend is confusing *Brychan*'s genetic offspring with the spiritual 'children' whom he sent out from the religious centre that he had founded to evangelise other lands, especially Cornwall. Whatever the truth of it, *Dwynwen* was one of *Brychan*'s daughters.

As the years passed, *Dwynwen* grew into a very beautiful young woman. One day when her father had some guests visiting in his great hall she met one of them, a handsome young man called *Maelon Dafodrill*, and as soon as she clapped eyes on him, she fell deeply and utterly in love. Fortunately, when *Maelon* caught sight of his host's young daughter, he also fell hopelessly in love with her.

The passing of time did not diminish the young couple's feelings for each other and eventually they decided to ask for *Brychan*'s blessing on their marriage. But when *Brychan* heard their request he flew into a rage, forbade the young couple to ever marry and just to make sure, the furious prince banished *Maelon* from his kingdom! *Brychan* had other much more important plans for his beautiful daughter, for he wanted to marry her to a much older and more powerful neighbouring prince.

Distraught, *Dwynwen* rushed out into the forest. She aimlessly wandered, heartbroken by her father's cruelty, until she came to the banks of a gurgling stream. Here *Dwynwen* sank down into the lush grass to drink some of the sparkling water and ease her throat, which was parched from much weeping. She bathed her sore, red eyes and, utterly exhausted, she eventually fell into a deep sleep.

While *Dwynwen* slept a magnificent angel took pity on her and appeared to her in her dreams. The angel gave *Dwynwen* a sweet magical potion to drink which would erase all memory of *Maelon* and turn him to a block of ice. But *Dwynwen* was also granted three wishes. First she wished that *Maelon* be thawed and returned to life. Secondly she wished that God would meet the hopes and dreams of all true lovers. Thirdly, *Dwynwen* wished that she would never marry. She received the promise that all three wishes would be granted and as a mark of her thanks, *Dwynwen* vowed to devote the rest of her life to the service of God.

The name *Dwynwen* literally means 'she who leads a blessed life'. The young girl became a religious woman, travelling many miles away from her family and her home, until she came to the banks of the Menai Strait, where she took the ferry and crossed the turbulent water over to the Isle of Anglesey. Carefully she sought just the right location until she found a tiny tidal island where she founded a church and religious order and spent the rest of her life in the loving service of God, who had come to her aid and salvation. The fact that she is also the local patron saint of farm beasts and sick animals perhaps throws some light onto just what kind of service and work she and her sister acolytes might have been engaged in. Here in Wales, Dwynwen will always be known best for protecting and blessing lovers.

Dwynwen lived a long life, only dying in the year AD 465. But after her death the island became a place of pilgrimage, just as it continues to be today, and is known as the island of Llanddwyn, literally meaning the 'island of the church of Dwynwen'. The remains of her holy settlement can still be seen today, as well as Dwynwen's well where, allegedly, a sacred fish (or eel) swims and by its movements predicts the future fortunes and relationships of the various couples who go there. It is also said that if the water 'boils' when a visitor is present, that person will have good fortune.

THE SCENT OF CHANGE

As previously mentioned, we often leave our Winter Tree standing long after the other decorations have been taken down. Sometime after Twelfth Night we remove the more obviously Christmas-themed decorations from its branches so that it may truly become a tree of winter, stark and frosty in its glitter and fading evergreens. But as Saint Dwynwen's day approaches, it can take on a new lease of life and a whole new emphasis. It is freshly hung with heart-shaped baubles in softest shades of pink and white and blue. Other synthetic flowers are gradually attached to its boughs... pretty little snowdrops and deep gold and purple crocus garnered from previous Christmas displays at the garden centre. Or, you may wish to make paper flowers and red hearts cut from cardboard.

Our branch and tree have now been with us since Winter first put in an appearance back at the end of October. They have illustrated the withering life of late autumn, the bare depths of Winter, the joy of frost and snow, the return of the Sun and colourful human celebration, and finally the return to the barren starkness of dark January days. Now, although the days are still short, the quality of light is different... lighter and brighter somehow, with more presence and purpose. The birds are beginning to bustle and sing and it is possible to see that Winter's days are now definitely numbered. Time to remove whatever decorations and vestiges of Midwinter / Christmas / Winter we may still have literally hanging about the house!

DOWN WITH THE DECORATIONS!

When I was a child my heart would break when it came time to dismantle the tree and put everything away until the following year. For this reason, my endlessly kind and patiently understanding mother would allow the decorations to remain long after 5th January, when the Twelfth Night party had been enjoyed by everyone, the Lord of Misrule had removed his coloured, bell-behung hat and our faces had once more turned towards a steadier mode of life. It was often not until the end of January or even early February, when the strengthening sunlight streamed in through the back windows of the cottage proclaiming that Winter would soon be over, that I finally, reluctantly, would allow the now pathetically dusty gaudiness and dry shrivelled greenery to be removed. Much as my parents adored Christmas themselves, it must have driven them to distraction to have such unseasonal decorations hanging around for so long. Just another example of their deep love and respect for me and my childhood wishes.

Even I felt a joyful relief when all the rooms were clean and tidy once more, with the odd stark feelings that the bare walls and beams and empty bowls and jugs brought. But our cottage took on a beautiful simplicity and happy anticipation turned to thoughts of spring. The same happens now in our family home. Perhaps a little sherry glass will be filled with the first snowdrop, or a tiny bowl will appear on the hall table containing the first rich colour of the natural year; deep golden and royal purple crocus, or even a pot of the first earliest yellow narcissi. Then there are vases of softest silver pussy willow and lamb's tail catkins with their dainty golden fairy dust upon the dining-room table where, until only recently, the little musical tree stood to play 'Silent Night'.

Even now, much as I love spring – my most favourite season of the year – I still shed a little sentimental tear as everything is packed away, and inevitably catch myself thinking, 'Oh well, only another nine months till the start of the *next* Midwinter / Christmas season!'

AND SO TO SPRING

As we approach the beginning of February the season turns and we lift our faces to the coming spring. Traditionally this is the time when *Gwyl Ffraid* (in Wales), *Imbolc* (in Ireland) and Candlemas in the Christian church is celebrated. Still a time for hearth and home – for the weather at the onset of the second month of the year can be more perilous and wild than the rest of the winter put together! This is the time to honour the Goddess, Woman and the Land. It is the season of the very young maiden, Brighid (Irish) or Ffraid (Welsh), who is patron of healing, the arts, fertility, inspiration and metalwork and to whom many fresh clear springs of water are dedicated.

Acknowledge the reawakening of spring, recognise the growing of the light, celebrate the new lambing season – and historically the arrival of all-important fresh milk. It is a time to light white candles (which mimic the strengthening and lengthening daylight), to initiate fresh projects and to come together in community, sitting around the metaphorical hearth to enjoy poetry, music and song.

But this is also a time to begin to focus our attention on the outdoors again. As well as gatherings under the protection of four walls and a roof, it is the perfect time to venture out into the woods and fields and seek the first signs of spring; to breathe deeply and fill our lungs with clean tangy air, to raise our faces to the sky with anticipation of the long light months ahead and the joy of simply being alive.

It is particularly appropriate to go in search of a sacred healing spring (of which there are many, along with the remains of accommodation and protection for the visiting sick, scattered across our landscape); bathe your hands and face in their refreshing waters, cleanse your mind and spirit of unworthy thoughts and anger, and raise your heart to meet sparkling new challenges.

A FINAL WORD

Looking back on the winter months just passed, you may ultimately try out lots of ideas, but will eventually discover which you are repeatedly drawn to, which resonate with you most and which you look forward to. Others may feature in your annual calendar for a while and then drop by the wayside, to be naturally replaced with other, more relevant activities as your life unfolds, evolves and progresses. Just remember – and I cannot stress this enough – that whatever you do with and in your life, each and every day, every moment, is special. It will never come again, so make the very most of it – not just at Midwinter, but throughout your entire life... SO ENJOY!

Endmatter

The Winter Calendar

One kind word can warm three winter months.

JAPANESE PROVERB

THE FOLLOWING IS a month-by-month list of some of the special days and dates that occur during the months of Winter. You might like to use some of them for inspiration, or to base some of your Winter festivities around. This is by no means definitive. I am sure that there are many other special days around the world which fall within the Winter season, in both the Northern and Southern Hemispheres. There are also bound to be localised celebrations and anniversaries within your own area. See what there is, use it to inspire, and then utilise what appeals or feels most right for you, adding your own ideas and interpretations as applicable.

Do not think that I am suggesting that you celebrate ALL these dates! You can follow up as many or as few as you like. Celebrate one or two different ones each year, or simply as the fancy takes you. Keep things fresh and inspiring and try not to get bogged down in repetitive tradition. We all celebrate Winter each year in one way or another, but it helps to sharpen our focus and intent, and more thoroughly enjoy ourselves, if we don't merely repeat the same process year in and year out.

OCTOBER

<table>
<tr><td>End October / early November</td><td>Diwali</td></tr>
<tr><td>31st</td><td>Calan Gaeaf, Samhain, Hallowe'en. Ending of autumn. The Ancestors. On this date and for a couple of days before and after it.</td></tr>
</table>

NOVEMBER

<table>
<tr><td>1st</td><td>All Saints' day.</td></tr>
<tr><td>2nd</td><td>All Souls' day.</td></tr>
<tr><td>5th</td><td>Guy Fawkes night; bonfire, fireworks, seasonal games, storytelling.</td></tr>
<tr><td>11th</td><td>Saint Martin's day; old start of winter; the traditional slaughter of the animals.</td></tr>
<tr><td>22nd</td><td>Saint Cecilia's day; celebration of music.</td></tr>
<tr><td>23rd</td><td>Saint Clement's day; smith craft, metalwork and citrus fruits.</td></tr>
</table>

25th	Saint Catherine's day; celebration of learning, the written word, books, libraries, students, philosophers and teachers.
Fourth Thursday in November	Thanksgiving
First Sunday of Advent	Usually last Sunday in November. Also Stir Up Sunday: traditional day to bake your Christmas cakes.
30th	Saint Andrew's day / night; Patron saint of Scotland, but also celebrated in Cyprus, Greece, Russia, Ukraine, Romania, Barbados, Sicily, Prussia in Germany, Amalfi in Italy, Patras in Greece. All things Scottish – music, foods, poetry, storytelling, dancing, wearing the kilt.

DECEMBER

1st	Time to begin opening Advent calendars.
4th	Saint Barbara's day; connection to wheat, fruit, harvests and prosperity; also divination of love.
6th	Saint Nicholas's day; children, gifts, balancing of duality of life.
13th	Saint Lucy's day; old Winter Solstice; light, candles.
17th	Start of the Roman Saturnalia.
21st	Astronomical Winter Solstice, beginning of the

'raw nights' and first of the 'smudging nights';
Saint Thomas's day.

22nd   Sun enters the zodiacal sign of Capricorn.

23rd   End of Roman Saturnalia; Saturday takes its
name from 'saturn day'.

24th   Christmas Eve; Mother's night, celebration of
your children, your mothers, of motherhood;
holy night, second 'smudging night', cleansing
of home / living / work space.

25th   Christmas Day; rebirth of the Sun / Son; birthday
of Jesus, Mithras, Osiris, Apollo, Mabon, Sol
Invictus; celebration of the rebirth of Light.

26th   Saint Stephen's day, Boxing Day; charity to
others, gifts, giving to others... to people... to
the land... to wildlife... to yourself... earmark
this as a day of rest! Also the day of horses,
death and rebirth.

28th   Holy Innocents' day; Children's day; celebrate
children and childhood, your own, your
children's or the children of other people. Share
memories, but best of all make memories – spend
quality time with your children, or young
relatives, or youngsters... whatever you do, do
it together – let the day and your thoughts and
activities revolve around them.

29th   Feast of Fools; ceremonial social reversal – fun,
capers and chaos! Safely let off steam. Reverse

the normal way of doing things, even by such a simple action as wearing your clothes back to front! Have a day when everyone is encouraged to act foolishly – play silly games, laugh and have fun, or have a fancy dress party.

30th Honouring the Boar; bringing the emphasis back to the importance of the Sun at this time of year. Celebratory meal, mask making, ceremonial construction and consumption of edible boar's head made from fruit.

31st New Year's Eve; third 'smudging night'; traditional day for presenting mumming plays. Parties, 'first-footing', fireworks, resolutions.

JANUARY

1st New Year's Day; wassailing the land and giving thanks for what we have; also remembering what has gone before and the hopeful optimism of what is to come. Making *Calennigs*, guising, *Mari Lwyd*. Lighting candles in windows to shine out to all the spirits and energies of the New Year.

4th Distaff day; ceremonial return to work – or school! Assessment of work and obligations; celebration of one or all of them. Perhaps

showing your appreciation of the fact that you
have a job, and possibly also celebrating and
showing gratitude for the fact that you are
healthy enough to do it.

5th   Twelfth Night, fourth and final 'smudging night'
and end of the 'raw nights', eve of Epiphany.
Removal of Midwinter decorations. Assessment
of giving and receiving; your wants, but more
importantly, your *needs*. Time to decide on a
course of action to achieve / fulfil even just one
of your personal needs.

6th   Epiphany; Three Kings' day, old Christmas Day,
birthday of Dionysus, Greek god of wine,
vegetation and ecstasy.

Plough Monday   The first Monday after Twelfth Night and the
official return to work after the Midwinter
revelry, the beginning of the agricultural year.

17th   Alternative day for wassailing.

25th   Saint *Dwynwen*'s day; Welsh patron saint of
lovers, love and loving.

FEBRUARY

1st   Celebration of *Gwyl Ffraid*, *Imbolc*; the end
of deep winter and the beginning of early
(Celtic) spring.

2nd   Candlemas; official end of the Christmas
          season; time of light processions and rituals
          performed to promote and protect the fertility
          of the land.

I will honour Christmas in my heart, and try to keep it all the year.
CHARLES DICKENS

Alternative Carols

AS IN ALL seasons, there are times throughout Midwinter when it is good to be alone in your own company, but more often than not, Winter is a time for coming together, for companionship, for socialising, for friends, community and sharing. Making music is a most effective way of engendering that feeling of togetherness. Nearly everyone can sing to some degree of basic proficiency. Even a couple of songs give a core purpose to coming together, whether it is around a blazing Midwinter bonfire, sitting cosily in your living room with all the fairy lights twinkling and a dainty seasonal afternoon tea or around the kitchen table with steaming mugs of hot chocolate in your hands.

However, you may find that the words to existing Christmas carols do not resonate well with you, or truly reflect your Midwinter beliefs. So why not take your favourite carol tunes and write your own words? It really is not difficult. Many of us know the tunes, so everyone can easily join in. This way, not only can you have carols which better describe your own feelings and attitude to Midwinter, but you can make them as personal as you wish, including your family names and individual local or family customs or events. Perhaps this is something that your whole family might like to be involved in doing, or maybe each family member could take a different tune and see what they come up with.

Children – or those less eager to use their voices – might like to accompany you with percussion instruments. Bells and drums give an age-old tone to your efforts, but you can also make your own shakers and rattles... one of the things you can do, either for yourself, or with children, in those wonderfully anticipatory days of late autumn or Advent, or on Saint Cecilia's day.

Making music and singing together helps to consolidate family or group identity, and as with so many aspects of Midwinter, the key words here are 'celebration' and 'togetherness'.

Midwinter comes to all parts of our world at some time in the yearly cycle, touching us all with its seasonal planetary relevance.

It is for ALL of us to share, celebrate and enjoy.

GOD REST YE MERRY DRUID* FOLK

(TO THE TUNE OF 'GOD REST YE MERRY GENTLEMEN')

God rest ye merry Druid folk,

Let nothing you dismay,

Midwinter's here to celebrate

Upon this Solstice day;

When Light will be reborn again

And Sun will have its sway,

Good tidings of comfort and joy,

Comfort and joy,

Good tidings of comfort and joy.

We gather here at sunrise,

Rejoice the birth of Light,

And here the Oak and Holly Kings

Once more will stand and fight!

But it is Oak to triumph now

He brings us back our Light!

Good tidings of comfort and joy,

Comfort and joy,

Good tidings of comfort and joy.

---

* I have written 'God Rest Ye Merry Druid Folk' because I am a Druid; but I could just as easily have written 'God Rest Ye Merry Quaker Folk' because I am a Quaker also. You might even wish to use 'Earthly Folk' or 'Human Folk' or 'Joyful Folk' and keep it as non-specific and inclusive as possible.

Rejoice that we stand here
Upon this beauteous ground,
To witness once again rebirth
And Light and Hope refound.
May friendship, peace and harmony
From this day hence abound!
Good tidings of comfort and joy,
Comfort and joy,
Good tidings of comfort and joy!

WE THREE GIFTS

(TO THE TUNE OF 'WE THREE KINGS')

We three gifts the Elements bring,
Earth and Air and Water all spring –
Succour ever, ceasing never,
Praises to Awen* sing.

CHORUS:
Oh Star of wonder, Star so bright!
Star who brings forth day from night!
Westward leading, still proceeding,
Bless us with your warmth and light!

Earth am I, who nourishes all,
Tiny seeds and oaks standing tall,
Food and flowers, leafy bowers,
Come and I grow you all.

Water clear, I ripple and gleam,
Oceans, rivers, bubbling streams,
Soft rain falling, is my calling,
Quenching your thirsts extreme.

---

* Awen is a Welsh word which is practically untranslatable, but roughly equates with divine spirit, divine inspiration, the energy flow of life... that which is within everything that exists and connects us all.

Here am I, the element Air,
Loud and angry, fresh or fair,
So you breathe, Life I bequeath,
Pure and free and fair.

THE HOLLY AND THE IVY

The Holly and the Ivy,
When they are both full grown,
Of all the trees that are in the wood,
The Holly wears the crown.

CHORUS:
Oh, the rising of the Sun,
and the running of the deer,
Herne is off a hunting in the woods,
While we sing aloud good cheer.

Oh, the Holly bears a blossom,
As white as lily flower,
And Mother Earth breathed life in us,
So we could rejoice this hour.

Oh, the Holly bears a berry,
As red as any blood,
And Mother Earth looked all around,
Smiling to see such good.

Oh, the Holly bears a prickle,
As sharp as any thorn,
And Mother Earth gave life to all,
To celebrate this morn.

Oh, the Holly bears a bark,
As bitter as any gall,
And Mother Earth is quickening now,
So rejoice us all.

Oh, the Holly and the Ivy,
Now they are both full grown,
Of all the trees that are in the wood,
The Holly wears the crown.

MOTHER'S NIGHT

(TO THE TUNE OF 'SILENT NIGHT')

Silent night, Mother's Night,
All is calm, all is right,
Soft the Midwinter's darkness falls,
Stirs the heart while the memory calls,
Seek our blessings from thee,
Children we all at thy knee.

Snow in the air, scents of the fir,
Mother we come, seeking the Sun,
Gathered at hearthside together we wait,
Reaching for you as the hour grows late,
Seeking our blessings from thee,
Children we all at thy knee.

Bringer of Life, cosmic 'Good Wife',
Grant us your love, joy from above,
Circle the world with your blessings and gifts,
Feed the starving and heal the rifts,
Children we all at thy knee,
Seek now our blessings from thee.

Ethical Gifts and Lending

And I thought how we covered up Christmas so deep with work that we hardly ever had time to get at the real Christmas down underneath.
NEIGHBOURHOOD STORIES, ZONA GALE

www.kiva.org – platform for connecting online lenders to entrepreneurs for as little as $25.

donate.worldvision.org/small-business-loan-for-a-woman – thanks to microloans such as these, women who once lived on the edge of survival now own successful small businesses running market stalls, grocery stores, sewing, etc.

www.oikocredit.coop – among other things they dispense small loans in countries such as India and Guatemala with the emphasis on rural areas and women.

www.lendwithcare.org/gift_vouchers

www.presentaid.org – ethical gifts from £4; goats, school books, tools, etc.

www.ethicalshop.org – ethical and fairtrade gifts and products to buy online.

Sites and Links of Interest

GENERAL INTEREST

www.traditionalcustomsandceremonies.wordpress.com

www. gathervictoria.com – information about the Deer Goddess.

www.druidnetwork.org – information about the ancient celebratory practices of Midwinter and humanity's connection to nature.

www.lavenderandlovage.com – Karen S. Burns-Booth, recipe for Lucy buns and much, much more.

www.whychristmas.com – general information about celebrating Christmas around the world.

SUPPLIERS OF LIVE CHRISTMAS TREES

www.welshchristmastrees.co.uk

www.pinesandneedles.com

www.realchristmastrees.co.uk

www.bctga.co.uk – British Christmas Tree Growers Association

WASSAILING

www.chepstowwassailmari.co.uk – advertised as Chepstow's premier winter event, with wassailing, mumming plays, ceilidh dancing and Morris dancing

stroudwassail.com

www.yardecider.co.uk/wassail.html – Devon wassailing

www.nationaltrust.org.uk – some National Trust places are now holding wassailing events and it is worth checking out properties local to your area

Bibliography and Further Reading

Cater, Karen, *The Shortest Day: A Little Book of the Winter Solstice*, Hedingham Fair, 2014.

Chandler, John, *A Country House Christmas*, compiled in association with the National Trust, Sutton Publishing in association with the National Trust, 1999.

Harrison, Michael, *The Story of Christmas: Its Growth and Development from the Earliest Times*, Odhams Press, London (no date).

Harrison, Michael and Stuart-Clark, Christopher (eds), *The Oxford Book of Christmas Poems*, Oxford University Press, 1983.

Hawkins, Paul, *Bad Santas: And Other Creepy Christmas Characters*, Simon and Schuster, London, New York, Sydney, Toronto, New Delhi, 2013.

Hill, Susan, *Through the Kitchen Window*, Hamish Hamilton, London, 1984.

Matthews, John, *The Winter Solstice: The Sacred Traditions of Christmas*, Thorson's, London, 1998.

Miles, Clement A., *Christmas Customs and Traditions: Their History and Significance*, Dover Publications, Inc., New York, 1976.

(Originally published by T. Fisher Unwin, 1912 under the title, *Christmas in Ritual and Tradition: Christian and Pagan*.)

Patel, Sonja, *The Christmas Companion: A Merry Little Book of Festive Fun and Trivia*, Think Books, 2008.

Rätsch, Christian and Muller-Ebeling, Claudia, *Pagan Christmas: The Plants, Spirits and Rituals at the Origins of Yuletide*, ATV AT Verlag, 2003. Translation: Inner Traditions International, Rachester, Vermont, 2006.

Scanlan, Patricia, *Winter Blessings: Thoughts and Poems to Warm Your Heart*, Hodder Headline, Ireland, 2005.

Siefker, Phyllis, *Santa Claus, Last of the Wild Men: The Origins and Evolution of Saint Nicholas, Spanning 50,000 Years*, McFarland and Co., Jefferson, North Carolina and London, 1997.

Simpson, Jacqueline and Round, Steve, *A Dictionary of English Folklore*, Oxford Reference Collection, Oxford University Press, reissued edition 2016.

Steiner, Rudolf, *Christmas: An Introductory Reader*, Rudolf Steiner Press by Sophia Books, Hillside House, The Square, Forest Row, RH18 5ES, 2007.

Struthers, Jane, *The Book of Christmas: Everything We Once Knew and Loved About Christmastime*, Ebury Press, 2012.

Wright, A. R. and Lane, T. E., *English Folklore*, Folklore Society, 1940, Trieste Publishing, reissued edition 2018.

Index

Unbound is the world's first crowdfunding publisher, established in 2011.

We believe that wonderful things can happen when you clear a path for people who share a passion. That's why we've built a platform that brings together readers and authors to crowdfund books they believe in – and give fresh ideas that don't fit the traditional mould the chance they deserve.

This book is in your hands because readers made it possible. Everyone who pledged their support is listed below. Join them by visiting unbound.com and supporting a book today.

Ali Burns

Ros Campbell

Ted Capstick

Harri Carmichael

Wren Carter

Tris Chadwick

Andi Chell

Brendan Cleverley

Louise Cliffe

Gina Collia

Kathy Cosgrove

Stephen Cropper

Neil Crosby

Elizabeth Darracott

Nancy Day

Hiranya de Alwis Jayasinghe

Philippe Demeur

Sue Denim

Katy Driver

Barbara A. Fletcher

Kate Fletcher

Ann Garner

Gina and Gail

Helen Groeger

Katy Guest

Rohantha Gunaratna

Alice Harvey

Rita Henderson

C & C Henry

Helen Hill

Marie Hodgson-Scott

Gillian Hubbard

Nia Hughes-Jones

Amanda Jacob

John Jeffrey

Carolyn Jones

Jennie Jones

Bea Kelsall

Christina Kennedy

Dan Kieran

Mandy Killaspy

Anne Kimberley

Helene Kreysa

Tony Laking

Maryline Leese

Jane Legge

Nikki Livingstone-Rothwell

Kate Macaulay

Jenn MacCormack

Cara Martin

June McAvoy

John Mitchinson

Dafydd Monks

John Murphy

Pauline Murray

Carlo Navato

Erik Nook

Lisa Obrien

Carol Ann Owen

John and Mari Owen

Linda Owen

Sheilagh Pattemore

Tanya Pentelow

Justin Pollard

Alison Powell

Dorothy Prosser

Keira Roth

Hazel Royles

Holly Shablack

Abigail Sherriff

Alison Sherriff

Jacoba Sherriff

Adam Tinworth

Greta Walker

Rachel Walker

Ruth Waterton

Alison Weetman

Roy West

Katie Weston

Jenny Williams

Naomi Williams

Samantha Willis-Hall

Denny & Cheryl Yetsko